THE INWARD

The Inward Gaze looks at men's fantasies and self-images from a wide range
of texts (notably boy's superhero comics, modernist literary classics, and a
Freudian case-study) to discuss the most recent theories of subjectivity,
masculinity and emotion.

Peter Middleton discusses the split between the experience-based claims
of the men's movement and the discourse theories of postmodernism. Does
this division reveal a continuing refusal of masculine self-awareness? Why
does postmodernist theory investigate desire and ignore emotion?

This is a ground-breaking and controversial book which seeks to reformu-
late the way we think about men's subjectivity. Its interdisciplinary
approach weaves together material from many different sources, and will be
of vital interest to students of literature, cultural studies, gender studies and
psychoanalysis.

Peter Middleton is currently Lecturer in English at the University of
Southampton.

THE INWARD GAZE

Masculinity and subjectivity in modern culture

Peter Middleton

London and New York

First published 1992
by Routledge
11 New Fetter Lane, London EC4P 4EE

Simultaneously published in the USA and Canada
by Routledge
a division of Routledge, Chapman and Hall, Inc.
29 West 35th Street, New York, NY 10001

Typeset in 10 on 12 point Garamond by
Florencetype Ltd, Kewstoke, Avon
Printed in Great Britain by
Redwood Press Ltd, Wiltshire

British Library Cataloguing in Publication Data
A CIP catalogue record for this book is available from the British Library

Library of Congress Cataloging in Publication Data
Middleton, Peter
The inward gaze : masculinity and subjectivity in modern culture /
Peter Middleton.
Includes bibliographical references and index.
1. English literature–Men authors–History and criticism.
2. American literature–Men authors–History and criticism.
3. Masculinity (Psychology) in literature. 4. Civilization,
Modern–20th century. 5. Subjectivity in literature.
6. Masculinity (Psychology) 7. Modernism (Literature) 8. Men in
literature. 9. Popular culture. I. Title.
PR120.M45M53   1992
820.9′9286–dc20   92-9321
CIP

ISBN 0-415-07328-6   ISBN 0-415-07327-8 (pbk)

CONTENTS

PREFACE

The arguments in this book first emerged during long, exciting conversations with the dancer and psychologist, John Colvin, as we tried unsuccessfully to construct an anthology of men's writings on changing masculinities. His patient, thoughtful and intuitive care for all aspects of men's lives showed me possibilities that have helped shape this book. My attempt to understand the difficulty men were having in writing about their gender for the anthology pushed me into thinking about the hindrances to men's self-analysis.

I also want to acknowledge three other influences on this book. For two years between 1979 and 1981 Mary Brind shared her perceptions of the feminist debates on the magazine *Spare Rib*. During the mid-1980s I was involved with re-evaluation co-counselling and learned much from various men's groups and men's workshops about the inner textures of men's lives. This work cleared up some of my earlier puzzlement about the relation of men to such feminisms as that at *Spare Rib*, and more importantly gave me a strong sense of how many of men's aspirations are repressed in public life. Throughout this period, the ascendancy of poststructuralist theory in the departments where I worked provided a resistance to the experiential emphasis of the men's movement, a problem that I only began to articulate while trying to put together the anthology with John Colvin. Theory seemed both enabling and myopically obstructive for men trying to comprehend the politics of their experience.

Those are the general influences. I owe a large debt to present and former colleagues in the Department of English at the University of Southampton for the intellectual environment they have helped create, an environment in which work like this can flourish. Students have also provided much stimulus. I am grateful to the many people who have generously read often very rough drafts of the material over several years, or discussed my arguments in illuminating ways. I particularly want to mention John Bowen, Andrew Bowie, Claire Buck, Erica Carter, Stephen Clark, Peter Dews, Elizabeth Guild, Paul Hamilton, Ken Hirschkop, Maria Lauret, David Leverenz, Rodney Livingstone, Laura Marcus, Richard Middleton, Paddy O'Brien,

Julian Roberts, Jonathan Sawday, Trudi Tate, Barrett Watten and Tim Woods. While I was writing this book I read early drafts of Jonathan Rutherford's *Men's Silences: Predicaments in Masculinity* (1992), and found his idea that the men's movement project was a reflexive one very helpful for my own research.

The Department of English at the University of Southampton, and the University itself, granted a period of unpaid leave and later a sabbatical leave during which most of the writing was done. I would like to thank them and acknowledge the burden that any leave, paid or unpaid, creates for colleagues.

Some of this material was published in an earlier form. I would like to thank the editors of these journals: *Fragmente*, *New Formations*, *News From Nowhere*, *The Oxford Literary Review*, *Radical Philosophy*, *Reality Studios*. Early drafts were given as papers, and I would like to thank those departments which gave me an opportunity to air the arguments as I went. I would especially like to thank the Department of English at the University of Florida, Gainesville, and the New Langton Street Arts Center, San Francisco, for inviting me to present papers on emotion and literature in April 1989.

Excerpts from *Collected Shorter Poems* by Ezra Pound are used by kind permission of Faber & Faber Ltd; excerpts from *Personae* by Ezra Pound are used by kind permission of Faber & Faber Ltd, New Directions, New York, and the Ezra Pound Literary Property Trust. Excerpts from 'The Hollow Men' and 'The Waste Land' in *Collected Poems 1909–1962* by T.S. Eliot are reproduced by kind permission of Faber & Faber Ltd and excerpts from 'In Memory of W.B. Yeats' in *Collected Shorter Poems* by W.H. Auden are used by kind permission of Faber & Faber Ltd and Random House. The excerpt from William Carlos Williams's 'Danse Russe' from *William Carlos Williams: Collected Poems. 1909–1939, Vol. I*, copyright 1938 by New Directions Publishing Corporation, is reprinted by permission of New Directions and Carcanet Press. Every attempt has been made to obtain permission to reproduce copyright material. If any proper acknowledgement has not been made, we would invite copyright holders to inform us of the oversight.

Books on sexual politics are appearing at a great rate, evidence of the vitality of this debate. Several books appeared too late for me to take them properly into account. In general, books appearing after summer 1991 have not been discussed.

To keep the book from being too long I have had to do without footnotes. Citations are keyed to the Bibliography at the end of the book, which lists all books and articles mentioned in the text, as well as a few to which implicit allusion is made. Comics cited in the text are somewhat arbitrarily listed according to either title or superhero. I have not listed my many debts to literary criticism of modernist writers, or to secondary material on the modern thinkers discussed here, due to considerations of space.

Wherever possible I have used widely available popular editions of the literary texts.

This book could not have been written at all without the love and support of Kate Baker, George Middleton Baker and Harriet Middleton Baker. This book is dedicated to them.

1

INTRODUCTION: THE INWARD MALE GAZE

REFLECTIONS

Writing about masculinity can be difficult. My first attempts were poems. My first discursive writing about masculinity was intended to be a prose fiction about the violence of writing. I was barely aware that it was also about men's relation to representation. Only when I finished this book did I realize that the story which follows, 'Abstract Paper', had been the introduction to it all along, as much as it had been an introduction for me to the possibilities of writing about men and masculinity.

ABSTRACT PAPER

At that time I wrote very little despite the strong desire to make a record of what was happening. Whenever I tried to write, the ball-point would dig deeper and deeper into the paper, incising the words and then tearing through. A written character with the force I wanted just obliterated itself in the act of writing. Of course I've learnt to write since, to restrain such violent incisiveness, and slide across the coated surfaces of quality papers. I use pencils and roller-ball pens that have little friction between point and whiteness. As I write, the pen moves just ahead of that slow uprushing pressure, fast enough to be always a word or two beyond the point where the pressure could start its destruction. Occasionally, because I am sleepy or have stared too long at memories outside the window, the force builds past the danger levels, the pen goes deeper and deeper in, and I feel myself disgusted at the ripped sheet. It has to be thrown away, and not in my wastepaper basket, in the swingbin out of sight, and if that's full, and the lid won't swing back but lodges on a tin and some dried-out baked beans spilling their guts out over the cartons and bottles, the liner has to be taken out, put into one of those plastic sacks provided by the city, into which no ashes must be put, tied at the top, and placed ready for collection outside. Once the paper is effectively out of sight I wonder where I am, but then go back to the window and think about the scrap paper I used to collect from a printer on the way to school. Offcuts in luxurious, extravagant thick piles if

1

you were lucky, green and pink as well as white. I don't remember using this paper, simply showing it off to my friends at break and comparing what we'd been given. I collected these empty sheets as carefully as I collected teacards or baseball cards at other times. When I had to write or paint on them the pleasure disappeared. My paintings were always diagrammatic and symmetrical, using symbols rather than paint textures for their effect. A house had an exact frontal view of doors and windows either side, up and down. Men were sticks. I didn't see them as sticks, or as combinations of zeros, ones and half Ms. I saw them as fully formed, moving human beings. My sticks showed how I supposed people were defined, by roads and cars and houses and tanks and guns. My greatest skill at drawing developed in pictures done for friends, of airplanes preparing to bomb their targets. I worked hard at the perspective of aircraft wings, foreshortened to indicate their length and right-angle position to the onlooker, who was also up in the air alongside, taking part in the battle. It was the shape of the wing that kept the plane in the air.

For a long time I couldn't write because no wording seemed sufficient for the head of pressure that had built up. I stared out of the window in various places at the roads and cars and houses. Sometimes I closed one eye, and aligned the road sign, the vertical strut in the window frame and my pencil in my other eye, but when I reopened my closed eye they fell back into their happy distances, and their colours and outlines looked like nothing that could be drawn up. This isn't the story of how I came to write or an illustration of its difficulties. This pencil slides so smoothly across the surface that I can't easily recall those violences any more. I was younger then and believed that everything had an explanation. There were days when words seemed so powerful they could carry a lifetime's experience over the thousands of years necessary to reach us from the earliest acts of writing. Words were the hiding places of the world's secrets. The problem was no paper was strong enough for them.

IDEALIZED SELF-IMAGES

This is a book about men's representations of their subjectivity and power as men. Men have written plenty about themselves as men; little of it consciously. When men are conscious of their gender they talk of heroic masculinity, of manhood and its vicissitudes. Writing self-consciously and self-critically about their gender has proved much more difficult, especially in response to feminism. But then if the only reason to write self-consciously about masculinity were feminist demands to do so, men's silence would be understandable, if not justifiable. Who wants to indulge in public self-criticism after all? But feminism isn't the only strong motivation for a politicized self-reflection by men on the conditions of their masculinities. Modern men have suffered greatly in a series of wars generated by largely masculine codes of behaviour whose close examination might be a useful step towards preventing their endless repetition. Manipulative images of masculinity pervade our culture. Manhood is used to sell everything from cigarettes and politicians to toilet cleaners and toys. Literary texts are dominated by it. Modern men writers have revelled in masculinity without ever quite naming it, in works as different as James Joyce's *Ulysses*, Thomas Pynchon's *Gravity's Rainbow*, Yeats's poetry or Charles Olson's *Maximus Poems*; manhood fascinates modern men writers even if they don't quite own up to it. In fact, there seem to be many good reasons for men to reflect upon their gender. The usual reason given for men's lack of both political discourse and academic scholarship, when compared to feminism, is that men have a vested interest in silence. I think there is another reason for men's silence, the lack of a language for such reflection. Masculine bias in many existing concepts of subjectivity and power is an obstacle to such gender reflection. Men after all have written plenty about their subjectivity and power, but they have constantly universalized it at the same time, and assumed that the rationality of their approach was the sum total of rationality. Universality and rationalism were built into these concepts to avoid such disturbing self-examination by men. Men's self-reflection is blocked at various points along the route. Getting past these obstacles to create an emancipatory men's discourse requires a constant checking of the very process of turning analysis back on the analyst. In this book I have identified one main site of blocked reflexivity as emotion, and in that way concurred with the dominant views of the men's movement, but it will quickly become clear that the ordinary assumptions about what we mean by emotion are part of the problem.

I have already used several terms which raise fierce objections in contemporary debate. Even interiority itself may be a 'pure superstition' (Barthes 1977:144). No one can innocently use terms like 'men', 'representation', 'subjectivity', 'emancipatory', 'discourse' or 'emotion'. These are cruxes of contemporary debate which signal not only intellectual disagreement but institutional, political and national differences. They are also, I shall argue in the course of this book, all terms whose contribution to existing masculinities needs more analysis. For the time being I will let them stand. In the remainder of this introduction I shall discuss the difficulties of producing an emancipatory men's discourse as if it were simply a problem of reflexivity, in order to map out the dimensions of the discussion to follow (in doing so I am echoing Jonathan Rutherford's idea of describing the men's movement project as a reflexive one, outlined in his book *Men's Silences*). Later in the book I shall show that these difficulties are closely connected to other modern debates about reflexivity, desire and modernity. Here I shall be asking a seemingly simple question. What happens when men reflect on their gender? I shall take this question literally for a moment and ask: what does a 'real man' see when he looks inward? A 'real man' is of course a fantasy ideal representing aspirations neither realizable, nor necessarily desirable if they were. Like many fantasies, the 'real man' fantasy ideal reveals to analysis psychic structures otherwise hard to see. I have chosen two such fantasy figures here, one a superhero from popular culture, and one an artist from high culture, in examples where the inwardness produced by self-reflection is very much on show.

My first example, 'The Super-Key to Fort Superman' (Superman 1987), published by DC Comics in 1958, is a portrait of that minor deity of American imperialist manhood, Superman, in his spare time. He spends his off-duty hours on 'hobbies and self-improvement', at a polar fortress hidden under the Arctic snow. His super fallout shelter provides a compelling image of a defensive masculine subjectivity, and evokes the apocalyptic mood of that time. In 1958 most Americans had fallout shelters on their minds. Offices and bigger stores all had shelters in the basement, and there were signs everywhere telling you how to find them. School drills and Conelrad radio broadcasts added to the impression that a nuclear attack was imminent. When a jet crashed the sound barrier I remember thinking – 'this is it'. The threat of total annihilation was a Communist threat, and not for example the ultimate in male violence, as feminist peace campaigners were later to claim. It is not surprising that in 1958 Superman makes sure he has a secure underground bunker, and what better symbolic location than the pole, the point on which the earth turns? Yet it ought to be surprising. Superman is supposed to be invulnerable. In the story he reviews a collection of presents to be sent to his friends if he dies, and this improbable awareness of self-limitation underlines the paradoxical vulnerability embodied by this cold-war ideal. The subjectivity projected by the image of the bunker is both a type of masculine defence and a national political condition. Masculine subjectivities have socio-political significance.

Inside, the secret hide-away is a mixture of museum, zoo and laboratory, full of trophies, robots, extraterrestrial beasts and, oddest of all, eerie life-size wax simulacra, not only of friends like Batman and Lois Lane, but also of his Mr Everyman alter ego, Clark Kent. The inner, unconscious world of this 'real man' is populated with exotic bestial passions, externally control-ling forces and narcissistic introjections, all sealed off from any contact with the outer world. On one of his days off, Superman arrives at the bunker to find writing glowing on the inside wall announcing an intruder. The panel art makes this penetration of the impenetrable fortress seem frightening. Inscribed in his subjectivity is the awful recognition that his autism is unsustainable. Eventually Superman tricks the intruder into revealing his identity. He pretends to need rescuing from a dangerous dose of Kryptonite radiation released after an earthquake (which in reality Superman caused). Kryptonite destroys his powers, so he is apparently helpless. Out of the shadows steps Batman. He hid himself by pretending to be a waxwork and Superman didn't even notice. Batman's excuse for this invasion of

Superman's private space is that he wanted to give Superman a birthday present, and decided to make a birthday puzzle out of his uninvited presence. At first Superman is not happy about this and, instead of thanking him, complains that he trusted Batman completely, trusted him not to enter (with all its connotations) his intimate world. Then the only physical violence in this unusually tame story occurs. The earthquake had sealed the room shut and Superman punches an exit in a burst of displaced rage and homophobia, a destructive, retaliatory phallic thrust, freeing him from excessive intimacy and unwanted homosexual desire. A moment earlier, when he was pretending to be stricken by Kryptonite, he was shown lying full-length on the ground, propped up on one elbow like some male Maja Vestida (and more than halfway to Desnuda because of those briefs he wears) for Batman's benefit.

But why does Superman go to the fortress anyway? What is all this self-improvement for? Why should Superman, this paragon of every masculine attribute (all those muscles, brains, X-ray vision and the power of flight), have room for improvement? Is it because this ideal of masculinity falls short even on its own terms? The contrast between Batman and Superman seems to suggest that it does. Batman is not omnipotent, he can't rescue Superman when he seems to have succumbed to Kryptonite, yet he has the edge over Superman, as if his greater vulnerability actually gave him greater resources. The diagrammatic opposition between life world (the remarkably lifeless private world of the snowbound fortress) and the public sphere (of heroic law enforcement) in the Superman story is slowly challenged through the intrusion of Batman, and the consequent deconstruction of Superman's fortress subjectivity. Batman is more socially adept because his masculinity is not threatened when he does 'feminine' tasks. In one panel we see Batman shopping (something it is hard to imagine in Superman's life), and at the end of the narrative Batman gives Superman a cake he has baked. Batman's care for Superman, his willingness to shop, bake, bring friendship into the fortress despite Superman's terrible paranoia and homophobia, propose new possibilities for transforming 'male homosocial desire' (Sedgwick 1985). Birthday cakes and puzzles belong more to the imaginative world of young boys (the main target group of these comics) than to men. This is a fantasy which blends manhood and boyishness, and therefore negotiates between men and boys.

In the opening full-page panel we see Superman engraving a metal diary with his X-ray vision using a 'language no one else in the universe knows', the language of the planet Krypton, destroyed not long after he was born. This private language belongs to the time in infancy when a child begins the transition from wholly private pre-linguistic bonds with nurturing adults, to the public languages of separateness. Superman's private language represents an uncompleted emergence from such bonds. Emotional experience remains inarticulate because it has not been translated into the public self-

5

representations of adult subjectivity. Perhaps that is why Batman announces his presence by making the walls glow into words (like God's warning to Belshazzar). Superman's inturned ego is inscribed against its will within the otherness of language.

The Superman story offers an amusing, vivid image of a defensive masculine subjectivity. Its inwardness is on show but it cannot look inward itself. Despite being the possessor of the ultimate male gaze that can see through all concealment, Superman doesn't see his masculinity, even if Batman does. But what Batman sees, according to the panel art, is a desirable man, and this at first confirms Superman's need for safe isolation. The story holds the danger at bay with a fantasy of having it both ways. The simulacrum Batman can come to life in the inner world without destroying its hermeticism. Superman can have the fortress ego and the friendship. During the cold war the 'real man' looks inward at himself only at great danger to his reality and manhood. The story splits the act of self-reflexivity into the two heroes, one of whom first secretly and then openly gazes at the other, and thereby generates a homoeroticism in need of containment. The plot is the story of that containment. In more general terms the storyline consists of the vicissitudes of Superman's subjectivity and it works so long as a reader doesn't interpret Superman's well-stocked fortress as an image of subjectivity. In this way the story is typical of the genre. Only its explicitness about the significance of the plot is unusual. As I shall confirm in the next chapter, most of these superhero stories are about threats to the sovereignty of masculine subjectivity, threats projected onto external forces. Similarly, if Superman were to become self-reflexive the plot rationale would vanish. The story's possibility depends on Superman's own lack of introspective capacity, especially the lack of any way of looking at himself as a man. The nearest Superman gets to inwardness is his diary in Kryptonese and that may be risky, as his vulnerability to fragments of the lost planet shows. Kryptonite represents childhood cathexes, and if those reach consciousness their regressive pull may destroy his manhood completely. It is not surprising that the discovery of Batman is followed immediately by Superman's supposed collapse because of the Kryptonite. The active presence of a man who stirs affectionate feelings in Superman's imaginary triggers emasculating, regressive longings for parental love. Superman's power depends on its hermetic isolation from his subjectivity.

Perhaps Batman's cake will change Superman and he will begin to be able to think about his masculinity after all. If he had wanted to in the late 1950s he would have found little to enlighten him. Only now after more than two decades of feminism are men finally beginning to respond with extensive analyses of their own gender. New books on men and masculinity have at last begun to appear regularly. Robert Bly's mythopoeic account of the transition from boyhood to manhood, *Iron John: A Book about Men*, has become a bestseller. In books like *How Men Feel* (Astrachan 1986), *Men*

Freeing Men (Baumli 1985), *Rediscovering Masculinity* (Seidler 1989), *Being a Man* (Cohen 1990), *Men's Lives* (Kimmel and Messner 1989) and *Men and Intimacy* (Abbott 1990), or *Gender and Power* (Connell 1987), *Masculinity and Power* (Brittan 1989) and *The Gender of Oppression* (Hearn 1987), men write about their experience as men and respond to feminist critiques of men's power. The titles suggest that it is hard to do both at once, just as it was in the story. The problem facing men when they try to reflect upon themselves, without self-deception, is that they use the same intellectual methods that once justified men's power. It is then especially hard to interrelate subjectivity and power without either exaggerating the ease with which men can change, or denying culpability. Political self-analysis can easily disappear into the cultivation of emotional sensibility, or into the submergence of individuality into transpersonal 'super-subjects' (Smith 1989:88) such as power and language. These welcome new books on men and masculinity handle the problems with varying degrees of success. Most men, however supportive of feminism, still find the political and personal barriers to the development of an emancipatory discourse on masculinity insurmountable. Men, as well as women, have doubts about the very possibility of a radical discourse of masculinity. If men still have power denied to women how can these male oppressors produce an emancipatory political discourse on masculinity, and subvert their own dominance? Isn't this more likely to be some kind of face-saving exercise than a radical political project?

Laura Mulvey's (1985) influential image of men's power as the male gaze offers one possible way of exploring the problem, because it triangulates vision, knowledge and power. The act of looking is overdetermined as an act of knowing (epistemology has habitually used metaphors of vision), an act of scopophilia, and as the establishment of the boundary between the subject and its other. Feminists have argued that even if the gaze is not intrinsically male, most actual gazes are. Mulvey's image of men's power turns the gaze back onto itself, making it visible and, at that moment, disturbing it. What happens when men respond to such feminist reflexivity and turn their gaze inward on themselves and their power? The Superman story suggests that this gaze will meet resistance, and the titles of the recent men's books (which I shall discuss in Chapter 5) hint that the problem may have something to do with the apparent incompatibility of theoretical representations of power and subjectivity.

The Superman story shows us powerful images of a super-man's inner world, but he has not begun to develop the kind of self-awareness of his masculinity that a male gaze might produce if directed back on itself. The real man in his popular fantasy form looks inward only with difficulty. The story is wiser than its hero and contains criticism that could lead to a change in the bunker mentality. This Superman is an ideal for 1950s popular culture. What does a high-culture ideal of masculinity look like? One typical modernist representation of an idealized but suspect masculinity can be found in the source of my title, 'the inward gaze' – Ezra Pound's poem about a failed modernist, *Hugh Selwyn Mauberley: Life and Contacts*. Mauberley, fictive parody of Pound's earlier poetic self now sloughed off at the Great War's end, spent too much time preoccupied with the 'obscure reveries' of introspection, instead of looking outward and making images to reflect modern society to itself. The poem is too long to quote in its entirety. These three sections give the tone of its terse, elegant summing up of the artist Mauberley's condition. This tone constructs a poet-critic who knows better than Mauberley what to do:

> For three years, out of key with his time,
> He strove to resuscitate the dead art
> Of poetry; to maintain 'the sublime'
> In the old sense. Wrong from the start –
>
> ***
>
> [the song of the sirens]
> Caught in the unstopped ear;
> Giving the rocks small lee-way
> The chopped seas held him, therefore, that year.
>
> His true Penelope was Flaubert,
> He fished by obstinate isles;
> Observed the elegance of Circe's hair
> Rather than the mottoes on sundials.
>
> ***
>
> The age demanded an image
> Of its accelerated grimace,
> Something for the modern stage,
> Not, at any rate, an Attic grace;
>
> Not, not certainly, the obscure reveries
> Of the inward gaze;
> Better mendacities
> Than the classics in paraphrase!
>
> (Pound 1977: 98–9)

This failed modernist is more interested in maintaining the old-fashioned sublime and misses the possibilities of future modern and postmodern sublimes. And what does it mean to maintain the sublime? At first sight this sounds like some kind of curatorial job, looking after what Pound's former employer, the poet William Butler Yeats, called the 'monuments of unageing intellect' (Yeats 1984: 193). The sublime, however, is different. The sublime is not simply equivalent to great works of art, although they may stimulate it, it is an effect of intensified subjectivity, and produces what the historian of aesthetics, Peter de Bolla (1989: 102) describes as a 'self-authenticating subject'. This self-authentication could be said to be Mauberley's inward gaze at imaginary masculine heroics, for which the classics provide the image of Ulysses. The failed modernist is not an inward stay-at-home. In his mind he is the adventurous Ulysses, crossing the seas, hearing the sirens, and loving the witch Circe. Nevertheless he longs for home: 'His true Penelope was Flaubert.' All the time his devoted wife Penelope waits for him, which in terms of this aesthetic allegory means that Flaubert and the Art he represents are his point of origin. Most women are wild and dangerous, but fortunately at home, out of the way, waiting at this ultimate goal, is the wife. Or is she? Isn't this Penelope a man in drag, a man writer? Perhaps that is why the inward traveller stays away; perhaps he doesn't want to confront this ambiguity of his art. His true goal is not only dedication to art, but unacknowledged intimacy with another man.

In his mind the failed modernist may be able to fantasize that he is a real man, but in the world's eyes his fantasy ideal, Ulysses, is no longer a paragon of masculinity. Now they go for knaves or, worse, men who lack even the basic equipment to be men: 'All men, in law, are equals./ Free of Pisistratus,/ We choose a knave or an eunuch/ To rule over us.' Modern life is emasculated: 'Christ follows Dionysus,/ Phallic and ambrosial/ Made way for macerations' (Pound 1977: 99). The classical world of 'real men' has been replaced by a Christian world of soft, limp men and self-abuse, where Mauberley's fantasied masculine exploits aren't sufficient to make him a poet. He really is a long way from Flaubert. The modern world doesn't want such fantasies, nor does it value the inward gaze. Instead it values what a later section of the poem calls a 'vacant gaze', the feminine gaze of one of Burne-Jones's Pre-Raphaelite maidens. The poet's own gaze falters and despite his 'full gaze' (ibid.: 108) he doesn't see the bright externals of his world's 'wide-banded irides'. Mauberley is unconscious, anaesthetized by his retreat into the 'isolation' of an inner fortress full of 'selected perceptions' (the aesthetic equivalent of extraterrestrial beasts). Yet a suspicion remains that the modern world may not value the inward gaze because it is sceptical of what this inward male gaze reveals. 'Obscure reveries' may be masculine fantasies on the royal road not to high art or even the unconscious, but simply to male sovereignty. Is the inward gaze no more than masculine self-aggrandizement, in which masculine subjectivity fantasizes hypermasculine exploits, inflates itself into sublimity, turns women into witches, and appropriates femininity for men's art? Pound's poem of transition, *Hugh Selwyn Mauberley*, both celebrates and ironizes the inward gaze of self-reflexivity on which so much post-Romantic verse had been based. The real poet, the truly masculine poet, may after all have to discard the inward gaze and the old sublime for a new, not yet identified, masculinity, and a much more hands-on approach to the world.

It turns out that the 'real man' of popular culture is not so different to the 'real man' of high art. When the artist looks inward he becomes a kind of super-hero and develops this inwardness into aesthetic withdrawal. Just as the initially anonymous Batman ends Superman's pure isolation, so the anonymous poetic critic of Mauberley's life pronounces his masculine aestheticism dead. Literary modernism is as preoccupied with masculine subjectivity as popular culture, and finds the relation between subjectivity and power just as difficult to articulate. The large difference is that the literary modernist is much more self-conscious about the problems of gender awareness. The artist's problem is that his kind of inwardness is no longer respected and all he can blame is a modern state of emasculation. He cannot blame the difficulty on masculinity itself. Masculinity still cannot be named and in that sense the inward male gaze is a vacant one. There is no masculinity to be seen, because it is hiding in its bunker or trapped by the 'chopped seas' (readable as a pun on chopped 'sees' – interrupted gazes – perhaps?) of heroic escapism.

METHODS

Men have carefully avoided constituting their own gender as a field of study, and masculinity is rarely acknowledged in contemporary men's theory. The questions I ask here cut across many existing academic fields of enquiry, fields whose methods, objects of study, forms of validity and styles of self-presentation are often incommensurable. Some of the material I use here may well be very familiar to readers from one specialism and yet unfamiliar to those outside it. Inevitably I have ventured into areas in which I have less competence than I would wish. I have been constantly aware of the vast amount of research, theory, history and literature that bear on my argument, and equally aware of my own limitations. Anyone who has ventured to explore men's consciousness of themselves as men will know what I mean. I believe that the attempt to clarify the political and cultural issues is important enough to warrant the speculation that seems inevitable if we are to make headway.

To exemplify the issues in an accessible manner I have deliberately taken my illustrative materials from literary and cultural texts. I am far from wishing to claim that they are the only ones that matter, yet I do have a polemical point to make as well, one which led to the choice of Ezra Pound and Superman as introductory figures. Literary and cultural studies have always been centrally concerned with subjectivity, and recently with power relations. There is another reason why such texts can help us understand masculinity. Literary and cultural texts are one of the means by which our societies generate their knowledges of self, society and the natural world. Literature was once believed to delight and instruct. In our time most literary criticism, as well as commonplace assumption, neglects the instruction, or considers it mere propaganda, forgetting that our most important scientific discoveries are presented as 'instruction'. Literary texts have much to contribute to our understandings of all the issues with which our other knowledges are engaged, if they are allowed to contribute as primary and not secondary sources. Texts are not just symptoms, but proposed cures, pre-figurative arguments as well as ideology: 'Works of art tend to be prospective symbols of one's personal synthesis and of men's future and not merely regressive symptoms of the artist's unresolved conflicts' (Ricoeur 1970: 521). Even the Superman story contained some proposals for change. We can also read representations of consciousness, self-consciousness, articulacy and inarticulacy in men's texts as claims about men's subjectivity, and examine them for consequent aporias. To give literary texts such respect requires as detailed an attention to the workings of what they say as to any complex argument. We need to recognize that it may sometimes be possible to read men's texts as transfigurative proposals as well as exposures of ideology, because at times men's texts are trying to initiate processes which require further development. Such a project would include the rereading of gay writers and their placement at the centre of new literary histories. It would also involve reflexive attention to the masculine anxieties of authorship, and to the ways in which criticism as practised at all levels from the institutional career to the furthest reaches of theory is part of the production of masculini-ties, as well as their self-analysis. That is why I have used such awkward locutions as 'men's modernism' and 'men writers' throughout this book. Doing so underlines the possibly masculine character of many of what Genevieve Lloyd calls 'cultural ideals of reason' (1984: 109). The unfamiliar use of the word 'men' in these contexts will and should provoke the reaction by men that their gender is not important, but with it, I hope, will grow the recognition that the transparency of gender needs to be argued for in each instance, not assumed to be generally the case for all men's productions. Women writers know there are men writers, and black writers know there are white men writers but we white men writers (I want to include myself for a moment very clearly) often don't see our own condition. Michael Kimmel expressed this condition vividly in a newspaper interview: 'When I look in the mirror . . . I see a human being – a white middle-class male – gender is invisible to me because that is where *I* am privileged. I am the norm. I believe that most men do not know they have a gender' (quoted by Brenda Polan in an interview in the *Guardian*, 29 August 1988). Reflexivity works imperfectly for men because they don't see what they are seeing when they see themselves.

In this book I am talking about the men and masculinity of the two cultures I know best, Britain and the United States. I do not want to claim for this study that it speaks for all men, indeed I don't want to claim that I speak for other men in that sense of representation at all. This study is offered in the spirit of dialogue, not representation. It is largely concerned with existing dominant cultural representations and theoretical conceptions of men and gender, but even then my choice of materials is deliberately

Western. A valid political project can only emerge if we men from that culture examine ourselves and our history more closely than we have done. To do that it is important to speak of what we know and to recognize that this is a dialogue as well as a struggle. Other men, other cultures, will have other things to say to which we need to listen. Our ability to hear those men will be much greater if we understand our own masculinities more clearly.

Modern philosophy from Descartes to Hegel tells us that self-reflection constitutes self-consciousness and leads to self-knowledge. Descartes's formula, 'I think therefore I am', is its best-known statement. Postmodern, poststructuralist philosophy deconstructs this constitutive act of self-reflection, but sees infinite dispersion of the subject amongst its signifiers as the only alternative. According to these discourses the inward gaze may not be capable of seeing all that occurs in self-consciousness. Critics of post-structuralism have argued that self-consciousness is not equivalent to self-reflection, thus opening up the possibility that there are different processes of self-consciousness. When men try to look at their power they are already caught up in a problem that has names other than masculinity and power, names like modernity and postmodernism. This is not the only difficulty. Not only is the political gesture of self-reflection caught in complex theoretical debates, it presents practical difficulties too. Any man writing about men and masculinity quickly realizes that this is a most self-conscious project, an almost self-consuming process in which the discourse he uses constantly asks itself if its productions are yet more versions of masculine self-promotion. It can seem as if every claim, every strategy, every concept is yet more Ulyssean fantasy or addition to the ego bunker. Writing about masculinity can seem to demand an extreme deconstruction, an interminable exordium considering the conditions of the statements always about to be, but never quite, made. The only way out of the infinite regress that threatens attempts to write about masculinity is to make the gesture of reflexivity itself the subject of preliminary enquiry. This is especially necessary because the politics of men's self-reflection has moral implications as well. The man writing about masculinity can seem to be adopting a higher moral position than other men, as if he were more right-on than those men whose academic theorizing leaves the theme alone. Even reflecting explicitly upon these claims could itself constitute a kind of claim to moral superiority. There is no way out of this, but we can at least explore the dilemma by making the workings of this recent political process of men's self-examination more visible. I shall do this by offering a theoretical framework for one central feature of the new disclosures by men, their focus on emotion. Doing so will show that far from being a simple issue, men's difficult relation to the emotional dimensions of everyday life has many far-reaching and unexpected consequences. My argument here will be that masculine subjectivities can only begin to be comprehensible if men rethink existing concepts of gender and identity in terms of the relations between society, reason and emotion. It is that third term, common enough in everyday discourse, and now widely researched in mainstream philosophy, psychology and sociology, but neglected within both gender studies and literary and cultural studies, which will prove the most necessary and the most resistant to reconsideration.

The book is divided into two sections. In the first I discuss boys' superhero comics, several men's modernist texts and Freud's case study of the Rat Man. These heterogeneous texts are all marked with modern masculinities. I trace their inscription within representations of self-consciousness, especially those moments when self-representation breaks down in sublime moments of withdrawal, and show that male violence is one of the recurrent causes of this limit condition of masculinity. In the second half of the book I discuss current attempts both by men and by feminists to theorize masculine subjectivity, and show the contradictions that beset attempts to discuss cathexis, desire and emotion. In the final section of the book I show that emotion is both rational and socially structured, and conclude by discussing canonical philosophical texts written by men, on which modern literary and cultural theories of language and subjectivity are largely based. Their importance has derived partly from their largely unacknowledged, rationalizing projection of masculine conditions. Such theories can be reread as phenomenologies of masculinity, in order to bring a gender awareness to contemporary theories of subjectivity. Throughout the book Superman makes repeated appearances. Deadly earnest for boys, he is merely comic to most adult men. This distance between seriousness and humour is a constant reminder of other formative distances between boys and men. Superman is a heuristic device, a reminder of the continuance of boyhood fantasy in so many modern masculinities, and a figure of the cultural unconsciousness of masculinity to which a politicizing self-aware men's gaze needs to be turned.

An expository book like this, that vouches for what is said through the fiction of the voice of a friendly, reasonable man (increasingly the literary standard of late twentieth-century writing in the humanities from New Historicism to Pragmatism, a style whose benefits are considerable, but whose blandishments need to be watched), and sustains its legitimacy with authoritative forms of argument, pays a price for the clarity that travels easily. The power of its voice is hard to question. Knots and tangles in our understanding, uncertainties, interwoven metaphors, thoughts too contextualized to be widely communicable, emotional nuances, all these and more, which might manage containment in a more wrought form like poetry or narrative, are bleached out in this standard expository style. This is a book on inward gazing which doesn't do too much inward gazing at itself (apart from the beginning of the next chapter, where I use my own recollections as test cases for a discussion of the aporetic difficulties of introspection). To do more would necessitate a literary style at odds with the demands of analysis, and probably become too experimental, and therefore restricted in readership, to serve its purpose. Like the poet who judges the failed modernist, I am reluctant to go too far on the inward Odyssey here. There are more pressing issues to convey. I hope that, unlike Pound, I have managed to do so with respect for the differences between men, women, cultures and histories.

Part I

Part I

2

BOYS WILL BE MEN: BOYS' SUPERHERO COMICS

INTROSPECTION AS METHOD

Where might we begin to find out about the formation of modern masculine subjectivities? We could begin with the question: how does a boy become a man? This question is asked by most current theories of masculine subjectivity (and has recently been made the central issue by *Iron John: A Book about Men* (Bly 1990) and the renewed interest in initiation rituals it has encouraged). These theories assume that by concentrating on what divides boys from men we may be able to learn more about adult masculinities. One way of answering these questions would be to turn our gaze inward, those of us who are men, or to look to the confessions of men, if we are women, and rely on introspection and memory. Surely men's histories and experiences could provide plenty of material for such an enquiry? Or can they? I shall begin this enquiry by putting two of my own stories to the test to consider the problems of using introspection as a method for developing a theory and politics of masculine subjectivities. The first is a recollection of boyhood, the second an anecdote about fatherhood.

My own boyhood, from the age of 8 to 12, now seems to have been dominated by intense, obsessive and serious pleasures. Some, like stamp and coin collecting, seem fairly intelligible still. Others like reading comics and 'trainspotting' provided pleasures that seem to be peculiar to that part of my life. The joy of watching trains all day seems especially remote. With other boys I sat on the edge of a path at the top of a grassy bank above the Birmingham to Bristol railway line, and wrote down the numbers of the engines as they passed. Long waits were punctuated by the intense excitement of trying to see the often dirty numberplate of a fast train. At home I underlined the numbers I had collected, in a special reference book, the 'combined edition', which listed all the current steam and diesel engines on British Railways. The memory of those 'combines', as we nicknamed them, is still powerful. I can still feel that one of these volumes would be valuable to own even though the information in it is of absolutely no interest to me now.

Sometimes I and my friends caught a train to the nearby city of

Gloucester, where we never left the platform. We took sandwiches and did a good day's work, watching the activities of the trains and engine sheds. At a station there was always the possibility of the greatest achievement of all, 'cabbing' an engine. Most railway workers ignored us or chased us away, but occasionally a friendly driver might let one or two of us climb up into the open cab of a steam locomotive waiting at the platform. How exposed the cab felt! We found it difficult to believe that all the coal needed for the journey was shovelled by one man into the boiler's incandescent mouth. That was a real man's labour. The shared pleasure of trainspotting was intense. I always travelled with friends to nearby stations. The days on platforms and railway banks were spent talking and speculating about the trains. Trainspotting satisfied a desire for independence, because it could take place outdoors away from parents and teachers, and much of the time in places unsupervised by adults. Yet none of these reasons would have been sufficient in itself to make trainspotting the centre of my life for nearly three years. I think its great attraction lay in an unconscious fantasy of access to men's power, a fantasy made possible by the tangible power of the loco-motives and their highly visible male drivers. Cabbing a locomotive was exciting because we were stepping into the mysterious place where men derived their power from real work. For a moment we were men too.

The best engines were those that had names: Corfe Castle, Leckampton Hall. Some Western Region engines had been given a name, written in an arch of brass letters on the side of the engine beside the boiler, that referred to country houses and castles in the west country. A geography of social power in the region thundered past us. I could not have put into words then why these engines so fascinated me. The intense feelings they aroused lay outside the logic of ordinary consciousness, just as the excitement of comics did. Now I can say that these engines seemed to embody the power of the places they were named after, but then the connection felt real and immediate. The engine was the estate. That was how I understood the nature of social power. The names conveyed a sense of the great British heritage, helped by glimpses of other rarer locomotives which didn't come along our line and could be seen only if we went to faraway stations, engines named after kings, princesses, earls and so forth.

Steam engines have highly visible pistons and crankshafts. They are colourful, large, powerful but simple forms of machinery, visibly engaged in acts of speed and power. Their independent mobility makes them good symbols for animate power. This force is visually available in readily sym-bolized form and controlled by men. It would be a mistake immediately to call this power phallic, because such a label too readily converts itself into some kind of visual equation between engine and male sexuality, when it is men's social and political power, as well as the power of adult men's bodies as perceived by a boy, which the engine is made to represent. Power is usually understood as potential for the future, but in these engines we also

18

saw the power of history. An entire recent history of men's achievements was figured by the locomotives, a history fuelled by the knowledge that many of these engines were much older than we were. They belonged, like the men who drove them, to the adult world, a specifically male adult world whose history they made tantalizingly visible and inaccessible. All we could do was watch it, excluded, and daydream about our eventual assumption of its power. Trainspotting was our way of negotiating with the world of manhood which lay all about us outside the home, so mysteriously powerful and remote. Trainspotting was a bricolage of accessible, visible elements of the adult men's world, out of which we could form rituals to provide the space for us to understand our current exclusion and eventual arrival in that world. Perhaps the dream of seeing all the locomotives on the railway, 'copping' every single number listed in our combined volumes of engine numbers, was a symbol of that achievement. At that point introspection fails me. I shall turn to another kind of introspection, less vulnerable to the vicissitudes of memory, a recent anecdote. Once you begin looking, moments exemplary of the relations between boys and men seem to occur everywhere.

One afternoon in early 1990, I took my two children to the playpark in a double buggy. I had wanted to go to the shops but my 2-year-old son insisted we go to the park first. Fortunately my 5-month-old daughter was fast asleep, and stayed asleep the whole time we were in the playground. She doesn't like to be left in an unmoving buggy too long if she's awake. When we arrived at the park I felt apprehensive and embarrassed. Six youths were sitting on the benches and equipment in the toddlers' section of the play-park. As I arrived at the gate they all fell silent and watched me from their perches. I looked back at them. Then without a word or any sign of acknowledgement they got up together and walked off to find somewhere else to sit. It was half term and they had no school to keep them busy. They seemed embarrassed to be found in a playground, but then so was I, despite my determination to spend time during the day with my children, embarrassed to be witnessed pushing a pram and cuddling a little boy.

My son began to ride one of the wooden motorcycles mounted on a large spring. Another older boy of about 8 ran up and began to ride the other one. I said something to him by way of hello and he quickly became chatty. He showed my son and me his tricks. He stood up on the wobbling platform; he made it weave from side to side. My son thought this was very funny. The boy then got off and told me he had made a sword out of a stick, using his penknife. Turning out his pocket to show it to me, he held out his other prize possessions as well. What caught my eye besides the knife in the little heap in his hand were a miniature gun and a plastic female figure with a tuft of hair, all of which seemed to belong on a chain of some kind. After proudly showing me the gun's workings, he told me about his secret den, and about his friend, who could be very 'naughty'. The friend cycled up, and the boy said, 'Do you want to play?' only to receive a daunting reply, a curt, suspicious, mannered 'What?'. These two certainly gave the impression that they wanted to avoid too much familiarity between themselves, at least in front of a man. They may have felt extra pressure to do this because only their behaviour identified them as male. Both had long hair, and the other boy could have been a girl if not for his manner, which was self-consciously masculine and 'tough'. After some talk the boys went off together, having told me that they had to be home respectively at four and seven. These return times were apparently significant measures of their status, because the 'naughty' boy who didn't have to be back until seven was clearly one up on the other. The more independent you were the better.

The incident stuck in my mind because it seemed to sum up something about boys and men. The only boy who played there unselfconsciously was my 2-year-old son. The boys of 8 or so were willing to play but very self-conscious about it, and the teenage youths were there almost nostalgically, as if it was a secure, familiar place where they could talk seriously about what was on their minds, even if they couldn't quite be seen to be enjoying the playground. And above all the boy's pocket contents fascinated me. They were so perfectly symbolic. A knife, a gun and a female fetish seemed to symbolize both what the boy wanted, and the violence to which this play version of manhood could be a prelude. The boy was fascinated in his turn by me, and what he seemed to want was some kind of approval of his symbols. Just before his friend appeared he tried to enlist my help searching for something he had lost in the shrubbery nearby. He wouldn't say what. I was a little suspicious and refused. I think now that the help he wanted was symbolic approval by a man, something he had trouble finding. All of us males except my 2-year-old son felt awkward about seeming to enjoy the pleasures of play, especially in the presence of other males. Only a serious masculine purpose could legitimate it. Two themes emerge from this anecdote, which I shall pursue further. One is the way the fantasy of manhood seems to be created out of a bricolage of fragments from the masculine public world, and the other is the difficulties that males, especially males of different ages, have articulating their relations with one another.

This anecdotal illustration of one alleged feature of contemporary masculinities can, I believe, be substantiated by both empirical and theoretical methods. Yet problems arise even before the anecdote itself begins. The collective pronoun in the opening sentences of this chapter shifted uneasily from the collective readership of this text, to the entirety of those who are male and female, and back again, blurring distinctions of all kinds which might make any such larger 'us' a fantasy. Even the conventional collective pronoun for the readership and writer is obviously subject to some conflict, as the fourth and fifth sentences indicate. So the apparent ease of the appeal to experience hides a potentially manipulative levelling of differences. But there is worse. My story contains a fairly obvious subtext: 'I am able to be both an academic and a good parent, a father who can do what are traditionally a mother's tasks.' It would be much more difficult for a woman academic to tell this story because it would be received very differently, perhaps as 'women's talk', something at the opposite extreme from an intellectually respectable conclusion based on close scientific observation. My anecdote also has traces of the confessional narrative that has been an element of a large part of the autobiographical writing on masculinity. This imposes on the story a subsequent, more informed, more worked-out viewpoint. Indeed the more self-critical the tone of such writing, paradoxically the more virtuous the narrator will appear. In feminist writing, confessional narratives commonly work in reverse because they show a progress towards the recognition that self-criticism was internalized oppression. Criticism within the narrative will be counterposed with an understanding critical of that criticism, and the process will have a complex and self-adjusting dialectic likely to be unavailable to a man writing such material. Moreover, existing models of women's writing lend themselves to adaptation for such purposes (think of the women novelists on whom feminists can now draw). For men, the existing models of heroic acquisition of manhood are likely to appear part of the problem they are addressing.

Similar problems adhere to the use of childhood recollections. Such personal memories will be resonant for some readers, but they cannot claim representative status. This introspective analysis of my trainspotting memories leaves a lot assumed or unexplored. I have added the emotions and desires retrospectively to the presentation of my memories, in a form which then colludes closely with interpretation. A fuller account would be something more like prose fiction. Desires would be embedded in the narrative in such a way that they were not wholly dependent on my interpolated framework of interpretation. A more general difficulty will have occurred to anyone familiar with contemporary literary and cultural theory. Experience, it is argued, is never simply given to us, but comes structured by ideology and discourses. Class, race, history and gender itself are determinants whose effects are likely to be largely unconscious. Such experiential material as this needs to be interpreted within some other, wider framework which is then subject to analysis, but it is questionable whether the same author can both write autobiographically and present a self-analysis. That it can be done is clear. Freud provides a famous modern example, and an indication of the difficulty. We are not all such polymaths, and are unlikely to have or perhaps even to want to develop a complex system of thought such as psychoanalysis. This doesn't mean confessional writing is worthless. Far from it. Much of the impetus towards a better understanding of masculinity by men has come from just such confessional material. The courage and acuity of such writing are impressive, and will remain important. Alongside it we need to develop more articulate insight into the inner life of masculinity than the strictly autobiographical form makes possible. A better model is modern prose and poetry where the presentation of introspection about manhood, sexuality and modernity can call on the widest linguistic resources. Such work, which I will discuss later in this book, precludes, in all but exceptional cases, the kind of argumentative analysis central to my project here. Therefore the remainder of this book will largely eschew personal writing because it is not yet possible to produce such writing and have it mesh with theoretical analysis in the way feminism has demonstrated. One day it may be possible, when men's movements and self-awareness of gender amongst men have generated languages and occasions for such discussion. For now a man writer discussing the inner dimensions of masculinity faces a choice between theoretical analysis and autobiography. I shall occasionally make personal observations but I shall not try and ground my arguments in any more general personal narrative.

The other obvious place to look for an account of masculine subjectivities would be that dominant form of contemporary investigation in the social sciences, the interview. Ask men about themselves in questions which foreground their gender, and then analyse the record. Such work accounts for most of the remainder of what is currently available about masculine subjectivity. Interviewing men about themselves has become widespread. Collections of representative interviews by journalists, the massive narrativized sampling of questionnaires in Shere Hite's (1981) work, and the more cautious, empirical work of academic sociology, have given us a wealth of material. Almost all of this work necessarily relies on the subject representing himself in a speech which is not only conscious but to some extent self-aware of gender politics. Masculinity, however, as feminists have repeatedly demonstrated, is often unaware of its areas of blindness. Any method that relies on articulate speech in a dialogue, even with the anonymous questionnaire, will be limited in its access to the field of subjectivity. Analysis of unconscious features may circumvent this limitation, but much will remain untouched by such ready-made narratives of self-explanation. Less conscious, less articulated and less resolved areas of masculine subjectivities are likely to remain unexamined by the subject's verbalized self-analysis. For a wider investigation of masculine subjectivities we need to look at symbolic forms, at fantasies, inarticulate experience and the activities of what has been called the unconscious, but might be more precisely called an unconscious, in modern men.

Childhood is both a condition and a history. The condition of childhood continues in our own and others' children, whose presence can help us recover and recapitulate our own historical childhood, but cannot entirely overcome its increasing remoteness. Our physical shape has changed, especially our size, and with it, our environment and its scale. We are now a part of the adult world, however far from its centres of power. All that remains of childhood are memories and compulsions which lie in the foundations of our being, out of sight and apparently beyond control. Indeed they are what

22

control us according to many modern psychologies. Hume's dictum that reason is the slave of the passions has been slightly rewritten. Now in a post-psychoanalytic age we believe that reason is the slave of childhood passions. Psychoanalytic study of these primary materials has made us aware of how such processes make us what we are, even when we cannot quite put this knowledge to work in our own specific histories. Infant desire and its reawakening in adolescent sexuality draw us back to the world of the under-5s and the over-12s. In between is a life which remains remote in a quite different way, seemingly not of interest to such theoretical representation. Between 5 and 12 is a spell of consciousness and dormant sexuality in which other pleasures dominated our lives, pleasures whose seriousness makes them now seem more remote than the stirrings of Oedipal desire. It is not that we cannot remember what we did then. My own memories of that period of my life seem exceptionally clear. Subjectively I felt more rational and intelligent than at any other time before or since. Those pleasures of later childhood are not repressed or forgotten but displaced into another economy of desire whose lack of the familiar teleologies of sexual behaviour can make it seem both attractive and irrelevant to adults for whom sexual priorities determine lives.

BOYS AND COMICS

Trainspotting is just one of many boyhood rituals whose significance is hard to assess because it leaves so few visible traces. Boys construct a symbolic universe and its ritual actions out of a chosen set of activities and objects, which have little do with the adult socioeconomic purposes of rail transport, and, like some cargo cult, create an almost metaphysical negotiation with what is to them a seemingly transcendent power. Boys have many such rituals and they will always be changing, local and much of the time invisible to the adult world. Some, like sport, produce more direct relations between men and boys, but they probably do so because sport itself is a game deliberately set aside from the productive processes of economics and daily life (this may be one reason why games have provided men philosophers with attractive paradigms for language and aesthetics). Boys are excluded from the activities which define men in the public and domestic sphere. At present there are few ways that boys can find a dignified and respected entry into the men's worlds of defining work. For me, and for most boys still, the only access lay through the media.

Film, television and comics provide armatures on which boys can wind all kinds of fantasy. Comics, relatively low-budget, highly targeted and visually simple, offer a useful means of analysing the pre-emptive structures of fantasy which I am suggesting can be found in most boyhood rituals of entry into manhood. Martin Barker (1989) has pointed out that comics provide the analyst of popular culture and ideology with an easier point of reference than many other forms because comics are easily described and presented. For this discussion, the comic fantasies of masculinity and hypermasculinity have the advantage of being presented in a less censored form than in many other kinds of popular culture. The reality principle is also less evident. For this reason larger claims can be made for the comics' importance as a medium of fantasy. Without wishing to endorse Wiley Lee Umphlett's theory of nostalgia neurosis – 'an undermining of self-actualization by compelling us to retreat into our private dream world' (Umphlett 1983: 17) which impairs people's ability to see their environment and past at all clearly – I think that his claim about the comic book is worth taking seriously:

> Thus the comic book persists as both a psychological and sociological expression of the times that produce it, substantiating my interpretation of the medium as thriving on the nostalgia neurosis of our popular culture. The comic book, because of its obsession with the exploration and dramatization of fantasy, is capable of plumbing the depths of both our psychic wish fufilments and dreads as no other medium can, with the possible exception of the movies.
>
> (1983: 104)

Fantasy, however, cannot just be read off like a simple code. Its addressees and its hierarchy of structures, from individual panels to entire narratives, need to be considered.

The panels of sketchily drawn figures give desires a space for fantasies of manhood which can go beyond the machinery of masculinity to its fears, angers and imperatives in a private moment of imaginary privilege. Cartoon images are often highly expressive. Both speech and imagery can be so clear and well outlined that they become resonant in the way a short poem can. Terse, forceful expressions of desire and images of the human body at full stretch often have that ironic quality which pop artists isolated in the 1960s for their canvases. Said and shown with such self-certainty, these moments reveal their suppositions as an excess of assertion which becomes funny. Into that humour rushes an intellectual awareness that doesn't conceal the seriousness of the dilemmas they present, but can recognize and rethink it.

What follows is not a history of comics nor a study of representative cartoon strips, but an analysis of psychological structures within extracts chosen to demonstrate a thesis about men, boys and masculinities. Most of my examples and generalizations are drawn from the various genres of science fiction action comics, especially the American Marvel and DC comics, and the British comics *2000AD*, and *Eagle*. My choice of comics has some representative status, but I shall not try to demonstrate that. Instead I shall focus on developing a picture of masculinities which can then provide a route into the more theoretical chapters that follow. Comics are of limited value but the visibility of those limits makes them valuable for this discussion precisely because they are so visible. Their simplicities can illuminate the greater complexities to be found elsewhere.

Comics are commercially produced for profit by adults. Their appeal rests on several features. They offer powerful fantasies in a graphic mode which doesn't intrude too much disruptive reality either in the storyline or in the sketchy visual representation. The combination of visual and written material is both easy to read and, like other mixed media, more powerful than either would be on its own. Comics are also transgressive, in the way that pop music and films can be. Their content is not controlled or monitored in quite the way that most of the material accessible to children is. Fantasies of violence against other males and against property, which would be unacceptable in photographic realism, can be left uncensored. Unlike school books and 'good' literature for children, nothing is expected of these comic books. Printing techniques make it possible to produce comics cheaply, so children can buy them themselves, and therefore have some economic control over their pleasure. Above all, comics offer the inside story on the adult world. Hypermasculine action comics are offered to boys as the inside information on men's lives, information that they find hard to get from anywhere else. The marginal, slightly disreputable status of comics helps make them all the more attractive to their readers, who are likely to trust them more than something more official or more sanctioned.

One of the most revealing images of men I have ever seen appeared in *2000AD*, a futuristic action comic, which is popular with boys of all ages (*2000AD* 1987). This picture shows a battle-scarred man, the hero of the strip, with his allies, a robot and a fierce animal on a chain. The hero's enormous automatic rifle, enlarged by perspective to alarming size, rests on his hip and points out at the enemy and the reader. This mechanical phallus threatens the reader as if he were a potential enemy, as if just the reader's gaze were a threatening challenge. The man's monolithic, rock-like body is wrapped in bullets, guns and a chain. His granite face is expressionless except for bared teeth. An eyepatch and facial scars make him look angry, fearful and dangerous. The machinery of war has become a machine-man in the figure of the robot behind him. Its large robotic teeth, sightless eyes and enormous spiked barrel chest, bigger even than the large chest of the soldier in front of it, make it a parody of a man. The spanner strapped to its chest is a comic reminder that this is a machine, and can be controlled by whoever wields the tools. Perhaps there is even a parody of castration.

According to Aristotle (1948: 8), 'the man who is isolated . . . is no part of the polis, and must therefore be either a beast or a god.' The modern spectrum of masculine possibility has replaced gods with machines, but the cause of the limit cases is the same: isolation. Men who become self-sufficient cease to be men, as Batman appeared to be warning Superman in the story we read in the previous chapter. The picture of the ugly trio in *2000AD* offers an image of manhood pervasive in action comics. The man stands between the robot and the beast, caught between feeling like a wild animal completely mastered by his passions, and a robot incapable of feeling, totally under someone else's control. Both are degraded images of humanity. Between them is the man trying to restrain the fury of the beast, and overshadowed by the robot behind him. Robots and beasts are externalizations of inner experiences. In most of the stories they appear as the agents of destruction that must be destroyed or tamed (as our soldier has done). Robots and monsters are the extremes which manhood can easily attain, and which must be fought. The stories almost never present these threats as inner emotional or psychological struggles, but place them outside the protagonists, who can then use simple physical force to defeat the problem. This physical force is the gift and confirmation of manhood. Yet it entails a very destructive paradox. To save ourselves we have to go to war against embodiments of ourselves. Masculinity wars against itself.

This intestine war creates its own special verbal and visual codes in the comic strip as means of representing masculinities. Consider a typical issue of the revived *Eagle* of the 1980s, which employs a feature borrowed from its more violent American cousins (*Eagle* 1987). The comic is full of linguistic innovations. Bdam. Fwadooomf. Koff. Haaaaaaa. Eeeeek. Gnawwgh. Aaaowwgh. Wurrgghhh. Aaaaaaaaa. Graaaaach. Gaack. Yeaaaaaargh. Fzzzk. This sound poetry is of course the noise made by men in battle, by their cries and crashes. They are either neologisms uttered by the characters in extremes of stress, or the sound effects of violent action, both evidence of manhood's struggles. Why do the cartoon strips use such hard-to-pronounce neologisms, and what do they signify?

On the back page of the *Eagle* is that old favourite, Dan Dare. A rocket has kidnapped one of our heroes. Everyone looks stunned. Tremloc, a blue-skinned figure, not unlike the battered soldier who stood between the beast and the robot, aims another of these enormous rifles at the rocket ship. 'Relax lady! I'll soon bring that Treen snoop-bucket down to earth!', he cries. Dan Dare shouts back, 'No, you fool! Don't shoot!' In the next frame Dan Dare hits Tremloc, one of his own men, with his gun, to stop him shooting. 'You'll kill the boy!' he explains. We see Tremloc reeling from the blow, his mouth wide open, baring his teeth to show a bright red (bloody?) mouth. He utters one of these neologisms: 'Aaauulllgh!' Dan Dare and his team watch the rocket disappear as Tremloc crouches with his back to us, in suppliant posture, head bowed, and body obviously recovering from shock. One of the others says, 'It's moving off, Marshal! We've lost him!' Tremloc responds from his bowed position: 'And the Mekon has gained a prisoner! You may be a galactic marshal, Dare, but you'll always be an Earthie. . . .' In the final frame we see Tremloc from the front, head and neck raised assertively again, a red stain on his blue skull, saying, 'And that blasted soft heart of yours could foul up the whole mission! Just five minutes with the Mekon's torturers, and that kid is going to betray us all!' Tremloc is pointing a finger straight out of the frame at the reader, and presumably also at Dan Dare. We readers are accused of having feelings and, worse, showing them, and therefore being too soft like Dan Dare. We are in good company if we do have such feelings, but the narrative is warning us about their dangers. The casual treatment of Tremloc's injury sets the tone.

How is it that Tremloc not only accepts the blow which drew blood, but can speak of Dan Dare's 'softness' as the cause of this violence? Tremloc's cry, 'Aaauulllgh', is indicative of his pain at being hit, but why does he need this neologistic exclamation? Why could he not use a traditional interjection like 'ah' or 'ow'? The word he uses is effectively unpronounceable. No one would mistake it for English (or probably any other language). This word, like the words listed earlier, is not strictly a word at all. Such words make a sound but do not speak to us. This silence is made all the more poignant because the letters of each word are familiar, and insisted upon by their repetition, but instead of cohering into a word in the language that will form an utterance, even a one-word sentence, the letters never make it. The speaker remains inarticulate. Tremloc's pain remains unspoken. These words are not even phatic. They are moments of great emotion, great passion, which cannot speak. At these points the transition between cries and utterances has failed to occur.

Dan Dare is angry with Tremloc for preparing to shoot the rocket and thus endanger the young man who has been captured. Dan Dare is also probably scared and angry with his enemy, the Mekon. He is clearly very fond of the boy who has been kidnapped (boys don't often appear in boys' comics and when they do, appear to be a liability). All these feelings issue in the blow to Tremloc's head, not, as we might reasonably assume, in a command to stop trying to shoot down the escaping rocket. Tremloc is physically hurt by the blow, but he must also be grieved to be hurt so unexpectedly by the leader to whom he is loyal. This emotional hurt is buried under the inarticulate cry, 'Aaauulllgh', and so never allowed full expression. The emotional issues are not allowed to come into the open and be negotiated. Instead, his verbal response, once he has his breath back, is to use logic to argue with Dan Dare's strategy. Doing so, he translates his complex feelings of embarrassment, grief, shock, fear and anger into ideas which deliberately conflict with those of Dan Dare. What Tremloc cannot do is speak directly of what he feels about the incident, which is therefore left unresolved. The emotional mess will be left to clutter up their relationship.

These neologisms found everywhere in action comics are points where the languages of interaction have broken down. The strange stuttering repetition of letters hides emotional crises even as it indicates their inaccessible presence. What remains hidden is the complexity and relational nature of these feelings. All that can emerge is the meaningless cry, pre-linguistic and therefore impossible to have a dialogue with. Sometimes, when the sound effects of men's conflicts are written as neologisms across the space of their battle, it is the material environment which seems to cry out, in an even more dislocated repression of utterance. Cries and blows are the repeated climaxes of these plots, points beyond which the masculine narrative cannot go.

Anecdotal observation suggests that boys commonly use sound effects in their games, especially when they are fantasizing battle. The sounds are fun, clearly a release of energy, and never discussed. They often begin as attempts to mimic guns, engines and crashes, and then go beyond this to pure sound poetry. I suspect they function similarly to the sound effects in comics, but I am not sure. Such sound play also seems to differentiate boys from girls.

In action comics for boys the characters the reader is invited to identify with are already adult men. Boys rarely appear. When they do appear the strip is usually 'comic' in the ordinary sense of the word. The action comics are aimed almost exclusively at males. Androgynous British comics like *Beano* and *Dandy* show adults outwitted by clever children who finally have to submit to adult control of the world and its laws. The big difference occurs in comics exclusively aimed at girls. These tend to show girls learning to live in a world controlled by powerful but understandable adults in which they are already beginning to participate. Where boys want to read about men, the publishers appear to believe that girls want to read about girls more than women (although there have been signs that this is changing with the appearance of comics like *She Hulk*). Girls are usually the heroines. We could infer from this that manhood is much more exclusive than womanhood. Perhaps women welcome girls into their world in a way that men don't welcome boys.

'Your Best Friend', a story in the British girls' comic *Nikki* (*Nikki* 1986), demonstrates how this works. Compared to almost anything in a boys' comic it is a complex narrative. It begins with two girls writing an agony aunt column for their school magazine in which they offer advice to a girl who has trouble looking after her two younger brothers while her mother is at work. One of these writers, Sally, has an older sister who is a teenage 'hooligan'. Most of the strip is taken up with the responsibilities of looking after children on behalf of parents. The tables are turned on Sally when her father insists that she needs a babysitter and makes her older sister do the babysitting. Sally's sister brings round her punk friends and they follow her school magazine advice and play at cooking with her. As the cake mix flies and the punks turn boisterous Sally shouts, 'Stop it, Alison! Stop it!' We leave Sally sitting alone, downcast, saying, 'Mum and Dad's evening will be ruined if they come home to this lot! I'll have to try to clear up. Life's just not fair! Other people can ask "Your Best Friend" [the agony aunt column] for advice, but there's no one who can help me!' The loneliness is seen to have causes and remedies, unlike the isolation of characters like Spider Man (whose alter ego Peter Parker is often alone) and Hulk, and derives from a reflection on the nature of authority. The givers of advice may themselves need it. There can be no absolute solutions to problems. This strip is more emphatic about a girl's responsibilities than some but it is only a matter of degree. We see Sally learning about child care, expecting to take care of the environment when other people have made a mess (Peter Parker appears to live in a permanent mess and rarely does anything about it), and learning to negotiate with adults. She is not excluded from the adult world depicted in the strip, but expected to have a (minor) place in it. Significantly it is her father who thinks she is still a child and resists letting her have more responsibility. Her mother already treats her like a little woman. As the story shows, that has its own burdens. There is conflict which cannot be easily resolved, certainly not by the kind of violent solutions which action comics propose. Conflict is contained in words, as it is in almost all girls' comics, where there is rarely anything more than a smack to contend with. The most violent moment in this story occurs when plates of food are thrown around the kitchen.

The *Nikki* story shows a girl learning a task that adult women carry out. It is educative about human relations, and surprisingly subtle about emotions like pride and arrogance. Sally is shown to have overvalued the power of her good advice. Such subtlety is nowhere to be seen in boys' comics. Men in comics are strong, and fight other men when they are angry. There is no place for boys who are less than men, and therefore no way to negotiate the transition into adult responses and their responsibilities. At the end of the *Nikki* story, our heroine Sally has to recognize the unfairness of the world she lives in. It will not always conform to her wishes and ideals. The story ends with a personal sense of injustice met with both irritation and intelligent acceptance. She will clear up and think of her parents' needs (even though her father neglected hers). In this resolution we can see the emergent shape of the self-denial feminists have exposed as the enforced character of a girl's development, as well as a lesson in the complexity of justice. Boys' comics hardly ever show such understanding of injustice or the necessity to recognize that others' legitimate needs may conflict with one's own; they simply show anger against such needs, leading to violence. Dan Dare hits Tremloc; he doesn't try and understand Tremloc's feelings or point of view. This example from girls' comics suggests that the possibilities for showing the process of learning to become an adult, a woman, are likely to be greater than in boys' comics, although one example is only enough to hint at this.

BATMAN'S WAY OF SOLVING CONFLICT

Many action comics make justice a central mechanism in the plot. Crimes are committed by others and it is the duty of the superhero to bring them to justice. Their ability to become superheroes actually depends on this prior transgression of the law. Their powers spring into life when the rule of law breaks down. Then the criminals can be hunted down and brought to book.

The story will end with the excitement of their capture, not their trial or punishment, because the law itself is never examined. Exciting fight scenes depend completely on the unexamined assumption that the injustice is external. Even when one of our superheroes does momentarily go off the rails it always turns out to be the result of mind control or some similar form of external cause. No growth in self-knowledge or acknowledgement of complicity in transgression is necessary to end it, only physical contention against its source. These superheroes can be said to gain their power from the law. The resultant equation of law and manhood means that the law is the sole reason for manhood, its only purpose. In itself it is nothing. There is no story in 'Dr Robert Bruce Banner, Thoroughly Obsessed with Himself' (*Hulk* 1981: 7). It takes the challenge of giants from another planet to rouse him from his introspection and become his Mr Hyde self, Hulk, before the narrative can really begin, and it never returns to the original troubling introspection. In the *Nikki* story justice emerges from within the thoughts and behaviour of the heroine and her immediate circle. In the superhero comics justice exists independently of the hero, although he draws the power of his manhood from it. One ideological consequence is that this law is much too readily identifiable with the actual laws of the United States (since most of these comics come from the US). In the 'Justice League of America' comics this becomes explicit. The superheroes are simply special federal agents operating from a base in science fiction.

Not all agents of the law are so pure. Batman's popularity must surely have been the result of his relative independence of the law as well as his absence of superpowers. Not that he is a criminal but he is not simply an agent of city hall. In many of the stories he is at odds with the official handling of an investigation, and in that way very like a private eye. Batman also seems to have attracted the most explicit attempts to dramatize relations with boys, men and women. Robin is not just a teenage clone like Superboy or Supergirl. The Joker, who loves to pursue and torment Batman, is so camp it is almost redundant to say that he represents a homophobic portrait of gay culture. And Batman does get romantically entangled with women, perhaps because he is, strictly speaking, mortal. He may seem to fly, but there is always a grappling hook and some very tough climbing rope to help him on his way. The sense of his limits gives the stories much of their suspense, as is particularly evident in a story like 'The Joker's Five-way Revenge' (*Batman* 1990). In this story Batman is engaged in a battle of wits with a criminal who, like Moriarty in the Sherlock Holmes stories, reappears regularly to test the hero to his limits, knowing all his weaknesses. The Joker has escaped from the state hospital for the insane and is killing one by one all of his former gang members, because one of them betrayed him. The Joker delights in murder, and we see him kill one former colleague, Alby, with an exploding cigar, laughing as the man dies, saying, 'Rest in pieces, Alby' (ibid.: 171). We know that the Joker is dangerous because he has green hair, a mauve suit and a green shirt. He even wears lipstick. The Joker's face is very expressive, he smiles, laughs and uses his high cheekbones and narrow chin to great effect. No hero would have a face like that. Batman has a mask over his eyes to conceal any telltale expressiveness as well as his identity. His face is square, granite-jawed, and only expressive of anger when he bares his teeth or parts his lips.

Heroic men's faces in the hypermasculine comics are either expressionless, smooth undefined areas, or the teeth are bared in anger, and the ends of the lips droopy with sadness. The face is an important way of revealing emotion. We have very sensitive responses to the minutest changes of facial gesture, although we do not ordinarily translate what we see into a consciousness of these coded signs of character. These men in comics are giving little away. When they do show an emotion it is usually one that depends on bared teeth or a downturned mouth. Happiness, when it does make its rare appearance, is merely hinted at by showing the mouth in a slightly upturned crescent without any other facial signs at all. Sadness and anger are the most common emotions by far. Consider the face of the law. Judge Dredd, shown in profile, wears a mask that obscures any trace of the expressive part of his upper face (2000AD 1986). The deeply shadowed furrows of his cheek and chin describe a series of downward arcs. His lips are pursed together and fall a long way down at the ends in the classic image of sadness. His chin has a wonderful forward thrust, solid and stubbled, which counters this old terrain of suffering. This map of repressed pain is the face he wears when confronting a murderer at the end of the story (called with typical irony, 'Sob Story'). Part of the narrative tension of the comics derives from the strain of concealing emotion according to the codes of manhood at times when the pressure to let it out is very great. Facial gestures are not something an individual graphic artist has much liberty to invent. For readers to understand the expression, the facial pattern must be fairly close to codes they can understand and which find support in their culture. The art work cannot always rely on the additional support of the words in the bubbles to give them a clear interpretation. These comic-book faces are the male faces of a code that boys learn to recognize and then expect to see and emulate in their own lives.

The Joker may wear a suit to go to work, but no respectable hero would wear anything so concealing. Batman wears a cape that falls almost to the ground, but, like a flasher, wears only trunks underneath. His large muscular body strains and stretches as he fights the villains. Comic men are tall and square-shouldered. Only the foolish or the bad have bodies which don't conform to this stereotype. Roundedness or fatness or any sign of effeminacy are all clear indications of weakness. A code as rigid as phrenology is at work. Much the commonest form of the heroic male figure depends on an almost erotic exaggeration of the male physique, especially in the superhero comics. Wearing clothes that reveal as much of their bodies as possible, these

31

muscular but sexless characters are displayed in every possible pose. The male body is on display (a display able to bypass the ego's censorship because, as one artist puts it, 'readers saw our pictures only out of the corners of their eyes' (Abbott 1986: 171) – a glance like that of the fetishist) and it is rippling with muscles apparently unconscious of their sexual potential.

These are the bodies of boyhood homoerotic desire. They have as much and as little sex as the boys who read them. They are ideal figures of what the male reader would like to be: strong, tall, handsome and awesomely powerful. Heavy shading on the drawings outlines their tense muscles. Many of them look like the men in photos of body builders. To achieve the muscle definition such photos require, the men in the pictures have to tense their muscles very hard. Hence the various odd poses taken up by body builders in competition. The muscle definition shown in the comics is the result not only of muscular power but also of tension. The high rounded calves, the long bulging thighs, the layers of finely detailed stomach muscle are the result of postures which embody extremes of tension. These are bodies ill at ease with themselves, either in the middle of some violent action or ready to perform one. Above all they are bodies to be looked at. A whole history could be written about the subtle changes in the idealization of the body. The earliest superhero comics show a Superman, for example, who is not especially impressive. Marvel went for much more muscular development until they reached an apogee of monstrous beefcake which the newer cartoonists, like those on *2000AD*, often seem to be caricaturing. Judge Dredd's epaulettes emphasize that his shoulder width owes more to tailoring than muscle.

The action-comic image of the male body is of one reduced to its basic motor functions. These bodies kick, punch, stretch, with the maximum use of the limbs and maximum occupancy of space (by contrast girls' comics allow a much greater range of human capacities to be made visible). The exaggerated emphasis on motor functions seems to lead naturally to superhuman attributes in many of the action-comic narratives. After reading a few of these comics you have to remind yourself that men can't fly, because such abilities are so commonly taken for granted. The artists fly with their heroes, surveying the world from the height of superior power and vision, yet the superheroes never fly just for pleasure, as the readers do. They are purposefully on their way to the scene of trouble, flying into action against the foe, and because they can fly they are freed from the ordinary bothersome constraints of travel and all the social obligations earthbound movement requires. Money, vehicles, timetables, tickets and inquisitive companions who don't understand why you are in your underwear can be avoided. Not surprisingly, when a story does explore the consequences of a superhero being brought to earth by a temporary cessation of superpowers yet still required to rush to the scene of the action, it is a woman, Supergirl, whom we see riding a bus across town (*Supergirl* 1973: 5). Thanks to the power to fly, the usual plot and its hero can concentrate on what really matters, the violent masculine action.

Batman has no superpowers but paradoxically he thereby becomes even more effectively the embodiment of complete manhood. In 'The Joker's Five-way Revenge' he wrestles a shark as well as several more human enemies. At first the Joker gets the better of him with a punch, and knocks him out with a well-aimed kick (the Joker would never be able to win with a manly punch). But then standing over him, the Joker relents, saying he wished to win after a 'cunning struggle', not as the result of 'mere luck' (*Batman* 1990: 175). He lets Batman go, later traps him in a tank with a shark, and then unluckily succumbs to a knockout punch from Batman after slipping on oily sand as he tries to make his getaway. For Batman, mere luck is good enough if he can get in his punch. The other common attribute of hypermasculinity is superhuman strength, a fantasy of masculine bodily omnipotence. Batman may not be a 'man of steel' like the invincible Superman, but he is still one of the best fighters around, as his first opponent in the story, a former pugilist, acknowledges: 'The manly art of pugilism lost a champ when ya put on your mask, fella!' (ibid.: 169). All disputes are settled by the matching of physical force, along with any amount of legitimate weaponry which can be counted as an extension of one's own personal power. To see how marked this is we need to stand back, as we did with the Dan Dare strip, and ask ourselves how this conflict could have been settled by some other means. Fortunately most disputes in our own lives are resolved by discussion and negotiation, not violence. In these comics, language is seemingly not available for conflict resolution; the best method is to smash your opponent. We might suspect therefore that the real motive for the violence is not the resolution of conflict at all, but the release of anger, because the fighting is apparently such a satisfactory means of emotional catharsis. The use of violence, especially by young males, would be a dangerous move in most real circumstances. According to Peter N. Stearns, American public perceptions of the acceptability of anger have changed over the past century and a half. From the late nineteenth century until the 1940s anger was recognized to have a limited place as a motive for political and commercial drive. But in the 1940s this waned, and advice for parents became less and less tolerant of male anger, especially male anger in the home. Similar changes occurred in the workplace (Stearns 1987: 87). Comics may have offered a fantasy fulfilment for the cathartic release of anger during such changes.

To make the fantasy work the hero with whom the reader can identify therefore needs the additional safeguard of superhuman strength in the face of such risks. Now we can really weigh in without hesitation and hit our enemy hard. For this reason the stories are usually coy about the degree of invulnerability of the superheroes. The heroes must have some vulnerability or there would be no satisfaction in the overcoming of danger because there would be no threat of hurt or death. Hence narrative moments of weakness abound (Superman is always bumping into Kryptonite) but our heroes rarely sustain a lasting injury from their fisticuffs.

Strength is crucial to the hero. Almost all the stories are tests of physical strength. Outwitting an opponent is fine as long as it is not a substitute for sheer physical power. The only options these comics recognize are physical attack and defence, a simplification which is part of that inarticulacy signalled by the neologistic cries. There is no language for such negotiations. The body has to carry all the force of expression, and is apparently only allowed to express anger. Yet these drawings of men flying into action in extremes of physical tension could represent men in extremes of physical passion. The male body is used as a signifier of states of emotion which cannot otherwise be articulated. Strong taboos against men showing certain kinds of affection for each other, and the widespread homophobia in our society, make the depiction of men as objects of desire nearly impossible. The comics show what is possible for men. These heroes can't keep their hands off one another, but when they touch their desire turns to blows.

The Batman/Joker stories come close to thematizing this homoeroticism. Batman is an isolated figure in the story. His isolation, his withdrawn demeanour, his identification with the law, and the importance of physical combat for him, are related to his attraction to and fear of other men. The Joker says, 'The caped crusader will locate me! He always does! However, I will be ready for him!' (*Batman* 1990: 170). He manages to make it sound like an obsession of Batman's. The Joker takes pleasure in violence, just like the heroes, but they always have to appear to be engaged in angry righteous execution of the law. He simply takes a sensual pleasure in violence, and always signs it with a play on words. He repeatedly emphasizes that he is mad, and happily so ('it's my most charming trait' (ibid.: 180)). The Joker has all the fun, all the jokes, because he has reneged on manhood, but manhood can't keep its hands off him. The Joker is a homophobic portrait of homosexuality as a feared part of the hero's personality. If beasts and robots are the images of internal and external control which need to be defeated, the Joker is an image of homoeroticism run wild. The Joker represents the fear that manhood will come to love what it ought to be doing solely to maintain the law, the killing of other men, and contains that fear by showing that loving men too much will kill them.

THE HULK

An apparent exception to the celebration of justice occurs in the *Hulk* series of comics. In most cases the superhero has an easy relation with his own superpowers. Difficulties only arise in ordinary life where his true identity must be kept secret, and he is not devoted solely to the pursuit of lawbreakers, human or alien. Violence and destruction are permissible during the active pursuit of justice because they are presented as necessary means for halting the violence already initiated by the men and monsters who have threatened the social order. The superhero takes pleasure in defeating the enemy, and therefore indirectly in the violence he uses, but that pleasure is not presented as a problem. The *Hulk* series makes the split between ordinary man (boy) and superhero (manhood) its central theme, showing that what this division symbolizes is not the easy partnership represented by such images as Clark Kent's telephone booth transformations. Bruce Banner could never just pop into a phone booth as if to get in touch with his super alter ego. Hulk would tear it apart. The Hulk stories suggest how close the heroes are to terrorists. The destruction of the urban environment which became popular in comics and then moved into the action movie (in *Terminator* for example) has more in common with terrorism and counter-terrorism than fisticuffs and one-to-one combat. But following that up would take us away from the case of the Hulk.

Hulk began in May 1962, the creation of the brilliant team of Stan Lee and Jack Kirby at Marvel (Maurice Horn (1982: 429) describes Kirby as the 'most accomplished of all comic book creators' and he is widely credited for having helped sustain the development of comic books for several decades). Like the Superman series, the Hulk stories centre on an endlessly repeated origin myth, but whereas the Superman story is one of separation from the father, the Hulk story derives from the threat of nuclear destruction. Every issue of *The Hulk* retells the story. Dr Bruce Banner was about to test a deadly new weapon, a 'gamma bomb', when a young man, Rick Jones, strayed into the test area at the crucial moment. Banner managed to save his friend by pushing him clear as the bomb exploded but he was heavily irradiated himself. Now he has not just an alter ego but an alter body, Hulk. When Banner is in danger his body spontaneously undergoes a mysterious transformation. A large green man tears his way out of Banner's sober clothing and goes on what Banner himself describes as 'mindless murderous rampages'. Hulk actually began grey, but between a very early issue in 1962 when he was greened, and a temporary reversion to grey in the late 1980s, Hulk was synonymous with greenness. The temporary colour change also signalled a change to a more intelligent Hulk, one capable of fairly sophisti-cated dialogue. My guess is that one reason for the attempted colour change was the political validation of green as a very positive colour. Once super-markets began selling green products, another colour might have seemed needed to signify elemental fury and opposition to human culture, but readers didn't think so and green returned. Unlike Bruce Banner, who represents the good sense of masculine reason, the *Hulk* comics are ambiva-lent about the rampages, and both condemn and condone this violence. One part of the series ('another untold episode of those early days when the Rampaging Hulk first made his gamma-powered presence known to a fearful and awestruck world' (*Hulk* 1978), even appeared in what was called *Rampage Monthly* as if in celebration of Hulk's behaviour.

Hulk's massive green body is that of a muscular green giant, an idiot, wild descendant of the virile, moral spirit of the landscape who tested Sir Gawain's knighthood in the medieval poem, *Gawain and the Green Knight*. For most of the series Hulk is childlike and simple-minded. All he understands is pain, his own or someone else's. Otherwise in his own words, 'Hulk wants to be alone' (*Hulk* 1978: 29) (he often refers to himself in the third person as if he had little self-awareness). Hulk is a body whose drives are all rages. Hulk fights and fights, saying 'anyone . . . anything . . . can be smashed' (ibid.: 28). Bruce Banner by contrast is an uncertain, gentle, bespectacled scientist. This division between the two sides of this male persona is frequently explained in the stories as a mind/body split.

The origin myth suggests a different meaning. Perhaps the division is integral not to a Cartesian subject but to a masculine subject. Hulk is the result of an accidental nuclear irradiation in the process of weapons testing. Nuclear threat is both embodied and contained (but only just) by Hulk. If he had not split into two personae Banner would presumably have died from the radiation. All the irrational fear, hatred and anger symbolized by the explosion of nuclear weapons is made visible as the image of an uncontrollable raging male. His greenness is an allusion to the force of nature, and also to the deadliness of perverted murderous science which turns the flesh a deathly green. This origin myth begins with the dilemma posed by nuclear weapons. They are the ultimate embodiment of the forces of justice and law, but their power, uncontrollability and excessive destructiveness hint at forces out of control in men's psyches as well as in nature. Has men's law produced a rampaging mutant?

Hulk is as strongly contrasted with his host body as could be. Other superheroes sometimes express a little concern about the relationship between the demands of their ordinary life (if they can manage to have one) and their omnipotent persona, but Hulk presents a big problem. He is too large, and lacks the taut graceful lines of other heroes. You could never bring him home to dinner. He is green. Worst of all in this world of exacting codes of justice and style, he doesn't comb his hair and wears unfashionably torn trousers. But perhaps we ought to think of Hulk as the host body (there is certainly more of him). Is Bruce Banner really the problem, and does Hulk find himself embarrassed by this paragon of reason, science and restraint? What does this division signify?

In one story Banner is about to marry (*Hulk* 1986). Each page splits the storyline between the wedding preparations and a parallel but not obviously related plotline, in which Hulk (who has an autonomous but connected existence at this point in their history) fights for his life against 'Hulk hunters'. Meanwhile Banner, his friend Rick Jones, and the bride-to-be, discuss the disappearance of her father. The contrast between the violence and apparent harmony of the two plotlines is made more evident in the strong contrast between the maleness of the two alter egos. Banner's border-line masculinity is signalled by his prominent glasses, toothless mouth (Hulk bares his teeth at every opportunity) and short chin. As we read the story of Banner's wedding (there is not much story to Hulk's fight), the two sets of plotlines seem to have nothing in common, but their juxtaposition (like an Eisenstein montage) offers an implicit comment on both. The passionate violence of the green man becomes what cannot be spoken by the mild, friendly men in the other strip. Something is being left out of the emotional life of the husband-to-be. And something is left out of Hulk's story. Yet none of this is made explicit in the two narratives.

Such splitting is a common device in the comic books. The ordinary guy/superhero split is fundamental to many of them even before other less conscious narrative fissions take place. Alan Moore's virtuoso Superman story 'For the Man Who Has Everything' (1985), reprinted in the DC Comics anthology of best Superman stories (*Superman* 1987), also uses it. Superman has been attacked by a strange plant-like creature which attaches itself to his chest and induces paralysis and a hallucination of what the monster, Mongul, who has used it as a weapon, calls the victim's 'heart's desire' (ibid.: 282). Moore's Superman is shown dreaming of a planet Krypton that never blew up, a Krypton undergoing a slow breakdown of social order. Meanwhile the monster from outer space responsible for the attack on Superman is personally fighting Superman's friends, Batman, Robin and Wonder Woman, one by one. Mongul is shown engaged in violent combat, breaking up the floors and walls, hurtling back and forth as the battle rages. Batman frees Superman from the creature that induces hallucinations, only to fall prey to it himself. Superman meanwhile ignores Batman and concentrates on the real action, replacing Wonder Woman at the front, and carrying on the fight against Mongul. Finally Mongul is over-come, the dream-inducing creature is attached to him and he safely dreams the total destruction of the entire universe. The cleverness of the Alan Moore story lies in its projection of the internal structures of fantasy, and its suggestion that figures like Superman must be fundamentally unhappy to live as they do. The splitting of the narrative between battle with a monster and super-civilized life on Krypton can be read as a symbolic projection of the emotion generated by the dream, especially the father-son relations. In the dream world, Superman has a son, with whom he drives across the city, after a visit to his own father. The affection (and mild conflicts) between father and son are then projected into large-scale violent clashes between superheroes and Mongul. Splitting is repression, a moment when part of the psychic process goes underground and refuses consciousness. It is a counter-part to the neologistic cries which lie like buoys on the surface of what cannot be articulated and made visible between men.

The *Hulk* story about Banner's marriage is unusual for the degree of warmth that the two men show each other. In one frame Banner holds Rick at arm's length, hands on his shoulders, and they greet each other by looking affectionately into one another's eyes (*Hulk* 1986: 2). The next frame is double-size and shows a monstrously enraged Hulk, whose green body has been turned momentarily sallow by the glare of an explosion meant to kill him, roaring 'Rr-ahrr!' out of an irregular set of bared canines (this display of bad dental work reminds us how little care the excessively physical male takes of his physical needs). Banner's open affection for a man nearly destroys the Hulk. Such affection demands a high counterbalance of anger and fear. This schizophrenic narrative never addresses these emotional relations, but the ending, in which the friend is shot by the bride's father, indicates how dangerous it is for men to allow themselves to express love and friendship. The story shows us all the parts of the dilemma but offers no resolution to them. The best it can do is show us the whole picture, both sides of manhood, Hulk and Banner.

In the 1970s, comic-book heroes began to be much more reflective, in a style especially associated with the 'Amazing Spider Man' series, and its alter ego, Peter Parker. A series like 'Amazing Spider Man' or Hulk or Superman is drawn and written by many different artists and writers over the years, artists and writers who have a similar, possibly greater, freedom to that of the soap-opera script writer. There is a formula, a set of precedents and a history with which to maintain continuity, but the audience is tolerant and forgetful (*2000AD* in its monthly form recycles the weekly stories of about five years earlier, apparently assuming that there is a new set of readers ready for them), so innovation and transformation are always possible. Comic-book art is a reflexive, incremental form. Later stories can presuppose not only earlier stories but even earlier interpretations. The Peter David/Todd Macfarlane series of Hulk comics which appeared in the late 1980s made some of the issues I have discussed quite explicit. In one of their stories, Betty, who is pregnant, insists on staying with Bruce Banner until nightfall when he becomes the Hulk (*Hulk* 1988). Hulk and Betty have a long confrontation on a bleak snowy mountain peak, in which she insists, to Hulk's fury, that he and Banner are part of each other. 'I'm *not* Banner . . . never *was*, never *will* be' (ibid.: 27), shouts Hulk. But Betty fights back: 'You're *not* just anger and rage! You have Bruce's real *love* and *passion* locked in you too!' (ibid.: 29). Earlier she had described Bruce Banner as 'a man who considers emotions so *horrible* that he can only show them if it's through somebody . . . or something . . . else' (ellipses in original) (ibid.: 14). This exchange comes close to making explicit the very dynamic of the strip in such a way that its fantasy symbols might become redundant. A letter in the same issue goes even further:

We've already established, since issue no.312, for that matter, that Bruce Banner was a very emotionally disturbed child, and repressed all emotion. The Hulk, therefore, is a creature of emotion. We can go a step further and say this – the Hulk, because he is an alter-ego of Banner, can get away with nasty things that Banner cannot. The Hulk and Banner, then, are two separate people – they are the same person, but one acts out the will of the other. Hulk is the id, and Banner is the super-ego.

(ibid.: 31)

These developments show how close to allegory this work can get. The comic book can sustain a considerable weight of self-interpretation. What the letter does, however, is to equate emotion with anger, and use the misleading parallel of the late Freudian model with a set-up in which the Hulk/Banner division depends on a lack of consciousness on both sides. As Banner puts it to Betty:

'It's not that I'm *afraid* to show emotions, Betty, just what can happen . . . if they get out of *control*. Don't you *understand?* For me, getting upset or angry has always gone hand-in-hand with violence. . . . First with my *father*, and then with the *Hulk*.'

(ibid.: 14)

The clever panel art shows Banner's face cut off below the nose and above the eyes, hidden behind the reflective faces of his glasses. All we can see are those large sightless lenses where his eyes should be. The inward gaze turns all emotion backwards, because all it can see is anger and rage.

The Hulk comics show that the relations between the two forms of masculinity, boy and man, or wish and ideal, are not so easily justified as other narrative paradigms (Superman for example) tended to assume. Masculinity may not be justifiable, may even be redundant or, worse, destructive. A noticeable feature of Hulk's story is how little he wants – it is others who want things of him (as Hulk Hunters, lovers of Bruce Banner or tyrants who want to use his power for their own ends) and precipitate the plots. Hulk embodies an alarming if appealing redundancy in his very persona.

FROM BOYS TO MEN

It is men who write and draw these comics (recently a few women artists have begun to emerge – their presence is sure to make a difference). These are men's images, ideas and fantasies which are offered to boys, but they cannot be understood simply as the ideology of manhood imposed on young readers, as if this were a one-way process. The 'commercial production of symbolic violence' (Connell 1989: 198) is a negotiation between men and boys, which, however, is almost entirely absent from the storylines. One comic-book artist, Steve Englehart, comments in an interview:

If I had to put a label on it, which I never really did when I was doing

39

it, I think most of the readership of comics is young boys who are
having to come to terms with growing into manhood.

(Lanyi 1984: 143)

To the interviewer's interesting comment that perhaps 'it's a lack of father-
ing in the national soul that might be responsible for the invention of comics
here and our continued world leadership in their production' (ibid.: 144),
the artist seems to have no reply. His earlier disclaimer, 'I just write fantasy'
(ibid.: 142), is all he can say.

The stories are about being, not becoming, a man. Superheroes may lead
ordinary lives in disguise, but they can be transformed in a moment from boy
to man, from failed man to real man. Peter Parker may be modest, self-effacing
and easily dominated by his aunt, but the moment justice is threatened he can
become a real man of power, Spiderman. There is no long, arduous process of
learning the emotional, moral and intellectual requirements for manhood.
That is the beauty of it: power is all you need. These action-comic stories are
about the excitements of hypermasculinity, but they are substitutes for an
apprenticeship to manhood. For boys, Superman and Spiderman are as much
fantasy figures as they are for the men who produce them on behalf of men's
culture, but these fantasies are not given the same role in the psychic economy
of each side of the divide between men and boys. For a boy, the image of
Superman is an image of what he dreams of becoming. The necessity of that
dream lies in his present boyhood, but he dreams it as a possibility. It
represents an actual future for him. This is why so many of the superhero
comics overlay future and present (and sometimes past) in a bewildering
fashion. Technologies from the future are shown as if they already existed.
They signify the future projected for the child reading the comic, and the
imperialist success of the contemporary masculine order at maintaining itself.
For men this fantasy is a sign of failure. They have failed to become supermen,
and the fantasy is therefore an imaginary resolution of the difficulties their
failure to achieve this power of manhood appears to demand. Men are offering
an image of power which conceals a loss, to boys who are encouraged to
believe that this image of manhood is not just a fantasy; it is a symbol of their
destiny, thus ensuring the continuing reproduction of that failure. The more
powerful the muscles of the soaring hero, the greater the symbolic loss.

Yet these soaring fantasy compensations for the failure to achieve the ideal
of manhood are what redeem these comics. The celebration of manhood in
erotic physical display makes these comics one of the special areas of boys'
culture. Where else can they see their desires so openly revealed, and the
wonders of sheer physical maleness celebrated so fully? There is another plot
at work too. Those desires show up as homoerotic celebration of men's
power simply as men. That is why the muscles are much more important
than reason. The desire evoked by these comic pinups has to be paid for with
violent blows and the fiction of justice. Each blow is a caress. The anger at

themselves that such erotic excitement provokes then flies from scene to scene always ready for the next confrontation, in the confident knowledge that there will always be more enemy males longing to provide tests of manhood. Manhood will never become redundant. This is borne out by comments by the artists. Jack Kirby describes comic-book heroism in very positive terms: 'male heroism, to my mind, is the prelude to romantic love' (Lanyi 1983: 28). Frank Miller is even more emphatic:

> As a reader, I *love* to fall in love with characters, to get to know them, to see what they go through. I love to see heroics. And I love to see extravagant, wonderful things done by characters that are fascinating. I'm not at all attracted to doing comics with a specific intent to persuade people on political issues. Emotion is what I write about. I'm not trying to tell people how to vote or how to live.
>
> (1990: 31)

Jack Kirby's defence of comics – against the charge that they 'maim young sensibilities' by replacing attentiveness to quieter inner thought with head-long inner excitement – is to say that 'we're creatures of emotion' (Lanyi 1983: 28). These two artists, who between them are responsible for much of the look and feel of modern comics, testify to the importance of identification and emotion in the comic book. Falling in love with the superheroes is both a form of extreme identification and homoerotic fantasy. To say that 'we are creatures of emotion' is to say that men are dominated by emotion, made beasts by it. Only heroism can redeem such emotional thraldom.

Boys of course read comics for many reasons. I have emphasized two, both based on a lack. One is a desire to be powerful enough to act out one's anger and satisfy it. The other is a wish to know about the man's world. Many social critics have pointed out the absence of men in the lives of children but the full force of that absence on boys' conceptualization of their relation to men is not always recognized. Men's absence at work (or the substitutes which even the most unemployed men usually find) means that the defining activities of manhood are largely invisible, even as the scope and power of this masculine world are everywhere evident. The material world of man-made things is evidence enough. Meanwhile the small space of domestic life is the scene for at least some of a woman's defining activities as the culture represents them. Whatever her other work outside the home, her domestic work is seen by children as a central part of her adulthood because our societies assume that too. That is not so for men. Their defining activities take place elsewhere. Yet this elsewhere is vast and pervasive. Technology, factories, traffic, offices, all the apparatus of the human universe, seem to testify to the power of this world from which boys are excluded by their own sex, the same sex that is supposed to have created it. Men's work is a mystery, and mysteries create awe and longing (as many religious leaders have known). Comics are part of a culture which aims to satisfy that longing by translating manhood's awe-inspiring processes into images a boy can understand, images of hand-to-hand combat, guns, machines and the capture of criminals.

Men don't want boys in their world, so they give them a surrogate one because their admission into the world of manhood would force unacceptable changes. Men would have to care for the boys and this would mean sharing power with women and children, and transforming those laws which call comic manhood into being. For men, manhood must remain a separated condition, not one of emergence and dependency. Boys can be given by comics and other forms of this culture (such as television and cinema) fantasies of what manhood most desires: unlimited strength, unrestricted movement and unbounded space. Men exclude boys from their world, but give them comic-book adventure fantasies in which they are allowed to identify with manhood's adventures in return for something. What is it that boys have to trade with in this settlement? Their money certainly, and the child market is profitable, but something else is involved too. Boys trade their belief. In return for admission to the picture palace of men's exploits, they provide the credence which makes it possible. For this is the inner secret of manhood's relation to boyhood. This masculinity of pure motor drives fuelled by anger is sustained by the longing felt by boys excluded from acceptance as proper males by their elders. Manhood is a long-running fiction which men construct out of boyhood's worship generated by boyhood's exclusion – of idealized masculinities – just as the old gods needed worshippers to offer up their faith. But there never was such a manhood to be excluded from. What boys were excluded from was the loving care of adult males. Boys wanted it and needed to be reminded that real men hit one another. Every caress should be a blow. If such real men are a hit with boys it is because of the complex negotiation that goes on between boys and men over the fantasies of manhood.

The comic-book fantasies of masculinity are a symptom of the social structures of desire and emotion produced by the general absence of continuity between men and children. For boys this means not so much an absence of initiation rituals as an absence of everyday involvement largely formalized in the separation of work and the domestic sphere, and the sanctioned absence of men from most of the extended responsibilities of all care of children from infants to teenagers. Individual men resist these pressures but the separation of spheres continues. The action comics train boys in a code of manhood that is, however unfortunately, a necessary part of the social order as far as most men are concerned, and at times that even makes visible to boys some of its more obvious contradictions. Nevertheless, action comics for boys are certainly damaging because they offer false solutions to the difficulties of growing up which both sexes face. There are better ways to negotiate relations with other men than annihilating them and hoping that one's own invulnerability will triumph.

3

THE MARTIAN LANDSCAPES OF MODERNISM: JOYCE, YEATS, LAWRENCE

MEN'S LITERARY MODERNISM

Superman doesn't spend his spare time reading comics. Scientific research, painting and writing a diary keep him busy. Anyway he doesn't need to read comic books about the heroism of real men because he already lives there. In the 'Super Key to Fort Superman' we don't actually see him reading, probably because the contrast with the comic-book reader's choice of reading matter would suddenly become too evident. The nearest we get to literature is Superman's writing and painting. Superman paints like a surrealist (perhaps the Max Ernst of *Europe after the Rain*) but he is actually a realist: 'This isn't the result of my imagination – it's a realistic picture of a Martian landscape, as observed by my telescopic vision' (*Superman* 1987: 106). The Martian landscape represents Superman's origins from beyond ordinary reality, his superreality. We might hear an echo of sentiments widely held amongst modernists and wittily summed up by Paul Klee: 'Formerly we used to represent things visible on earth, things we either liked to look at or would have liked to see' (Bradbury and McFarlane 1976: 48). Superman can see places where ordinary human beings may go in the future. Indeed he embodies the gaze to the future so characteristic of the popular literature of the 1950s: science fiction. We must not forget, however, that the Martian landscape is a fantasy, and by showing this real man at work on it, and claiming that it is not the product of a feverish inner gaze, the story validates the reader's credence in the *Superman* narrative. The painting is both fantasy and reality, just like the comic book itself. What a relief Superman comically offers to all those readers who were afraid that modern art was reality 'as observed by' the inward gaze of the modern artist. Alien modernist works (James Joyce's later novels or Max Ernst's surrealist paintings) were not after all a turning away from men's commonsense visible reality to reflexive preoccupations with visual and verbal languages. The artists were depicting landscapes they could see with their equivalent of telescopic vision.

When Superman returns to the fortress after a short absence he is shocked to find that someone has completed his Martian painting: 'it's *not* a Martian landscape! I've never seen anything like that in all my travels through the solar system! It's weird – utterly weird' (*Superman* 1987: 109). Superman's landscape had green hands and forearms reaching out of the ground into the Martian atmosphere. Now there are also strange crystalline shapes in the sky and a spiky, improbably balanced crystalline tower on the ground. This unwitting artistic collaboration seems weird to Superman because another man has had a hand in it. Superman's hands wave from the ground as if signalling that a green man, another Hulk perhaps, is buried there. Batman's figures are angular, inhuman, soaring images. To Superman they are incomprehensible. He cannot recognize a cultural reality constructed by male co-operation. Now the Martian landscape really is Martian to him, yet its weirdness is the product of an uncomprehended cultural relation between men. Men's modernist culture is one means of sustaining modern masculinities. Its insistent strangeness, its fragmentation and alienation are in part the sign of unadmitted relations between men, relations which still have to be buried like the green man, or hidden like Batman in the shadows.

One modernist poet used his telescopic vision (and his wife's automatic writing) to compose a historical typology of man's character based on the 'circuits of sun and moon' (Yeats 1978). In answer to the question whether he actually believes in their existence, W.B. Yeats says:

> To such a question I can but answer that if sometimes overwhelmed by miracle as all men must be when in the midst of it, I have taken such periods literally, my reason has soon recovered; and now that the system stands out clearly in my imagination I regard them as stylistic arrangements of experience comparable to the cubes in the drawing of Wyndham Lewis and to the ovoids in the sculpture of Brancusi. They have helped me to hold in a single thought reality and justice.
>
> (ibid.: 25)

Sometimes he believes, like Superman, in the literal existence of these extraterrestrial landscapes, but in more rational moods he sees them as strategies for reintegrating the seemingly autonomous spheres of knowledge and morality (Superman is supposed to unite the three spheres of modernity in his own person; he stands for 'truth, justice and the American way' (Lang and Trimble 1990: 160)). The lunar, or Martian, quality of the work derives from its attempt to overcome the schizophrenia of modern subjectivity.

T.S. Eliot's waste landscapes have a distinctly Martian quality, filled with broken columns and stones. They are a 'broken jaw of our lost kingdoms' (Eliot 1963: 91). The strong chin of manhood is broken. The hollow men, like effigies of Guy Fawkes waiting to be immolated, have no eyes, no substance, and cannot even die. They have lost all power to gaze with the 'direct eyes' of those who have gone to 'death's other kingdom' (ibid.: 89). If they had eyes they would probably see towers 'upside down in air' (ibid.: 78) and other incomprehensibly Martian figures because Eliot insistently uses distorted, grotesque landscapes to represent distorted subjectivities, remaining in this a late Romantic.

If some modernist landscapes look Martian they do so more because of a projected decline of the West than an optimistic anticipation of future travel to other planets. The opportunities to gaze out over vast stretches of human history seemingly made possible by modern historical scholarship, and memorialized in works like those of Frazer, Toynbee and Spengler, brought with them a disturbing sense of loss. Hugh Kenner, celebrating the 'Pound Era' in terms similar to many apologists for modernism, claims that this gaze is its great achievement:

> Nothing we know the mind to have known has ever left us. Quickened by hints, the mind can know it again, and make it new. Romantic Time no longer thickens our sight, time receding, bearing visions away. Our books of cave paintings are the emblems of its abolition, perhaps the Pound Era's chief theme, and the literary consolidation of that theme stands as the era's achievement. Translation, for instance, after Ezra Pound, aims neither at dim ritual nor at lexicographic lockstep, but at seeming transparency, the vigors of the great original – Homer, Kung – not remote but at touching distance, though only to be touched with the help of all that we know.
>
> (1972: 554)

Crediting Pound (even if only as the signature of an era) with the idea that the deep structures of the mind remain constant over millennia and enable us to recapitulate the past, an idea widespread in anthropology and psycho-analysis, is a little excessive, but this humanistic appraisal is a good summary of modernist men's ambitions to gaze at all of human life from the summit of modernity. A sense of belatedness in the face of those old vigours under-mines the towering confidence embodied in such works as Ezra Pound's *The Cantos*. The result may be, as Maud Ellmann argues, a failure of the gaze:

> Pound himself has argued that one of the 'great maladies of modern criticism is that first rush to look for the person, and the corresponding failure EVER to look at the thing' (*ABC of Reading* 147). However, he has made his person so objectionable that his readers gladly turn their gazes to the thing.
>
> Yet no gaze could even quite take in *The Cantos*.
>
> (1987: 137)

These Martian landscapes are Art with a capital A. To render them requires an artist, as does the unifying of reality and justice, or the representation of the vigours of the past. Joyce's *A Portrait of the Artist as a Young Man*, which I shall discuss in the next section, depends on this high valuation of art for its resonance. Replace artist with businessman and one would suspect satire rather than gentle irony. Joyce is unable simply to accept that art is

45

synonymous with an achieved form of manhood, however. His portraits of Bloom and Stephen in *Ulysses* make a clear distinction between their different valuations of art: 'Were their views on some points divergent? Stephen dissented openly from Bloom's views on the importance of dietary and civic self-help while Bloom dissented tacitly from Stephen's views on the eternal affirmation of the spirit of man in literature.' (Joyce 1971: 587).

Reading this exchange in a feminist era we cannot help hearing the word 'man' in a limited sense to mean 'men', and therefore reading this as a criticism of Stephen's aesthetic universalizing of masculinity. Neither Bloom's political conservatism (the enterprise culture), nor Stephen's aestheticism, comes off well in this question-and-answer style, which by its very form assumes that questions have adequate answers, and that this is one of them.

The Martian landscapes are a figure of the strangeness of formal experiment in men's modernist writing, writing which claims to represent new worlds, but actually represents an uneasy subjectivity. Impersonality was one mask given to that unease by writers like Eliot and Pound, and in Maud Ellmann's words, 'impersonality was born conservative', masking a subjectivity with 'a passion for its own extinction' (1987: 198). Those extinctions can be traced in much high modernist writing, and I have chosen works by Joyce, Yeats and Lawrence in which the torments of self-consciousness are particularly evident, in order to trace the roots of this process further.

In the winters of the years 1913 to 1915 Ezra Pound worked for W.B. Yeats as a secretary and one of his tasks was to read to the master vigorous manly poetry like Morris's sagas and Browning's *Sordello* (Richard Ellmann 1949: 215). Pound later tried to begin his *Cantos* with Sordello, talking of Browning's desire:

> To set out so much thought, so much emotion;
> To paint, more real than any dead Sordello,
> The half or third of your intensest life
> And call that third *Sordello*.
>
> (Bush 1976: 54)

Pound imagines that Browning's reason for seizing on this historical figure is to fill it with the writer's own subjectivity, his own thought and emotion. The heroic, historical figure legitimates the artistic realization of subjectivity. Browning's representation of self-consciousness is in practice different from Pound's as a comparison of a passage from 'Bishop Blougram's Apology' (lines 764–9) with one from *Homage to Sextus Propertius* will show:

> Of course you are remarking all this time
> How narrowly and grossly I view life,
> Respect the creature-comforts, care to rule

The masses, and regard complacently
'The cabin', in our old phrase. Well, I do.
I act for, talk for, live for this world now
As this world prizes action, life and talk.

(Browning 1981: 636)

Persuasive as he is, Browning's Bishop is only an 'I' that acts as if it not only
lived for the world but were the world. Fully achieved, fully in possession of
its reason, the I can only demonstrate itself, at length. Ezra Pound's Sextus
Propertius might sound similarly self-achieved when he says to his friend
Lygdamus, 'I am swelled up with inane pleasurabilities and deceived by your
reference/ To things which you think I would like to believe' (Pound 1977:
84), but the comic image of self-inflation, and the hostility to state militarism, suggest some resistance to the extremes of self-aggrandizement which
sovereignty signifies: 'Thus much the fates have allotted me, and if,
Maecenas,/ I were able to lead heroes into armour, I would not,/ . . . I
should remember Caesar's affairs . . . for a background' (ibid.: 86). (The
irony of this rejection of fascist glory coming from the poet who lamented
the loss of Mussolini as 'the enormous tragedy of the dream in the peasant's
bent shoulders' (Pound 1975: 425) is palpable. It was in the 'Caesarial *ore
rotundos*' (ibid.: 87) rather than the genius 'no more than a girl' (ibid.: 86)
that Pound eventually found poetic authority.) Browning's poem assumes a
rational self all too resolvable into the material setting of the bishopric.
Pound's poem uses anachronisms and translator's puns to indicate the
degree of mimicry which results when the lyric self pretends to be
Propertius, and to demonstrate its self through the poetic props of the
Roman Empire. Despite the unease the mimicry induces in the sovereign
self, his poem signifies the power of the modern self to understand all past
epochs enough to make them speak, and speak in a language of the present
self, a self embodying an unquestionable, fully achieved, rational awareness,
fully aware of its lapses from control. Perhaps ruling the masses of the past
leads to a fascination with present-day autocracy.

Other male contemporaries of Pound decided to use the less exalted
authority of their own masculine positions, such as they were, to endorse
their circlings out from the first person. The New Jersey doctor would
surely be able to use an unadorned first person, even if he had to do it in the
privacy of his own room at dawn, and strip off all the clothes of personae in
his 'Danse Russe':

If I when my wife is sleeping
and the baby and Kathleen
are sleeping
and the sun is a flame-white disc
in silken mists
above shining trees, –

47

if I in my north room
dance naked, grotesquely . . .
Who shall say I am not
the happy genius of my household?

(Williams 1986: 86)

He is his own genius. In the naked dance the basic physical self revels
narcissistically in its existence apart from all ties. The male narcissism of
men's self-consciousness is literalized and in the process its dependence on
others (his wife and daughter are only asleep after all), and its limitations
(represented by the inherently playful comedy of this no doubt clumsy
naked revel in front of the mirror), made plain. The final rhetorical question
actually begs the question. There is no one to challenge this male arrogance
at the moment because everyone is asleep, but once the world is awake such
boasts will look hollow. Williams's poem shows how preoccupied modernist writers were with the question of the authority of their subjectivity, and
also reminds us how rare were such attempts at questioning its masculine
arrogance.

Williams's poem is itself limited by its presentation of subjectivity as fully
achieved. He uses the 'I' to found statements of what is already known,
already realized, but at least it is not to be read back as the explicable
'remarking' (to echo Blougram again) of a view of such a life. For modernist
men writers the presentation of self-consciousness was a primary and per-
plexing concern. Nothing so readily differentiates the women modernists
like Dorothy Richardson and Virginia Woolf from the men as this issue. The
women writers are much more flexible in their representation of self-
consciousness. For the men there is a kind of all or nothing quality to it,
either complete rational clarity or dark unconscious groping. The constantly
negotiated emergence of self-awareness in relationships, so subtly done in
Pilgrimage or *To the Lighthouse*, is hardly to be seen in the men writers. In
Ulysses Joyce has many devices for showing self-consciousness but they all
assume self-clarity.

In his earlier story 'The Dead' Joyce represents Gabriel Conroy's self-
consciousness about his wife's lost love like this:

> He had never felt like that himself towards any woman, but he knew
> that such a feeling must be love. The tears gathered more thickly in his
> eyes and in the partial darkness he imagined he saw the form of a
> young man standing under a dripping tree.

(Joyce 1988: 255)

The narrative seemingly cannot help being definite about Gabriel's self-
knowledge: 'he had *never* felt like that', 'he *knew* that'. Even if there were
qualifiers like 'possibly' or 'perhaps' the result would still be a framed
certainty. The partial darkness in which Gabriel imagines the young man

may symbolize the shadowiness of his thoughts but they remain distinctly represented to his consciousness by the form of the narrative. In *Ulysses* things seem to be different. The diversity of narrative forms separates out the subject and the style with the result that, as Franco Moretti puts it, the different styles are not directly motivated by the individual characters:

> The idea of an arbitrary literary style – that would dominate and determine its subject, and would not be simply its transparent and 'sensitive' representation – already belonged to the 'decadent' reaction to Hegelian aesthetics. . . . The various styles – and the ideological forms they embody – are all perfectly equivalent; all equally arbitrary, all equally incapable of imposing themselves. All therefore, are equally *irrelevant* as interpretations of reality or formalizations of literary language.
>
> (Moretti 1983: 206)

However, despite Moretti's claim that the result is a total separation, the mode of representing self-consciousness remains firmly based on self-reflection. The styles vary but the mode of self-reflection stays the same, each time presupposing a clear, rational ego to interpret the image produced by the particular discourse or style. This use of a discourse to reflect an already autonomous rational self to itself is evident in the following passage from *Ulysses*. The extract begins with phrases going through Stephen's mind, and comes from the Scylla and Charybdis section:

> And you who wrest old images from the burial earth! The brainsick words of sophists: Antisthenes. A lore of drugs. Orient and immortal wheat standing from everlasting to everlasting.
>
> Two old women fresh from their whiff of the briny trudged through Irishtown along London bridge road, one with a sanded umbrella, one with a midwife's bag in which eleven cockles rolled.
>
> The whirr of flapping leathern bands and hum of dynamoes from the powerhouse urged Stephen to be on. Beingless beings. Stop! Throb always without you and the throb always within. Your heart you sing of. I between them. Where? Between two roaring worlds where they swirl, I. Shatter them, one and both. But stun myself too in the blow.
>
> (Joyce 1971: 241)

The 'I' is trapped between the inner and outer worlds but separate from them, however much it is forced to use their words and rhythms to picture itself. Becoming fully itself would mean standing entirely clear of this 'swirl', yet the self fears that if it tries to punch a way out it will injure itself. The sense of the outer world providing words and images for the inward gaze is unusually explicit, but the mode is typical of the novel. Whatever the style of the second-hand words that flow through the consciousnesses of Stephen or Bloom, the inner self is always represented as speaking to itself, and listening to itself doing so at the same time. For this to be possible requires the same achieved self-definition evident in the passage from 'The Dead'. The self that hears the speech must be already self-aware or self-conscious. Moretti's diversity of styles has the effect not so much of putting the subject into question (as Colin MacCabe and others have argued) as representing a search for adequate representation of self-consciousness. *Ulysses* does not ask whether such self-consciousness might not be fully in the light. Yet the insistence on the proliferation of styles has the effect of disturbing the kind of masculine complacency exemplified by Gabriel Conroy's absolute conviction that he knows how his wife thinks and feels. In this way Joyce is ahead of humanist critics like the recent one who said that Eliot's first book of poems is more human than his later, more ambitious works, because 'empathy is balanced by judgement, solidarity by reserve' (Long 1988: 101). Joyce recognizes that modern masculine empathy has vicissitudes that are neither balanced nor solid.

The status of modernist writing depends on a widespread claim about its exposure of the linguistic formation of the subject. Julia Kristeva offers an interestingly extended version of this claim in an interview where she makes room for the body in addition to subjectivity: 'symbolic production's [e.g. modern art's] power to constitute *soma* and to give an identity is completely visible in modern texts' (cited in Lechte 1990: 25). The vicissitudes of soma, emotion, empathy and subjectivity are closely interrelated in modernist texts, but Kristeva's claim is a characteristically postmodern one: writing produces subjectivity. She goes further, however, by insisting not just on subjectivity, but on soma as well. When claims about the reflexivity of modern writing are made as strongly as this they can curiously reinforce older, pre-structuralist literary critical positions. Humanist criticism based on the work of Eliot, F.R. Leavis and the New Critics also argued that writing produced soma, although their soma had other names. One central tenet of New Critical humanism formed itself around a seemingly stray remark about emotion in T.S. Eliot's essay 'Hamlet'. In this tortuous discussion about 'some stuff that the writer could not drag to light' (where the generic word 'writer' instead of Shakespeare underlines how much Eliot wants to generalize the instance), Eliot said that emotion could only be adequately expressed in art through an 'objective correlative' (1975: 48), an object which would symbolize an emotion for both writer and reader. The problem with Shakespeare's play is that 'Hamlet (the man) is dominated by an emotion which is inexpressible, because it is in *excess* of the facts as they appear' (ibid.: 48), an emotion of disgust for his mother. Noting that Eliot blames the problem on Hamlet's relation to a woman, Jacqueline Rose links this essay to other men's meditations on the inscrutability of the feminine, and concludes that

what is in fact felt as inscrutable, unmanageable or even horrible

50

(ecstatic in both senses of the term) for an aesthetic theory which will only allow into its definition what can be controlled or managed by art is nothing other than femininity itself.

(Rose 1986: 128)

The modernist attempt to present self-consciousness breaks down when a man's self-consciousness cannot represent to itself what is not only other to itself, but also not simply presentable as a fully achieved state of rationality. At that point a man's self-consciousness is likely to feel that there is something dark in the corner of the mind, some stuff that one doesn't want to drag into the light. We cannot say that all moments of excess and instability are the result of failed engagements with the feminine, but as Rose shows us, these are certainly among the central areas of disturbed subjectivity. Some of those Martian landscapes are sites of oppressive relations with women.

Mars is the planet of the god of war, patron of violent masculinity. Mars has signified a possible world just beyond our ability to see clearly, ever since the 'canals' were first sighted through telescopes. Until recently our gaze was not quite good enough to decide whether the canals were natural formations or evidence of intelligent life. As a result, science fiction and fantasy writers from Edgar Rice Burroughs on have used Mars first as a site of alien life and then as an image of a technologically led future moving out into space. The Martian landscape signifies aliens, the future and, to a lesser extent, men's intramasculine violence. Modern artists, according to this image, are depicting otherness, temporally measurable transformation, and the territory of men's negations. Yet despite the preponderance of men in positions of power in the landscapes of modernist writing, Ulyssean, phallic, intellectual, capable of talking to gods and spirits, or gazing across all the centuries of human culture, modernist men writers rarely acknowledge that their subject is men. When they do, as Lawrence sometimes does, all sorts of special pleading for men's allegedly beleaguered phallicism comes into play. Mostly men's culture is simply assumed to be universal culture, men's issues simply human issues. Perhaps the landscapes of modern literary experiment are more like Superman's Martian landscape than men modernists and their supportive men critics have wanted to acknowledge for, as many recent feminist critics have shown us, modernist men writers were not as imperso-nal, impartial or pro-feminist as they represented themselves, and were subsequently represented, to be by several generations of men critics. T.S. Eliot might separate the man that suffers from the mind that creates, but both were masculine. Men's subjectivity in literature was not gender-free but a gendered and therefore highly partial male gaze wherever it was directed, at the throbs inside or outside. The feminist literary historians, Sandra Gilbert and Susan Gubar, call modernism a product of the 'sexual battle' between men and women. Men writers have adopted strategies which included:

51

mythologizing women to align them with dread prototypes, fictiona-
lizing them to dramatize their destructive influence; slandering them in
essays, memoirs, and poems; prescribing alternative ambitions for
them; appropriating their words in order to usurp or trivialize their
language; and ignoring or evading their achievements in critical texts.

(Gilbert and Gubar 1988: 149)

Modernist men's writing has much to tell us about men's subjectivity, both
because the representation of self-consciousness and its relations to emotion,
language, women and other men are obsessive preoccupations, and because
subsequent readers have had the kind of faith in it that Kristeva's claim
reveals. Indeed modernist writing has an importance for the formation of
men's subjectivity that we can approach through a consideration of what
Superman reads in his spare time (besides technical manuals). What does the
real man read? What do men graduate to from comics and popular culture (if
they do)? The real man would read the literary equivalent of the surrealist
landscape, that is to say men's modernist classics, for these help define the
well-read man. Contemporary novels, art films and theory may give more
pleasure, but few English-speaking male intellectuals would have no passing
acquaintance with any of the men modernist writers: James Joyce, William
Faulkner, D.H. Lawrence, Ezra Pound, T.S. Eliot, W.B. Yeats, William
Carlos Williams, Samuel Beckett or Ernest Hemingway. Such texts continue
to help form masculine cultures in Britain, America and countries with close
historical ties, in much the same way as comics, motorbikes, football and
popularized science do. At its best this culture can be intellectually and
emotionally complex, and potentially progressive, but as feminism has
shown, it is often far from that. This is a culture where men can define,
confirm and develop their subjectivity, and find a field of concerns where
they can sustain relationships with other men. Reading these texts we must
always remember that they have provided opportunities for men's discussions, self-understandings and politics (both through opposition and
assent). Such activities may build a long way up from the foundations this
literary culture helps provide, but these texts are still part of the discourse of
those other cultural levels.

The texts I have chosen for close analysis are central modernist texts but I
would not claim that they completely represent all aspects of men's modernism. My choice of these texts is only secondarily intended to make a case
about men's modernism, although I hope that the outlines of such a picture
are visible. My main aim is to choose texts which explore the dilemmas of
modern men's inward gaze sufficiently to lay a foundation for the theoretical
arguments that follow. The following readings of *A Portrait of the Artist as a
Young Man*, three poems by Yeats, and *The Rainbow*, locate images, narratives and theories of modern masculine subjectivities in which pre-linguistic
affectivity, impersonality, sublimity, envy of maternity and sexuality are

prominent. These readings should help make it easier to recognize generaliz-ations about modernism like the following, as men's modernist self-images – a heady mixture of Ulyssean adventure and confusions about inwardness:

> If it is an art of metamorphosis, a Daedalus voyage into unknown arts, it is also a sense of disorientation and nightmare, feeling the dangerous deathly magic in the creative impulse explored by Thomas Mann. . . . It is the literature of technology. It is the art consequent on the dis-establishing of communal reality and conventional notions of causa-lity, on the destruction of traditional notions of the wholeness of individual character, on the linguistic chaos that ensues when public notions of language have been discredited and when all realities have become subjective fictions.
>
> (Bradbury and McFarlane 1976: 26–7)

A great many men's modernist landscapes have become Martian.

I have decided somewhat reluctantly to leave out almost all reference to literary critics of Joyce, Yeats and Lawrence in what follows, due to the limits on space. Because, for the same reasons of space, the Bibliography is keyed to actual citations, much relevant work is not acknowledged there either. I hope readers who wish to will be able to place my interpretations in relation to other critical commentaries through the usual research resources. I could try to justify this by adding that little has yet been written directly on masculinities and modern writing. There is still a risk that I will appear to give too little credit to the feminist critics who have pioneered research into gender and modernism, so I will underline here that without such work this chapter could not have been written. I have acknowledged a few of those debts in the Bibliography even though the texts are not cited.

A PORTRAIT OF THE ARTS OF MAKING MEN

A Portrait of the Artist as a Young Man (Joyce 1988) can be read as a straightforward narrative of the development of an adult masculinity. It is constructed as a series of salient moments in the formation of the male artist. The choice of these formative moments is usually referred to the artist, but they can equally be read as constitutive of the young man. His arrival at the status of artist, and therefore man, occurs when the novel modulates from this realist objectivity into a new subjectivity signified by the articulate self-reflexive entries of a journal.

The novel begins with a rapid survey of the earliest memories of Stephen Dedalus, when women hold the power to enforce rules and threats. Fuller memories commence once he is away at an all-boys' school and women's domination ends. From then on it is men and other boys who train him to be a man. First he is taught to fear other boys. The opening scene at school is set during a football match full of 'struggling and groaning' (Joyce 1988: 9) during which Stephen wonders what it means to be a 'suck' (p. 11) while he malingers out of the way of the ball. Other males will either hurt you or love you in forbidden ways if you are not careful. Later he learns not to acknowledge his mother affectionately any longer, after he is teased about kissing her. When the school authorities accuse certain boys of an undivulged crime, flogging some and expelling others, the other boys all speculate about it in terms of the worst they can imagine – theft or the desecration of the eucharist. The reality is that the boys were caught in a homoerotic act, for which they can elect either violent punishment or expulsion. Symbolically they can choose between not being masculine as the school defines it, or being hurt by adult men in power over them, and then integrating the result of that male violence into their character. The confusion over the nature of the crime shows how a process of displacement is at work in the representation of a masculine desire for affection from other males. It is thought of first as a financial act, then as a religious act, and only belatedly as sexuality. Each is a crime, but money and religion are more acceptable displacements of men's affection for one another. Later in the novel Stephen will flirt with both finance and religion. At this early stage he has to deal with the immediate problem of male desire, in the form of its inverse, intermasculine violence, and he successfully resolves his fear as well as his sense of injustice by appealing to the highest authority, the rector at the school, symbolically re-establishing a link between punishment and reason. Violence is legitimized by the law, as it was in the comics.

Stephen tries out athletic masculinity with the coach Mike Flynn, but soon rejects it in favour of more aesthetic pursuits. We see him at his secondary school on the evening of the Whitsuntide play, now in his teens and in love with a girl, being teased by one his male peers, Heron: 'Dedalus is a model youth. He doesn't smoke and he doesn't go to bazaars and he doesn't flirt and he doesn't damn anything or damn all' (ibid.: 78). Heron tries to get him to admit that the girl with Stephen's father is a girl friend of Stephen's, and then teases Stephen by hitting him twice with a cane on the legs. The second time it stings, and the blow reminds Stephen of the violence held in check by the males around him. The hint of cruelty he can see in Heron's face recalls to mind a beating he received from his classmates for admiring Byron (whose notorious bisexuality was possibly an unconscious impetus to the trouble) in his first year at the school:

> At last after a fury of plunges he wrenched himself free. His tormentors set off towards Jones's Road, laughing and jeering at him, while he, torn and flushed and panting, stumbled after them, half blinded with tears, clenching his fists madly and sobbing.
>
> (ibid.: 84)

Once again the danger of too much closeness results in a violent parody of intimacy ('torn and flushed and panting'), in which Stephen is nearly blinded by the display of an emotion he should not be showing. Tears make you blind and they carry out the threat of women like Dante, who said 'eagles will come and pull out his eyes' (ibid.: 8) if the little Stephen did not apologize.

The Whitsun play episode culminates in what is experienced as unusual although it sounds as if it ought to be ordinary. Just as he is about to go on stage to play the part of the 'farcical pedagogue', he finds himself feeling 'whole': 'for one rare moment he seemed to be clothed in the real apparel of boyhood' (ibid.: 88). Only when pretending to be a tiresome man of the kind who has enforced the law of adult males for years can he feel himself as other to it. At the moment when the manhood by which he has been dominated is realized to be a fictitious costume, he can wear the real costume of boyhood and then perform as a man.

Stephen's brief life as a man and breadwinner follows, a time in which his prize monies enable him to create and lead a 'commonwealth' (ibid.: 100) within his own family. The expenditure of all the money is followed by the 'expense of spirit in a waste of shame', a spending of his body in a delirious pursuit of sexual fantasies and prostitutes, a kind of commonwealth of the body perhaps, but his 'savage desire' and 'secret riots' (ibid.: 101) turn him into a 'baffled prowling beast' (ibid.: 102), metaphorically similar to the beast in the cartoon picture of a battered warrior with beast and robot. Stephen's solution to the dilemma will be to become a religous robot, his desires all controlled by the father confessor and the rules of the church.

As a beast he is unable to speak poetry any longer. Only 'inarticulate cries' and 'unspoken brutal words' (ibid.: 102) (like the comic-book neologisms) can mediate the new sexual desires of adolescence (a labelling quite unavailable to the consciousness of this sinner). Stephen has returned to the pre-linguistic, to the unsayable. What he wants of the prostitute is the physical affection he cannot get from men and last received from his mother, who is therefore strongly associated with the kissing to which the prostitute invites him:

> His lips would not bend to kiss her. He wanted to be held firmly in her arms, to be caressed slowly, slowly, slowly. In her arms he felt that he had suddenly become strong and fearless and sure of himself. But his lips would not bend to kiss her.
>
> (ibid.: 104)

The prostitute's physical caress makes him invulnerable to other males, by making him feel strong and fearless. Unfortunately a kiss would also signify maternalism and violate his fellow boys' rules. Stephen visualizes his relation to the prostitute in terms of a doll she displays in her room: 'A huge doll sat with her legs apart in the copious easychair beside the bed' (ibid.: 103). His male gaze turns this woman into a female form without consciousness.

Stephen's sexual confusion is followed by the long centrepiece of the novel, the retreat where he is converted from his sinful life to a harsh devotional piety thanks to the vivid depiction of the punishment for those who transgress God's laws. This hell results from a male anger: '*His* anger' (ibid.: 137 my emphasis), a boundless rage that creates 'an eternity of endless agony, of endless bodily and spiritual torment' (ibid.: 136) in those who call it forth. The male body becomes hell. This male God is a substitute mother: 'He made you out of nothing' (ibid.: 138), the priest tells the boys. Stephen willingly embraces Him therefore out of his need for the maternal, and out of fear of apocalyptic masculinity. In the spirit of this embrace he becomes so pious that he is approached to join the monastic order itself, an opportunity that presents itself to him as a chance to learn the names of forbidden desires and pleasures, in the perfect safety of projecting them into the sins of others. Stephen can only imagine a state of knowledge in which desire is absent and the nominalizing power of religious reason holds sway, but he rejects it nevertheless and opts for university.

Before he becomes immersed in university life he has a vision of femininity on the beach, after questioning himself about a major crisis in his development, the actual transition from boyhood to manhood: 'Where was his boyhood now? Where was the soul that had hung back from her destiny. . . . Or where was he? He was alone' (ibid.: 175). This questioning actually seems to call forth his vision of feminine loveliness, or at least to transfigure an ordinary encounter and stir up the worst excesses of late Victorian poetic language. His soul is female, boyhood has disappeared, but no other masculinity has yet finally formed itself. He does not know how and when he will become a man. The sight of the girl takes place in a wordless swoon, the 'holy silence of his ecstasy' (ibid.: 176). For Stephen this seems like a vocation announcing itself from this pre-linguistic, unsayable realm of passion. Stephen sees her as a bird, a crane (a transformed Heron), in the middle of the current of watery life where he is standing. Like a magical creature met in a Native American puberty fasting rite, she gives him to himself, at a moment when he is between boyhood and manhood and temporarily away from human society. The transition to manhood requires a woman who does not kiss, make love, threaten him, or compete with the angers of masculinity. Her avian appearance makes her even less of a threat (she may not be a human female at all, only a bird). Her greatest gift is the gift of creation, the call to 'recreate life out of life' (ibid.: 176). Now he will be able to develop an art based on a masculinity capable of maternal creative power, taken from this vision of femininity. Feminine beauty disarmed of all maternal power will make possible a purposive manhood as an artist.

At university Stephen develops this aesthetic in a mock Platonic dialogue with his friend Lynch on the streets of Dublin. Stephen plays cleverly with the Thomist ideas of his Catholic upbringing by conflating them with Hegelian ideas which by the end of the nineteenth century had come to dominate philosophy. Unlike the Platonic dialogues which often start with homoerotic desire, this dialogue circles around their sexual attraction to women and the problems it faces them with. Their aesthetic is a theory of their male heterosexuality. To illustrate the separation of the aesthetic from the utilitarian, Stephen ridicules the idea that 'every physical quality admired by men in women is in direct connection with the manifold functions of women for the propagation of the species' (ibid.: 213). Such a denial of aesthetic autonomy 'tells you that you admired the great flanks of Venus because you felt that she would bear you burly offspring and admired her great breasts because you felt that she would give good milk to her children and yours' (ibid.: 213). It would never do to think that female beauty was maternal in some way. Aesthetics becomes a means of denying this now dreadful possibility.

Aesthetics offers avoidance of the perceived threat of relations of dependence on women, by creating a state of mind of neither desire nor utilitarian calculation:

> Beauty expressed by the artist cannot awaken in us an emotion which is kinetic or a sensation which is purely physical. It awakens, or ought to awaken, or induces, or ought to induce, an esthetic stasis, an ideal pity or an ideal terror, a stasis called forth, prolonged and at last dissolved by what I call the rhythm of beauty.
>
> (ibid.: 210)

At the climax of his dialogue Stephen describes this state as 'the luminous silent stasis of esthetic pleasure', and it occurs because one perceives 'the *whatness* of a thing' (ibid.: 217). The mind has been 'arrested', a term which echoes the Kantian sublime, a sublime about which I shall have more to say later. Here I want to note that the possibility that men's desire might be a sexuality both pragmatic and moved by beauty, and therefore a sexuality articulated through relations with what is other, without being silenced by that other or trying to silence it, is blocked by the introduction of this version of the sublime. The result of this sublimity is a condition in which the mind is suspended in a stasis where connections or relations are not possible. The young man has developed an art whereby he can suspend verbal consciousness in a state of bearable passion ('ideal pity'). Manhood is equated with the production and mastery of what is experienced as the body, the unconscious and the unnameable. The result is a masculinity in awe of its power to overwhelm all that is other to it.

Stephen's dialogue concludes with the impersonality of the artist:

> The personality of the artist, at first a cry or a cadence or a mood and then a fluid and lambent narrative, finally refines itself out of existence, impersonalises itself, so to speak. The esthetic image in the dramatic form is life purified in and reprojected from the human imagination.
>
> (ibid.: 219)

This is also a theory of psychic development. You begin with emotional cries, progress to ego-centred sentences and finally vanish into the universality of language and its arts. Masculinity steps aside and like 'the artist, like the God of the creation, remains within or behind or beyond or above his handiwork, invisible, refined out of existence, indifferent, paring his fingernails' (ibid.: 219). The artist/author disappears altogether at the end of the novel when Stephen's own diary entries take over, and he reports on a quarrel with Cranley about mothers: 'tried to imagine his mother: cannot' (ibid.: 252). But is it just Cranley's mother or is the problem really mothers? Are mothers now unimaginable because their maternity represents a power beyond that of the arts of masculinity? The novel ends with a prayer of his mother's, then the hope that he will be able to give birth in masculine fashion ('forge in the smithy of my soul'), and finally his own prayer, an apostrophe to the ultimate male artist ('old father, old artificer') (ibid.: 217). The ultimate masculinity is artifice, a fiction of fatherhood, but even as Stephen prays his language betrays him. He may after all only be asking to produce forgeries of birth and life, even forgeries of manhood. The artificer may be forging chains, not freedom, for Stephen.

This reading of the novel as a series of key episodes in the formation of a dominant masculinity both clarifies the choice of scenes and throws light on the wider issue of the formation of masculinity and the transition from boyhood to manhood. It is a very literal reading, however. To do justice to the narrative strategies of the novel it needs to be reinflected through the aesthetic impersonality Stephen praises, an impersonality enacted by the entire novel. All these episodes are refracted through the distantiating medium of sublime emotional stasis, in which the act of authorship is as hidden as maternity is by the punitive eyes of the boys watching for signs of mother love, the angry Jehovah, or the new Thomist aesthetic. Stephen's annunciatory vocation on the beach can be reread as merely adolescent sexual and spiritual inflation, since the language is so obviously a discourse of decayed romanticism. The slightly teasing presentation of Stephen, the faint hints of ridicule which dance around him like Lynch or cling to him like the seaweed on the beach, are the traces of that masculinity which will not appear in bodily form. This faint ridicule is the masculine distantiation from boyhood, and in that way too the novel offers an exemplary presentation of the making of masculinity. The making of the portrait is the making and masking of masculinity.

YEATS'S MASCULINE SUBLIME

Eliot and Joyce have become synonymous with modernism. Yeats, however, has occupied a slightly different position. Harold Bloom (1976: 205) describes him as the 'most canonized poet of the twentieth century', but he means that critical reading of his poetry is commonly overawed by its power to force the critic to his or her knees. I shall suggest that this canonization owes as much to the masculinity of his sublimity as to that sublimity itself as Bloom argues. Superficially less modernist than Eliot's more experimental and less unitary poetry, Yeats's poetics relies heavily on repeated reinscription of contemporary myths and images within an explicit rhetoric. Since many of his starting points are specifically masculine dilemmas, the result is often a subtle understanding of men's relation to modernity. A reading of masculinity's artifices in his poems suggests that a developing literary theory which tries to make explicit the gendered construction of men's writing needs to think its way slowly through the poems, rather than elicit summaries or a few poetic touchstones as adequate representations of their effect. The result could be a very useful account of the strategies men were toying with as all around them the older structures of domestic and public life were changing, and when the attractions of military and fascist solutions were strong. In this brief reading of three poems I want to propose a histology of masculine aesthetic artifice, because despite the claims to a disembodied art, the body remains, hidden by a language which would disown its affective vectors.

'A Dialogue of Self and Soul' (Yeats 1984: 234–6) can be read in terms of a specifically masculine splitting, where 'My Soul' speaks for the pre-linguistic, and 'My Self' for the ordinary condition of self-rationalizing manhood. Manhood, the poem claims, is slow to overcome boyhood and stand free. Boyhood is something to be discarded, but unlike Stephen Dedalus the actor, the poem finds it hard to shed this apparel. This is a hard process because of the 'ignominy of boyhood' and 'the distress/ Of boyhood changing into man'. Once 'finished', a man is likely to find himself amongst 'enemies', other finished men who want to finish him off. Further problems await him. There is 'the folly that man does/ Or must suffer, if he woos/ A proud woman not kindred of his soul', and this lack of a female counterpart may be worsened by male hostility. Other men may create a 'mirror of malicious eyes' in which the man sees a self-image that misrepresents the self to itself (the poem doesn't gender the 'enemies', but women are rarely given the public and political importance 'enemies' have). There seems to be no escape from this mismirrored shape the mirror of other men 'casts upon his eyes until at last/ He thinks that shape must be his shape'. A similar mirroring also affects 'the unfinished man and his pain/ Brought face to face with his own clumsiness'. The unfinished (but therefore living) man painfully confronts that which is unfinished in himself as somehow other to himself, because the incompletion produces a splitting of the masculine subject. The finished man (who may be finished in the more deathly sense) is brought face to face with another kind of clumsiness, a distortion of his achieved manhood produced by other hostile males, who do this simply because he is now a man.

The Soul begins the poem by an act of spiritual summons, almost conjuration, in which the Self is invited to climb the circular staircase to the sky and contemplate the darkness which represents the Soul, and 'where all thought is done'. The Soul identifies itself as the terminus and termination of thought. The Soul is therefore spokesman for some pre-linguistic and pre-conceptual condition; the prefix suggests something prior whereas the poem talks of what could better be called post-linguistic. Are the two states really the same? In this condition to which the Soul invites the active, conscious man, 'intellect no longer knows/ *Is* from the *Ought*, or *Knower* from the *Known*'. This invitation to catatonia sounds almost like a renunciation of mainstream philosophy, of Hume's argument about prescriptive language, and Kant's definition of things-in-themselves. In this condition there are no separations of knower and known because the subject and its objects coincide in an absolute immediacy, just as morality and truth cease to be vexatiously distinct. Each now produces the other. The Soul is inviting the Self to a resolution of the insoluble problems of Western rationality. This tempting prospect of relinquishing authoritative rationality occurs in a poem where manhood is an explicit theme, so it could be said that this is an invitation to give up a dominant masculinity. In 'Among School Children' (1984: 215–17), a poem from the earlier volume *The Tower* (1928), Yeats questions the relations between masculinity and philosophy even more explicitly. Plato, the poem jokes, thought that nature wasn't very real, a sort of scarecrow (like the old man Yeats). Aristotle was himself a teacher, albeit of a special infant. He had the honour to have 'played the taws/ Upon the bottom of a king of kings', mixing reason and male violence in his contribution to history. The word 'play' deliberately echoes what the spume of nature does 'Upon a ghostly paradigm of things' in Plato's philosophy. Male violence, used to train a boy to be a man, is paralleled with the action of nature on the ideal Forms. The Ideals are like the adult Alexander, the male warrior par excellence, who kills and conquers other men (as well as women and children). The poem implies that Alexander's warriorhood is formed by this conjunction of reason and male force. The Ideals are similarly both played with and beaten by nature, and perhaps they too will be as murderously and gloriously all-powerful. The poem is as fascinated as it is wary of such power as Alexander's.

The masculine Self in 'A Dialogue of Self and Soul' is not impressed by any of the soul talk. The Self is much more interested in an old knife and its makeshift scabbard, a piece of a lady's dress, icons dismissed by the Soul as 'things that are/ Emblematical of love and war'. The knife blade, according to the Self, is 'still like a looking-glass', a mirror like that of the other males, but this time able to produce an image 'Unspotted by the centuries'. A knife is more reliable than other men because it gives you a truer image of yourself. Wound round it, protecting it, is a piece of something 'torn/ From some court-lady's dress'. The violence of the verb 'torn' hints that the protection of this blade may only have been achieved at the lady's expense. Common sense tells us that the cloth probably came from a discarded dress, but the emphasis on tearing hints at sexual violence as the premiss for this protection. The blade's ability to mirror the man's Self depends on this earlier act of tearing, and the protection which her dress, with its association with fertility and beauty, 'flowering, silken, old embroidery', gives it. The old male Self wishes for such flowering in his old age also.

The Self wants to carry on living, both now and later after a temporary transmigration, so it says that it will 'claim as by a soldier's right/ A charter to commit the crime once more'. Life is a crime, and manhood a form of militarism. To this claim the Soul responds with the promise of a resolution to all the metaphysical conflicts I have just discussed, but then lapses awkwardly into the very silence it espouses: 'Only the dead can be forgiven;/ But when I think of that my tongue's a stone.' Since the Soul has been celebrating the condition where tongues cannot speak, and all sensations and perception are arrested in a kind of permanent 'époche', the implied regret of this is surprising. Why should the idea that only the dead can be forgiven induce inarticulacy and silence?

This silence is contrasted with the celebration of the self-conscious transformation the Self makes in the final stanza, when it claims that forgiveness can dispel the miseries of manhood. The poem ends with an ecstatic transformation of the mirror's barrier into a transparent state of being, in which: 'We are blest by everything/ Everything we look upon is blest.' Trace every action and idea to its source, and then you can forgive yourself totally, eliminating remorse. That is the obvious paraphrase, but the preceding lines make these celebratory conclusions slightly more complex:

> I am content to follow to its source,
> Every event in action or in thought;
> Measure the lot; forgive myself the lot!
> When such as I cast out remorse
> So great a sweetness flows into the breast
> We must laugh and we must sing.

Yeats replaced the word 'misery' with the word 'event' during composition (Finneran 1983: 19) to try to pull the poem free of a narcissistic masculine self-pity. The totality of this masculine self-examination still has to be bolstered up by a fantasy of male self-nurture. In this new state, 'sweetness flows into the breast' like milk in a breastfeeding woman, so the man achieves some maternal ability to nurture, perhaps with something like the 'milk of human kindness'. What brings this about? Explicitly it is the casting out of remorse, the repossession of that other casting ('casts upon his eyes until at last/ He thinks that shape must be his shape') the male enemies threatened. Remorse (humiliation might be a more familiar term here) is the name of this mirror created by other life-threatening men. At last it can be discarded. The new power to discard it comes from the painstaking labour of following all the actions and thoughts to their source. In one sense the source is simply the initial cause (a mood, belief, external pressure), but in another it is precisely source as maternal beginning. Source is a very different term to the ugly 'frog-spawn of a blind-man's ditch' used to represent unfinished men (according to the poem's logic) and, because of their appearance, the power of male generation, sperm. The poem tries to replace the image of a man as no more than a sperm with that of a man as nurturing maternal creator. This fantasy arises from an angry dismissal of what appears to be the only alternative form of manhood, competitive violence, rather than simply from the desire to appropriate feminine potential.

'I am content to follow to its source'. The subliminal pun on 'content' signals an emotional commitment to this project of self, and says that the 'I' is itself a sufficient content, a being substantive enough to be followed back to its source. Thus the masculine 'I' becomes a project to be traced to its source. The redemptive process includes not just forgiveness but judgement, 'measure'. The measures of the poem are part of this measurement, but so equally are intellectual analysis and the emotional act of forgiveness. By this affirmation of substantive being, whose source yields a transcendence in which the promise of the soul that all the paradoxes of reason will be resolved is decisively bettered, the paradoxes and pains of manhood are resolved. Yet what is this natural blessing but the perfect reflection of the blade?

The poem's affirmation does not replace the necessity of the cycle of birth, ignominious boyhood and the adult life of 'A blind man battering blind men'. That will go on. What is offered is a way of altering its relation to itself once achieved. Masculinity is shown by the poem to have two faces: a pre-linguistic, pre-rational harmony unable to communicate, and an achieved manhood which cannot bear to see itself in the mirror of rational reflection. The final affirmation suggests that the only resolution is a form of self-engendering, not by becoming womanly, but by discovering that the crimes all do have a source. Masculinity can be transformed into a nurturing manhood by recognizing the 'I' as itself source and content, and not relying on other men for its form, so that the pull back into uncommunicative isolation is forever resisted.

As so often in Yeats's poems, when the uncertainty of this 'setting forth' of the problems is the primary field of the poem, this is a precarious recognition. The contemplation of blade and silken sheath may be either a 'following to the source' or it may be a return to violence against others, men and women, in war and sex. The blessings at the end flow from everything, not everyone. This mutual circuit of blessing is not necessarily human. And that finally is the difficulty here. The affirmation is a positive transformation of a masculinity of late manhood, but forms another kind of isolation in which the gaze of the male other has no power of mismirroring because it has no place. The I only sees itself. The Self only talks to its Soul. A further stage of transformation, the blessing of others, remains undone. In other poems such as 'Among School Children' Yeats had more to say about such transformations. In this poem babies emerge surprisingly as 'self born mockers of men's enterprise'. They are new lives brought into being independently of men's bodily existence (except as 'frog-spawn'), and the priorities they establish would seem to mock 'men's enterprise', depending as it does on a system of public institutions independent of that form of human re-creation. Men's enterprise culture looks pretty empty from this standpoint.

Maybe that was why as Yeats composed the materials for 'Sailing to Byzantium' he dropped an early reference to a Christ-like 'infant sleeping on his Mother's knees' (Melchiori 1970: 69). He wanted a more inclusive relation to childhood than such a Madonna and Child could represent. An image of childhood less ruled over by that 'old artificer' was needed: 'By mobilizing all our childhood stages, all our archaisms, by embodying itself in the oneiric, the poetic keeps men's cultural existence from being simply a huge artifice, a futile "artefact", a Leviathan without a nature and against nature' (Ricoeur 1970: 524).

Paul Ricoeur's summary of the way regressive libidinal impulses and prospective impulses (especially social structures of feeling not constituted by libidinal cathexis) interact might have been written to describe the dilemma outlined in Yeats's 'Sailing to Byzantium' (Yeats 1984: 193–4). Like 'Among School Children', this poem also begins with a sense of acute displacement, this time because the poem's protagonist does not belong in the sphere of libidinal impulses and procreation. The poet responds to his exclusion by repudiating the country of 'birds in the trees', and life lived through the immediate desires of the senses, and then invoking a sacred process of transformation to turn bodily self into transcendental art, only to finish up a mechanical bird-like artefact singing in a tree about the cycle of life. Prompted by Sturge Moore's queries, Yeats himself seems to have acceded to the desire to clearly visualize the resultant transformation as a bird in the later poem 'Byzantium', where he speaks of the 'miracle, bird or golden handiwork/ More miracle than bird or handiwork' (ibid.: 248). In the earlier poem the form which the poet takes is deliberately without a living referent, a form which is definitely a sign but not an icon. The pull towards iconicity is that towards an art based on natural mimesis, envy and lack. For this is a poem very definitely about envy and lack. This poem is the narrative of an old man whose age renders him hardly a man, forced to watch all the young lovers singing about love, unless he himself begins to sing.

Extended metaphor is characteristic of Yeats's later poetry, and frequently these extended metaphors lack referents, as the Grecian goldsmith's construction lacks a natural counterpart. Song is one of the most important of these complex metaphors. In 'Sailing to Byzantium' every living thing (and some dead and inanimate things, according to the poet) can sing. Some singing appears to be co-terminous with the process of living itself, and some is more specialized, but all singing is a form of expressive commentary. The birds may usually sing their passions directly, much as the young utter cries of love, but all of them also manage the more descriptive task of commendation. To commend is not only to praise but also to entrust to the charge of an authority that which is commended. The world of those ruled by desire and appetite is not simply dismissed, as by both Aristotelian and Christian philosophers, although the poem reminds us that those so ruled pay a high price for their trust in desire: they die. They do so because they neglect the 'monuments of unageing intellect'. Nothing in the poem explicitly genders these monuments but the irresistible association with cenotaphs and more grandiose memorials to the heroic or regal dead implies masculine endeavours in battles for ideals, whether fought on battlefields or in books. The birds are part of the dying generations born as if only to sing and die, and this link with birth, as well as with the great intellectual achievements of the past (which will be almost by definition the works of men, since at the time Yeats is writing great intellectual achievements were not usually attributed to women), suggests that a gender division is at work here. Yet these great works require not just reading but singing, not intellect, at least not intellect alone, but passion too.

Lyric poetry itself has often been considered the purest form of subjectivity, so this would not be surprising if it were not for the poet's admitted inability to sing. Lyrics are the nearest poetry can approach to pure song. The poet of the first two stanzas is not yet able to sing, and therefore not able to write such a poem as this, and has had to go off on a long voyage in time and space to find a teacher so that he can transform himself into a singer. When he arrives, the poem shifts to apostrophe. The very ritual which will begin the transformation is spoken, and overheard by the reader, who might for a heady moment identify with those sages who can relieve a man of his broken manhood and transmute him into pure art. Can we help the poet in his dilemma and restore his manhood in some way? Or is this the trace or, better, the map of a route by which the reader could follow the poet into art, like some map of lost treasure? As we read this stanza it is quickly clear that the poet knows exactly what he wants, unlike his heart which 'knows not what it is'. Kant said that 'I have no *knowledge* of myself as I am but merely as I appear to myself. The consciousness of self is thus very far from being a knowledge of the self' (Kant 1933: 169). Such knowledge would require 'another self-intuition which gives the *determining* in me . . . prior to the act of *determination*', but such a self-intuition of what gives no consciousness would then entail the transcendence of time. Consciousness is a temporal act of constructing relationships. Kant is talking about the mind. Yeats would seem to both follow this logic of the impossibility of self-grounding reason, and at the same time shift the issue into the affective realm. The emotions cannot ground themselves either. Emotions are not origins.

Once the sages have emerged from their place in iconography they have strict instructions to get rid of the male body, and especially to 'consume' the heart. This cannibalism of the heart by these hypermasculine figures of art, religion and wisdom all rolled into one will purge the heart of passion, and give it that true knowledge of itself which it now lacks. The illness brought on by male desire will be cured by true understanding. The final stanza imagines a paradox, a man able to speak after his death, a precursor to other male voices who have been able finally to stop having to report, like Wittgenstein's imaginary novelist, on their bodies: Beckett's Unnameable, Eliot's speaker eaten by the leopards in 'Ash Wednesday', Thomas Pynchon's various characters leading a 'new otherside existence' like Walter Rathenau in *Gravity's Rainbow* (Pynchon 1975: 164) are only a few of a considerable company of male spirits. Out of nature and therefore wholly undetermined by any form of material causality, this free spirit, now more invulnerable than the most powerful comic-book superhero, can choose his own identity. Invulnerability is a repeated feature of certain kinds of masculinity, which might seem to derive from childish autism, but could also derive from class-based ideologies. In *The Wings of the Dove*, Henry James suggests that this idea of immortality has its origins in class. Lord Mark, the novel's most patrician male, holds a view of himself similar to that to which the poet of 'Sailing to Byzantium' aspires:

> It was one of his merits, to which she [Kate Croy] did justice too, that both his native and his acquired notion of behaviour rested on the general assumption that nothing – nothing to make a deadly difference for him – ever *could* happen. It was socially, a working view like another.
>
> (James 1978: 273)

For the aristocrat this 'working view' is about as close to work as he gets. This glimpse of aristocratic masculine invulnerability as a form of upper-class status is a reminder that class has a psychological function as well as an economic one, and that the fantasies we have been recognizing in comics and literature are tied to socioeconomic formations as well.

The first three lines of 'Sailing to Byzantium' insist that this is a process of thoughtful choice. A new identity is the sign of the renewal of manhood in this aesthetic heaven. A thoroughly modern man who can choose any identity, the poet confides that he will sit on a golden branch and sing, doubly protected from death thanks to this theft from James Frazer of the apotropaic golden bough. This identity, this form, is something the poet will 'take', as if taking over and possessing what he previously lacked. Since this act was precisely that which Romantic subjectivity constantly enjoined, the act whereby the external object was simultaneously consumed of all social meaning and given the refashioned symbolic fullness of poetic interiority, the poet is recognizing that lyric expression always begins with what is already art and culture. This recognition is represented as requiring the death of ordinary manhood. The recognition of the other as itself a subject rather than an object of appropriation requires the symbolic death of a certain kind of masculinity.

Why does this new identity sing both prophetically and historically, and what form of identity is it? That second question is unanswerable by any determinate referent, but that is the point. A form of death in art, this identity results from the production of a pure form of Romantic expressivity which has merged with the pure expressivity of another artist, the Grecian goldsmith. Two men have united in a work of art, in an act quite different to that miscasting which afflicted the Self in 'A Dialogue of Self and Soul', when other men tried to destroy his image, his art. This fantasy is one found in many modern and postmodern writers, in *Spurs*, Jacques Derrida's (1979) reading of Nietzsche, for example, and it is the other, forgotten side of Harold Bloom's (1976) picture of the struggle between new poet and strong precursors. Read regressively, this would reduce to a homoerotic fantasy of replacing the mother in the father's affections as Freud does in the Rat Man case (I shall discuss this in the next chapter). But I think we should register it also as a desire to reconfigure the public sphere. In his elegy for Yeats, W.H. Auden canvasses both possibilities. Auden visualizes Yeats's death like this:

the current of his feeling failed; he became his admirers.

Now he is scattered among a hundred cities
And wholly given over to unfamiliar affections.

(Auden 1966: 141)

Those unfamiliar (non-familial, non-heterosexist?) affections in which Yeats is now interactive form bonds between men and women that represent the highest achievement of poetry. Auden imagines Yeats's dream of the two men, the artist and artisan, united in a way which teases its homosocial unease into the light, and punningly revalues that homosociality by admitting its homosexuality as well as its sociality.

Let us return to the song. Western thought has commonly assumed that speech, not writing, is the direct expression of consciousness. Song is the emotive counterpart of speech, the direct expression of the passions. 'Sailing to Byzantium' is the story of a man who cannot sing, who cannot utter his passions in the supposedly direct fashion available to those who neglect male rationality's claim to universality and the invulnerability of the soul's immortality. This is why the third stanza begins with a traditional poetic interjection. J.H. Prynne argues that the English poetic tradition uses interjections to balance expression and apostrophe. Like their wild brothers, the comic-book neologisms, interjections are neither inside nor outside language. Lexicographers have found 'Oh' especially difficult to place. After reviewing usage and definition, Prynne offers a summary of their performance as a series of questions:

What is the action of these exclamatory interjections? Are they markers for the emphatical compunction of a lost sacred language over-pitched in secular vacancy? Are they part of the rhetorical apparatus for elevating the tone towards sublimity, for laying claim to the power of a primal *planctus*? Are they simply language breaking away into some prelinguistic expressivity, a vocalized pang or response to imaginative pain as if directly connected to the involuntary reflexes?

(Prynne 1988: 166)

All these possibilities are to be found in 'Sailing to Byzantium'. Yeats's invocatory 'O' to the sages is a moment both of passionate inarticulate feeling and of a recognition of a 'possible truth', however much its dialectic might seem contradictory. At the moment of saying 'O', the poet begins to sing because passion enters the voice in the moment of request. Only by articulating this desire will the sages hear it. The invocation is essential. The poem cannot continue as narrative. Its result may be (because the final stanza is a figure of that utopian alternative which an aesthetic of Romantic subjectivity offers) the new possibility of being in another male artist's arms, sustained in a form of his making. There the poet will be able to sing, and manhood will be restored. The only problem with this poetic solution is the loss of the male body. The final stanza affirms the need for some kind of bodily form, otherwise the singing would have no source, but this body is no longer the male animal body of desire and self-opacity. It is an ingenious solution and shows as fully as any modernist text the dilemmas of masculine pre-linguistic passion. Is it sublime, animal or art? Yeats's later poetry shows that it is all of these and therefore unstable and still in need of transformation.

THE DEVELOPMENT OF MEN'S SELF-CONSCIOUSNESS IN *THE RAINBOW*

An original account of modern men's relation to pre-linguistic fields of desire, and to the only partially articulate patterns of emotion, is to be found in one of the most philosophic novels written in English this century, D.H. Lawrence's *The Rainbow*. Its peculiar originality has largely been overlooked, because its philosophical terminology belongs more to the late Hegelianisms of the nineteenth century than the positivisms of the twentieth. Only now that literary theory has reminded us of the contribution to aesthetics made by Hegel and the German Idealists is it really possible to retrace this novel's remarkable representations of the emergence of masculinity and language within modernity. *The Rainbow* (published 1915) was banned almost immediately after it was published, and not made available until after the First World War in America, and only later in Britain. By that time a great shift in intellectual paradigms had taken place, and its innovative phenomenologies found few informed readers. From the beginning the novel signals its preoccupation with the history of consciousness, but its co-terminous family saga overlays the main outlines to such an extent that the philosophical history is not easily evident to readers who don't expect it.

Since the publication of Kate Millett's *Sexual Politics*, Lawrence's status as a significant modernist writer has fallen a long way. He loses out on two counts. His prose does not embrace polysemy or invite obvious 'writerly' participation, as does the work of the more linguistically innovative moder-nist writers. I doubt whether anyone has plans for a poststructuralist Lawrence. More significantly still, Lawrence is believed to be an almost unredeemable anti-feminist, misogynist and wholehearted celebrant of phal-lic energies. His work might be a clear symptom of pathological masculini-ties, goes the argument, but could not reflect self-critically on men's excesses. A recent collection of primary materials on modernism and gender uses two of Lawrence's newspaper articles from the last years of his life as representative texts (despite the editor's admission that 'Lawrence's most affirmative views of matriarchy and of women coming into their own identities are in *The Rainbow*' (Scott 1990: 220)). Reclaiming Lawrence is not my aim here. Since John Middleton Murry and F.R. Leavis both attacked and then partially recuperated Lawrence, that has been the paradig-matic move in Lawrence criticism. Lawrence also suffers from the system-building, single-author studies dominant in modern criticism. The pressing need for a biography (now fortunately being met by publication of the first volume of a series, John Worthen's (1991) excellent account of the young Lawrence) has not been fulfilled by critics placing the extensive reactionary writings into a Lawrentian psychological framework. The difficulty with Lawrence has been that the public debates and the dominant intellectual paradigms in which he oriented himself have often been forgotten or misre-presented, because as an outsider he rarely articulated them in terms im-mediately familiar to his contemporaries, let alone to future readers. At times the misogyny was certainly there but sometimes he was making contemporary prejudices more articulate than they were usually allowed to be, as is partially the case in the reprinted journalism, and sometimes, especially in the early work, he appropriated intellectual frameworks for his own revisionist and even revolutionary purposes. That was particularly the case with his use of phenomenological discourse in *The Rainbow*. If even a Bertrand Russell had only a shaky grasp of late Hegelianism (as his earliest writings demonstrate), a largely self-trained intellectual like Lawrence was likely to have an even more idiosyncratic hold on it. *The Rainbow* is not a text which demonstrates the tenets of poststructuralism at the lexical level, but it is a text permeated with the same philosophical speculation on subjectivity out of which poststructuralism emerged.

The Rainbow opens with the Brangwens living an almost solipsistic existence. The men are contented. It's the women of the family who are aware of limitations and a vital element missing from their lives – knowledge. Knowledge is what makes the vicar master over the farmer, 'not money, nor even class' (Lawrence 1981, 44). This dismissal of class and wealth as causative factors in the structure of power has extensive consequences in the novel, which effectively brackets out capitalism in order to see what human beings are capable of if they have no powerful material barriers to their development. The Brangwens are yeomen farmers. They have considerable class mobility because of their self-employment, enjoy relative freedom from material necessity, and so they face few of the barriers to development confronting the poor. This bracketing-out of money and class means that the novel is able to focus on the process of the emergence of awareness and knowledge with great subtlety. The risk is that individuals will be blamed for the shortcomings of their socioeconomic position. And power does depend on class and wealth as well as knowledge.

From the beginning of the novel different forms of conscious knowledge are shown to find embodiment as 'forms of life'. I have taken the phrase from Wittgenstein's *Philosophical Investigations*: 'human beings . . . agree in the *language* they use. That is not agreement in opinions but in forms of life' (Wittgenstein 1976: 88). Lawrence's novel shows people for whom a form of life is not merely a 'position in thought' (Lawrence 1981: 388), as Winifred Inger characterizes her outlook, but a way of thinking, feeling and living. In the course of the novel, everything from symbolism to nihilism is tested out. In true Hegelian fashion, the novel begins with the fundamental philosophical idea that we know the world directly through our senses, a position Hegel termed 'sense-certainty' (Hegel 1977: 58). On the farm the Brangwen men and women live different lives. The men exist in a merged state with the farm plants, animals and environment. In this state of 'sense-certainty' the lustre of the corn is known to the men without any mediation by language or consciousness: 'The young corn waved and was silken, and the lustre slid along the limbs of the men who saw it' (Lawrence 1981: 42). The men live a wholly unexamined, unconscious life within the knowledge of the senses and no more. Away from the day's work 'their brains were inert' (ibid.: 42). These men do have knowledge of a kind, they 'know in their blood' (ibid.: 43), and 'knew the intercourse between heaven and earth' (ibid.: 42), but what they know is only their immediate relation with the natural world, because they lack self-consciousness.

This interrelation is several times called intercourse: 'the women looked out from the heated, blind intercourse of farm-life, to the spoken world beyond' (ibid.: 42). The struggle for consciousness to emerge is presented largely in terms of what we would now call sexual relationships and so intercourse comes to be the governing metaphor for the novel's exploration of knowledge. The Brangwen men don't lack sexual intimacy; they lack verbal intimacy. They cannot articulate what they see and so in that sense remain blind. Whereas the vicar has access to 'the other, magic language' (ibid.: 43) of knowledge, and out on the frontiers of the unknown other men 'utter themselves' in their 'conquest' ('the woman . . . strained her eyes to see what man had done in fighting outwards to knowledge, she strained to hear how he uttered himself in his conquest' (ibid.: 43)), the Brangwen men are inarticulate. The novel proposes that the process of utterance, of putting experience into verbal form, is a difficult, slow emergence into self-consciousness. The use of masculine, military metaphors for the emergence into self-consciousness, which echoes Hegel's Master/Slave dialectic, is developed later in the novel in the character of Anton Skrebensky.

This opening is sometimes read as a pastoral golden age, an origin then criticized for its lack of historical validity, its illusory desirableness and its intellectual fallacy. Such sensual immediacy, it is argued, is impossible because language always intervenes. That argument presupposes an account of language different from *The Rainbow* and also repeats a mistake which Hegel's Preface to *The Phenomenology of Spirit* addressed (Hegel 1977: 2), that of dismissing a way of thinking and living because of its contradictions. Even the brisk pace of Hegel's own account of sense-certainty could read like a dismissal. Yet both Hegel and *The Rainbow* are proposing this form of life as valid on its own terms while containing the seeds of its own dissolution. In *The Rainbow* those seeds are the women's awareness of something other than farm life: the knowledge which education and language bring, and the power they confer. The pastoral form of life is already divided, divided by differences of awareness and gender, and it is these divisions which begin the novel proper, when Tom Brangwen, whose growing up is the subject of the first part, finds division within himself.

Tom Brangwen's failure at school and consequent dissatisfaction with his life as a farmer is only relieved by his marriage to Lydia, a woman from another world entirely, whom he experiences as an 'awful unknown next his heart' (Lawrence 1981: 94). His need for Lydia to represent the unknown for him is shown as a limitation, not a fundamental human need. *The Rainbow* suggests that Tom's construction of woman as other is the result of a failure of both his own upbringing and his formal education to offer a means to develop a manhood which is based on something other than dominant rationality and class ideologies. Education fails Tom not so much because of his own seeming inadequacy, but because the institutionalized education of the ruling classes suppresses the less articulate form of consciousness which Tom hangs on to. The novel is careful not to belittle or deride him for this. At school he may have been intellectually backward but his feelings were 'more discriminating' and he was more 'sensuously developed' than other boys (ibid.: 50). The alleged superiority is misleading; what matters is the insistence on the adequacy of his form of life. He is not weak or damaged in some way, but simply hasn't been able to develop rational thought beyond a certain basic point, in part because of a lack of interaction with others (a lack which the novel does not really explain).

His marriage to Lydia partially resolves this, although their relationship is experienced at a pre-verbal wordless level. In a retrospective account later in the novel we are told that 'there, on the farm with her, he lived through a mystery of life and death and creation, strange, profound ecstasies and incommunicable satisfactions, of which the rest of the world knew nothing' (ibid.: 141). Their married life is 'incommunicable', a 'deep inarticulate interchange' – 'The whole intercourse was wordless' (ibid.: 142). This is a definite limit for Tom, and also requires special novelistic means for presenting Tom's experience of this relation because it is so emphatically pre-verbal and sensual.

These novelistic devices have resulted in many confusions about the novel, especially the widespread idea that Lawrence is trying to celebrate some kind of atavistic *Lebenswelt*. When Tom 'falls in love' with Lydia there is no such language of love available to him. He could not say to himself that he had fallen in love. Instead he is only aware of a bodily change: 'A daze had come over his mind, he had another centre of consciousness. In his breast, or in his bowels, somewhere in his body, there had started another activity' (ibid.: 74). This process is experienced within the body, not as an idea or an emotion in the usual sense. When he decides to go and ask her to marry him the experience of awareness is decidedly physical: 'Queer little breaks of consciousness seemed to rise and burst like bubbles out of the depths of his stillness' (ibid.: 76). Consciousness is given to itself in the form of a sensation. Much of the strangeness of this early section of the novel lies in this presentation of Tom's awareness (and to a limited extent Lydia's) of his yearning for something new, and the fulfilment of this yearning in marriage. The yearning is presented as it is for Tom, as a complex set of sensations and emotions and occasional thoughts, but all of his thoughts are imbricated with an accompanying sensation.

At the time Lawrence wrote *The Rainbow* a shift in the way psychologists (and some philosophers) understood the workings of emotion was underway. Since Descartes, one dominant theory held that emotion was the soul's acknowledgement of the body's physiological response to an event. An emotion was assumed to be the subjective awareness of physiological changes, or feelings, passively undergone as the result of a response to some specific situation. At the time that Lawrence was writing this view was under reconsideration, with widely varying results. William James had reworked the dualism of the Cartesian model:

What kind of an emotion of fear would be left if the feeling neither of quickened heart-beats nor of shallow breathing, neither of trembling lips nor of weakened limbs, neither of goose-flesh nor of visceral stirrings, were present, it is quite impossible for me to think. . . . For *us*, emotion dissociated from all bodily feeling is inconceivable. The more closely I scrutinize my states, the more persuaded I become that whatever moods, affections and passions I have are in very truth constituted by, and made up of, those bodily changes which we ordinarily call their expression or consequence; and the more it seems to me that if I were to become corporeally anaesthetic, I should be excluded from the life of the affections, harsh and tender alike, and drag out an existence of merely cognitive or intellectual form.

(James 1950: 452)

James's insistence on the physiological basis was taken further by behaviour-ial psychologists who dropped all emphasis on subjectivity. According to them, emotion was merely observable physiological reactions conforming to regular patterns. They argued that we can dispense with the inner registra-tion of emotion and equate it with the external actions of the human individual. Psychoanalysis meanwhile was rethinking psychic structure from the inside and reducing emotion to a byproduct of unconscious desire, whose workings were the proper focus of analysis. For a novelist interested in the narrative representation of subjectivity this was a contradictory set of contemporary authorities but Lawrence was unlikely to want his characters to drag out their existence in a state of corporeal anaesthesia even if the novelistic conventions seemed to allow little else.

Consider what the different novelistic implication of these theories would be. The Cartesian idea of emotion leads to the most familiar form of representation of emotion. The ordinary usages of 'I feel sad', 'I feel angry' or 'he felt anxious' are Cartesian. The subject is not talking of the physio-logical feeling but the subjective awareness of it independent of the feeling. The behaviourist would describe behaviour (e.g. 'He grew red and hit the table'). A writer following James might well write like this of love:

Then his mouth drew near, pressing open her mouth, a hot, drenching surge rose within her, she opened her lips to him, in pained, poignant eddies she drew him nearer, she let him come further, his lips came and surging, surging, soft, oh soft, yet oh, like the powerful surge of water, irresistible, till with a little blind cry, she broke away.

(Lawrence 1981: 345)

This sentence from *The Rainbow* follows not a logical but a temporal progression through the changing physical responses of Ursula Brangwen. The 'surge', 'eddies' and cry are all physiological conditions suggestive of an orgasm, but the physiological registration of consciousness is as significant as the sexual metaphor. At school Tom Brangwen is embarrassed by the difficulties he has:

But when, almost secretly and shamefully, he came to take the book himself, and began the words 'Oh wild west wind, thou breath of autumn's being', the very fact of the print caused a prickly sensation of

72

repulsion to go over his skin, the blood came to his face, his heart filled
with a bursting passion of rage and incompetence.

(ibid.: 51)

The registration of physiological responses tied to the emotion is quite exact.
His prickly skin, blushes and sense of a swelling heart are all physical
changes resulting directly resulting from his struggle to read the poem,
without any mediation of consciousness: 'The very fact of the print *caused* a
prickly sensation of repulsion'. This direct process, like the intercourse of
earlier Brangwen farmers and the land, bypasses the undeveloped self-
consciousness altogether. On the evidence of such examples we might think
that Lawrence has chosen to fully endorse William James' account, and that
like the behaviourists he is chary of positing any subjective awareness. I
think what Lawrence is doing is better understood as the presentation of a
limited form of subjectivity largely experienced at this wordless, physiological level. The novel is presenting a variant of the William James theory (now
generally known as the James-Lange theory) as if it were a way one might
actually be, as a form of being, and then showing its limitations. That is why
the text talks of Tom being 'sensuously developed' and having more 'refined'
instincts than other boys:

> In feeling he was developed, sensitive to the atmosphere around him,
> brutal perhaps, but at the same time delicate, very delicate. . . . But at
> the same time his feelings were more discriminating than those of most
> of the boys, and he was confused. He was more sensuously developed,
> more refined in instinct than they.

(ibid.: 50)

Neither the senses nor the instincts are usually thought of as capable of
development, almost by definition. That possibility belongs to reason. This
model of the psyche therefore represents a rethinking of the standard model
of a subject necessarily capable of developing identities and taking up subject
positions. Tom, a representative man, is shown as capable of a state in which
he flourishes within the pre-linguistic, and can develop psychic capacities
outside language and dominant rationality. This portrait of a subject capable
of rationality largely confined to the senses, instincts and emotions challenges our current dominant conceptions in literary theory that assume that
subject positions are necessarily constituted by discourses and the misrecog-
nitions of self-reflection.

Tom's pre-verbal state of sense-certainty depended on a willingness to
embrace the unknown – unknown because Tom has no means of becoming
conscious of it. His son-in-law, Will, is also in love with the unknown, but
his is a much more sophisticated stage in the development of thought,
because where Tom is wholly inarticulate, Will is at least 'half articulate'
(ibid.: 150). Will is a symbolist, an aesthete, but unfortunately for them

both, his wife Anna is a thoroughgoing materialist, whose outlook eventually dominates his. The account of their courtship and marriage is an
extended study of the relations between two consciousnesses, and the text is
therefore scrupulous in its presentation of experience as 'for' one or the
other. As they prepare for marriage the difference between Will and Anna is
made explicit.

> For her, he was the kernel of life, to touch him alone was bliss. But for him
> she was the essence of life. She existed as much when he was at his carving
> in his lodging in Ilkeston, as when she sat looking at him in the Marsh
> kitchen. In himself, he knew her. But his outward faculties seemed
> suspended. He did not see her with his eyes nor hear her with his voice.
>
> (ibid.: 168)

This odd use of 'voice' instead of 'ears' underlines the importance attached
to reciprocity; a voice that 'hears' is a voice that responds to what the other
is saying, not one that speaks in egoistic monologues. The difference between the metaphorical implications of 'kernel' and 'essence' sums this up.
Essences (as in perfume or the French word for petrol) are powerful
remnants of what was once living. A kernel is the still-living seed that has the
capacity to grow and flower all over again. Anna wants Will in the most
tangible way, to touch him. He has the awareness of her inside him and that
is enough. He does not crave a tangible relation because he has her already,
as an essence and so he can get on with his carving of the figure of Eve
because the creative impulse will emerge from this essence within him. Will
is someone for whom even his own senses can be unimportant and so he
undervalues, indeed at times doesn't even acknowledge, the ordinary world
around him. Will's Anna is an introjection which then becomes the foundation of a self-consciousness only expressive of its internal source.

Will is repeatedly described as someone who lives blindly in darkness
which even he begins to experience as a 'black, *violent* underworld' (ibid.:
192; my emphasis). Will and Anna feel that the conflict which develops
between them is absolute: 'Never had his soul felt so flayed and uncreated'
(ibid.: 192). To Anna 'he seemed a dark, almost evil thing' (ibid.: 192) whose
'negative insensitiveness' is 'clayey and ugly' (ibid.: 194) (this is the reaction
Ursula later has to Winifred Inger). The interaction between them is not a
'passionate struggle into conscious being' (Lawrence 1968: 276); it is not a
dialectical struggle out of which emerges a new articulation, but a silencing
of development, a silencing most evident in the aftermath of their struggle
over the meaning of the Christian church. Anna rejects the hermeneutics of
the church – the lamb that must symbolize something other than itself – and
compels Will to do so as well. She is a kind of Nietzschean thinker who
celebrates the phenomenal world and believes that the other world of
religious truths has been falsely added to it (Nietzsche 1968: 49). Will
worships symbols precisely because they are not intelligible: 'He preferred

things he could not understand with the mind. He loved the undiscovered and the undiscoverable' (Lawrence 1981: 205). Will wants no possibility of knowledgeable self-consciousness, although he does want acknowledgement from Anna, and feels that she does not respect him. This is true: 'she did not care for what he represented in himself' (ibid.: 212). Anna is not interested in representations of the sacred or the beyond as Will is. The symbolist and the materialist cannot agree. Will can read symbols but he cannot see what they are made of. His darkness is the experiential world of a metaphorically blind form of hermeneutic consciousness because for him the world of the senses is simply not real. What matters is the eternal, unknowable world religion reveals, and hence the symbolic meaning of what that world offers through its material forms.

Will Brangwen achieves a partial reconciliation with Anna through sexual activity. Lawrence's portrait of Will is one of the first important analyses of modern masculine sexuality in English writing. It shows how the logic of self-centred sexual gratification develops from the pre-linguistic stasis and how such a sexuality can paradoxically free such a man from the toils of inward preoccupation. At the same time the painful limitations of this sexuality are made very evident. The process begins when, as a result of a renewed passion, Will begins to see Anna as 'the vastness of the unknown sensual store of delights she was' (ibid.: 278). This odd syntactic inversion underlines the importance of its apparently infinite scope. Discovery and gratification become his total preoccupation. We are not told what Anna wanted. Knowing arises from desire and requires strength, both of which are brought into being by her beauty. He needs to make these delights known to himself because otherwise they may be lost for ever: 'the many little rapturous places sent him mad with delight, and with desire to be able to know more, to have strength to know more. For all was there' (ibid.: 279). Will's ultimate aim is 'Absolute Beauty' (ibid.: 279) which is, we are told in precise, phenomenological language, 'perceived by him in her through his senses' (ibid.: 279). Beauty is available through the man's gaze, and by implication not through the woman, Anna. Absolute Beauty (an odd term, showing Lawrence's bricolage of Hegelianism) is all-encompassing beauty but it is also comprehensible or knowable beauty (Robert Solomon (1983: 274) glosses 'The Absolute' in Hegel's terminology as 'the unified, compre- hensible whole – in plain terms, knowable reality'). This knowing takes place without language. Beauty emerges in the 'revelations' of contact between body and body, and knowing this beauty is 'almost death in itself'. Such knowledge is deathly, but what we could read as neo-Hegelian is the idea that such knowledge is death from its own perspective, since Hegel's complex form 'in itself' means not only that something is other than us but that it is unreflective, or at least limited in its perspective. This sensual mode of being entails its own demise. The passage continues by telling us that 'this was what their love had become, a sensuality violent and extreme as death.

They had no conscious intimacy, no tenderness of love' (Lawrence 1981: 280). For the man this form of sexuality is experienced as a form of suicide, because it destroys the only kind of subjectivity he has, that of the symbolist. His relation to the world is that of subject to language. Everything in the world is a sign of the other, 'real' world, which cannot otherwise be known, so the material world vanishes in its instantaneous mediation by the senses. Through intensive physical intimacy with his wife he tries to make known this beauty by carrying out this mediation (symbolization), but the immediacy of her presence keeps overwhelming him, and the result is an annihilation of his subjectivity, because it only exists in that process of mediation. Forced to touch the 'kernel', his hold on 'essences' is destroyed. He doesn't look for a knowledge that arises dialectically through a mutual interengagement of his self and Anna's, because although he desires the knowledge, he cannot bear to be altered by it.

As a whole, *The Rainbow* is not a novel about sex, despite the predominantly sexual field of most of the encounters, because its preoccupation is not sensation or morality but changes in reciprocal awareness. The physiological registration of emotion and thought is given great emphasis because these are realities of the encounters, or measures of them, just as colour, shape or texture are measures of objects. Consciousness is not thought of as a property wholly under the control of its subjects, so familiar novelistic devices like secrecy and limited awareness are of no interest to the novel. Such devices depend on the presupposition of an independent moral agent able to decide on the withholding of secrets or the refusal of understanding. Lawrence doesn't necessarily deny the possibility of at least a limited autonomy for such a conscious self but simply focuses on its dependence on the struggle between self and other.

At times the attempt to embody a form of thought fails, especially in the hurried passages of the final section of the book dealing with Ursula Brangwen's several relationships. Ursula's development begins with the tension between materialism and spiritual hermeneutics that existed between her parents and continues through a series of stages mostly marked by her relationships with men and women, but also engendered by her college training. This produces a new strain and complexity in the novel. She recapitulates most of the major forms of nineteenth-century thought in her development and even anticipates twentieth-century forms. The result is not so much implausibility as a sometimes laconic and therefore misleading account of the consciousness of these forms of life. Her affair with Winifred Inger is the most notable example. The earlier emphasis on the process of an emerging awareness based on the struggles of an intimate relationship traced in detail sometimes gets reduced to a very brief and stereotyped encounter. The novel begins to generate unresolvable difficulties with its basic premises as it moves with Ursula into a complex society and broader history.

The Rainbow is a narrative of the emergence of articulate modern subjectivity through the historical sequence of different relationships. In that way it is very close to Hegel's *Phenomenology of Spirit*. Lawrence's novel shows the lived consequences of different forms of thought – humanism, behaviourism, different kinds of morality, art and science – on a not quite believably small group of people over several generations. What it does demonstrate very clearly is the extreme difficulty experienced by modern men in achieving a balance between the social identity by which they are recognized as men, and their largely undeveloped self-consciousnesses. The novel shows that despite Hegel's equation of self-consciousness and desire, self-consciousness can take less conscious forms. The causes of that underdevelopment are only hinted at. War, industrialization and possibly some inherent failure are all proposed. The novel has to shift gender entirely even to begin to think through a form that such development might take. Underlying the entire novel is a radical challenge to the dominant class institutions which turn education into an ideological state apparatus and deny the value of emergent forms of pre-linguistic interaction of those like the Brangwens who are outside the dominant social classes. *The Rainbow* is an attempt to provide a new education. Its relative lack of success is in large measure due to the apparent impossibility of finding a contemporary public form for it. The dominant masculinities are alliances of the undeveloped darkness of masculine subjectivities with a rationality that serves the militaristic state. Art provides the only outlet, but that is too easily subsumed into another kind of self-restraint. *The Rainbow* is, however, not a pessimistic novel about men, because it poses the possibility of development. It leaves us wondering how to foster such change when all the young men seem to have gone off to war and imperialist duties, or, like her suitor Anthony Schofield, have apparently regressed to the wordless comforts of the unconscious. Ursula and her suitor look at the moon on a snowy, twilit evening: 'He did not see it. He was one with it. But she saw it, and was one with it. Her seeing separated them infinitely' (ibid.: 467). From the earliest Brangwens to this contemporary of Ursula's the men have terrible difficulty in forming an inward gaze. Even in Anton Skrebensky, the man with whom Ursula has the most extended relationship, it remains fragile and easily extinguished by the emotions his aggressive masculinity arouses.

4

ARE MEN RATS? FREUD'S HISTORY OF AN OBSESSIONAL NEUROSIS

THE RAT MAN'S ORDINARINESS

Gaze inward at the weekend artist, Superman, and you see a siege mentality making the inner life of its fortress ego tolerable with hobbies and self-improvement. One of these hobbies is painting worlds that transcend this one. In the previous chapter, the full-time modernist Art Man turned out to aspire to sublime states transcending the ditch of everyday life, where he saw no more than a 'blind man battering blind men', and all too often ended up living like the would-be aesthete, Will Brangwen or Superman, in an 'under-world refuge' (Lawrence 1981: 201). At times these Art Men seemed more like Wolf Men or Rat Men than artists with highly developed rational imaginations capable of reintegrating the divisions of modern life. The Art Man becomes a 'baffled prowling beast' (Joyce 1988: 102), or a 'frog-spawn' (Yeats 1984: 236), or seems to an observer like Anna Brangwen to be a hawk with 'naive and inhuman' eyes (Lawrence 1981: 203), or a 'leopard that had leapt on her, and fastened' (ibid.: 228). At best this theriomorphic recidivism is simply contained by some mechanical restraint like Yeats's golden mimic of a bird. As if recognizing regressive bestiality as a significant modern phenomenon, Freud came to call two of his case studies the Wolf Man and the Rat Man, giving us a chance to see what the modern science of subjecti-vity, psychoanalysis, has to say about the inner or underworld of these modern masculinities whose self-image is a beast rather than the ideal of a demi-god. The inward gaze of psychoanalysis turns on masculinity in these case studies and gives us an opportunity to measure its power to generate a self-critical masculine reflexivity.

Of the two focused on young men, the case of the Rat Man is an obvious one to choose in order to see how well psychoanalysis achieves this self-reflection. The Rat Man, who manages to pass examinations, do his military service, seduce women and slowly make his way in a career, is quite ordinary, despite his obsessional neuroses. He is ordinarily violent towards women, ordinarily competitive, ordinarily fearful of men. By comparison the Wolf Man is so disturbed that he is unable to carry on the everyday activities of life, and comes from a family in which a series of severe neurotic disorders had already led to the suicide of a sister. The Rat Man is in many ways typical of his class. He goes to prostitutes but doesn't much like them, preferring a lower-class woman, a dressmaker, for sex, and having no intention of marrying her. The young man is typical of his kind in that he separates sex and love, as is evident in another detail of the case, only found in the notes because Freud didn't think it significant to the final presentation. The young man's reaction to a story he heard from a waitress about her lover's death nearly prevented him going ahead with his plan of spending the night with her, because:

> He always sought to make a sharp distinction between relations which consisted only in copulation and everything that was called love; and the idea that she had been so deeply loved made her in his eyes an unsuitable object for his sensuality.
>
> (Freud 1955: 263)

'An unsuitable object': the Rat Man's objectification of women is not taken by Freud to be a serious pathology. Even when Freud acknowledges the significance of the young man's violence towards women he is reluctant to focus on the violence itself. A striking incidence of this is Freud's changing response to the confession that the young man had assaulted his sister after his father's death. Freud's brief remark in the case notes that these assaults 'must have been the explanation of his pathological changes' (ibid.: 278) is not followed up in the published case, nor is the Rat Man's habit of undressing his youngest sister to look at her body. None of this is understood by Freud as a problem to be addressed. Nor are the young man's military interests. This behaviour might be inconvenient but it seems to be contained within the boundaries of an ordinarily elastic masculine morality.

The Rat Man case is a brilliant presentation of Freud's work with a young man who has had two periods of intense obsession, once as a child and once as a young man. Both were times when he was obsessed by thoughts of death and sexuality. The first, in childhood, began when he was seduced by his governess. The second occurred when, after his father's death, his mother proposed an advantageous marriage arrangement. Both times women precipitated the problems. Freud's exposition is designed to show how difficult it is to reach a clear statement of this history, especially the recent bout of obsession about the return of a tiny loan of postage for a pair of pince-nez sent as replacements. Freud's aim is to help the young man rejoin the mainstream of public life ('he had wasted years . . . lost much ground in the course of his life' (ibid.: 39)). Something gets in the way, both of clarity (Freud's narrative becomes enmeshed in various versions of an obsession with train times for example) and the young man's wish for success in love and work.

The Rat Man case study reads like a novel. The comparison with fiction is a tribute to how well written it is, and to the way Freud's exposition partly takes the form of reported conversations with the patient, in which the general principles and conclusions are outlined. At first glance it seems more of a leisurely nineteenth-century account than a postmodern fiction (despite claims like those of Steven Marcus (1984) to the contrary), owing more to Conan Doyle than Thomas Pynchon. The gentleman investigator's interior world is entered by someone with a disturbing story to tell, a story whose disturbances of sanity, order and law are strongly contrasted with the tidy masculine enclave of the study/consulting room. Henry James uses this familiar motif in the opening section of *The Awkward Age* to make possible a free conversation between the two male protagonists, who look at photographs of the women whose fate the novel will follow. Freud uses the idea of a mystery to be solved and the image of the man's study as a metonymic sign of the masculine rationality that will enable this to happen, and to help legitimize his innovative blend of medical consultation, confession and detection. The narrator introduces the character, describes at length his meetings with him, and then proceeds to draw conclusions from what he learns. These conclusions are both specific to the young man and general observations on human psychic processes. The young man is both individual and representative. For the young man to exhibit these mental processes it must be the case, Freud assumes, that all human beings do so. The depiction of the young man as physically present to the narrator, who is represented as remembering this for the reader, is metonymic of scientific observation. The young man's discourse is the raw material of actuality which theory tries to explain as the workings of more general laws. The narrator is reciting this to the reader, who thereby occupies a privileged position (because this recital was initially therapeutic, aimed at the young man). This presupposes a reader who is not subject to such disturbances, a reader who is in full command of reason, communication and the symbolic sphere. Such command includes the possibility of understanding and expelling such obsessional neuroses as those of the young man.

Freud's relation with the young man depends on an already existing framework for a person consulting a professional man who represents the law. Psychoanalysis was such a new profession that the authority and structure of the relationship in the consulting room had to be borrowed from elsewhere, from medicine. This relationship is part of a more general form, the relation with priest, lawyer and government official (king or clerk as it were). The man of authority mediates between some body of law, divine, human or natural, with which the client wishes to negotiate. There is, however, something new in this relationship. What after all are the laws Freud represents? As a psychoanalyst he does not embody widely recognized cultural norms, norms which the professional both enforces and explains how to propitiate. To understand this new relation we need to consider also that although the case history is full of information about troop manoeuvres, individual manoeuvres and ritual obsessive manoeuvres, none of this matters in itself as data. If it did, then the analyst would want all the information about the young man that he could obtain. He might well go to great lengths to find out all that could be known about the young man, perhaps by interviewing his family and friends, keeping up analytic sessions as long as necessary (not the arbitrary cut-off of the analytic hour), and even employing investigators. This sounds absurd to our ears because we are so familiar with the ground rules of psychoanalysis that we rarely question the way it sets up the restrictions on what can be known about the patient. For Freud, the aim is not to know what the young man knows, or what others know about him, but the manner in which he knows what he knows – to get at the functioning of belief, not the belief itself. This implies that the beliefs, the memories and the knowledge the young man has don't matter in themselves. The abstract mental apparatus, independent of what is known, is all that matters. Not the contents (a favourite submerged metaphor for Freud) but the container is the focus of attention. So what sort of relation does Freud have with the patient? The modern answer would be that there is a transferential relation between analyst and patient in which the form of the young man's relation to Freud reveals the originating form of his relations to his parents as it was founded by the pattern of libidinal cathexes in his development up to the Oedipal repression. Another way of saying this is that all that matters is the form of the communicative relation between the two men in all its complex handling of the symbolic. The analyst becomes the representative of the laws of the symbolic. Freud assumes that there are such laws and that they can be so represented. This relation is therefore not concerned with contents, with an engagement with what is said, as is the case in friendship. It assumes that reflexivity of this transcendental kind is possible and that contents and container are separable, a thoroughly modern view. In making this separation, Freud sets boundaries to the relationship between analysand and analyst which reproduce the commonly enforced boundaries between men in the public world. The men meet on the common ground of the law. Their emotional connections are retranslated into in-stances of general laws. The Rat Man says that he believes 'self-reproach could only arise from a breach of a person's own inner moral principles and not from that of any external ones'; Freud concurs: 'I agreed, and said that the man who merely breaks an external law often regards himself as a hero' (Freud 1955: 57). Freud provides a discourse for the relation to the law in the masculine terms of heroism. Some masculine inward gazes will see a hero created by the transgression of the law. Others like the Rat Man's are directed at laws which cannot be broken with impunity. The real implication of Freud's response is that the transgression of inner moral principles is similar in structure to the heroic law-breaking even though the pursuit of manhood is rewarded not with a hero's welcome but calumny.

The interaction between the two men, analyst and analysand, on the ground of the inner law, is not allowed to have actual consequences. The power of this therapeutic reduction is widely acknowledged, and I am certainly not arguing that Freudian psychoanalysis is limited because it doesn't allow analysand and analyst to get close in some 'touchy-feely' way. But the Freudian reduction of relations unfortunately reproduces almost exactly a masculine social practice which defends certain masculine pathologies, especially organized male violence. Showing how this happens will require a detailed reading of the Rat Man case.

This modern relation between the two men depends on a further circumstance of the case. The young man is presented as an actor witnessed in real time. Frequent locutions like 'he then went on to say' underscore this. The young man is presented as at once both the embodiment of an inaccessible history and entirely open to our analysis of his present words and behaviour. His outside history is known only by what he will say of it. He is presented by Freud through a series of moments, sessions, cross-sections of his life. The words he utters and the visible gestures that accompany them are taken to be the only certainty available to the analyst. Everything else, everything we might interpret from his presence and speech, could be fantasy or misrepresentation. The young man's presence is a given. There he is, and what he says constitutes the data from which we have to begin. In that way this is a very modern piece of writing, because nothing is more modern than the assumption, now standard in most forms of novelistic writing, that what lies between quotation marks is not just a sign but a part of the person who spoke, a datum of his or her self-activity. This doesn't mean that we necessarily assume the words are original, or that the person controls their meaning in some logocentric fantasy, but simply that the words spoken are that person's relation to the world of others. It depends on a fantasy, however, a fantasy of unimpeded audition, as if hearing gave direct access to the certainty of what someone said, rather than producing an interpretation of what that person said. It presupposes a scientific neutrality in the transcription and presentation of these words which older grammatical forms of reported speech did not. This is a modern assumption because it brackets out all the possible other relations in which the persons might be embedded, and in which the words spoken might form clauses in larger and quite different structures, from religious and political traditions (in the sense that Alasdair MacIntyre has explored in his recent works), to complexities of intimate family life and friendships, to the unspoken relations, emotional, bodily and spatial, which are also part of this larger syntax. The linguistic metaphor breaks down here, because these are not all linguistic, and may not be fully comprehended in language.

What then does the difficulty evident in a case like the Rat Man's imply? Freud is listening to uncensored communication which is rarely made to anyone else. One obvious feature of the Rat Man's life is that most of what he tells Freud he has apparently told no one else (he has confided some of his more discussable obsessions with a friend whose influence has been beneficial). The result is that what is being said is a kind of emergent communication, at the very edge of articulation, and indeed bodily gesture (the young man walks about and is often restless or even cowers from the analyst). Hence the echo of Conan Doyle, the emphasis on the process of detection the narrator undertakes, and the way this parallels the transformation desired by the young man – the expulsion of the obsessions – as a coincident process. The rats desert the man and part one of the case ends as both narrative and therapy cease simultaneously: 'When we reached the solution that has been described above, the patient's rat delirium disappeared' (Freud 1955: 100).

Freud tells us that the young man's father was 'an excellent man'. One way of describing the young man's problem is that he has had great difficulties since his father's death in likewise becoming an excellent man. Military service, sexual initiation, a good job, seem to fail to bring him into that condition. Instead he is haunted with obsessions. The popular name of the case suggests something about this. A Rat Man is not quite a man. Children's story books (those of Richard Scarry for example) are full of animals behaving like people. Why? The animal character makes them not quite people and therefore beneath children in status and power. They make children feel safely powerful, and the children can have the same relation to the animals as parents to children. The animal nature also signifies that in the child which is not yet fully adult, not yet man or woman. With this in mind let us look at the rat theme more closely.

Published as 'Bemerkungen über einen Fall von Zwangsneurose' ('Notes upon a case of obsessional neurosis') in 1909, the case is now universally known as the 'Rat Man' (the young man's real name, Dr Ernst Lanzer (Mahony 1986: 2), was not generally known until recently – I shall continue to call him the Rat Man to retain the mythological quality of his psychoanalytic history). The need for confidentiality resulted, as it did with the case of the 'Wolf Man', in the creation of these mythic creatures, half men half animal, whose stories tell of their relations with both gods and men, back in the beginnings of the world, demi-gods like ravens and coyotes (a commentator like Muriel Gardiner (1973) finds nothing odd in talking about meeting the Wolf Man in Vienna, as if she had wandered into a werewolf story by accident). They are also like young Native American men who have identified their animate guardians, an animal clan adopted during an adolescent fasting rite. The young Native American man withdraws from the community as a boy and returns as a man. Like Stephen Dedalus who sees a crane, Freud's young men have found an animal spirit to guide them, but they have been unable to understand the spirit's words. Stephen was more fortunate. He was apparently able to understand without language:

Her image had passed into his soul for ever and no word had broken the holy silence of his ecstasy. Her eyes had called him and his soul had

leaped at the call. To live, to err, to fall, to triumph, to recreate life out
of life! A wild angel had appeared to him, the angel of mortal youth
and beauty, an envoy from the fair courts of life, to throw open before
him in an instant of ecstasy the gates of all the ways of error and glory.

(Joyce 1988: 176)

Stephen translates her call both into a Christian discourse of annunciation,
and the medievalizing poetics of late nineteenth-century Romanticism that
mythologized the 'fair courts of life' so thoroughly (as in Alfred Tennyson
and William Morris). Stephen, the Crane Man, seems to forget the bird as
soon as his hallucination disappears. The bird is a girl, and the ecstasy
adolescent sexual excitement. Freud's animal men are not so lucky. They are
haunted by their animals. Instead of life, death seems to beckon from the
eyes of the rats the Rat Man sees on his father's grave. He will need to have
this rat's call explained to him. The Rat Man's transition to manhood is
blocked, and so he cannot leave his animal visions behind and return to
society like the young Native American man.

Freud explains his association between the young man and a rat by linking
it to the young man's memory of seeing a 'big beast', which he took to be a
rat, walking over his father's grave, as if it had just been feeding on his
father's corpse. Freud then proposes that the young man actually identifies
with this hungry parricidal rat by recalling his own literary association of
rats with an episode in Goethe's *Faust*. Mephistopheles conjures up a rat in
order to break his way through a doorway guarded by a magic pentagram,
just as the young man does to get at his father. Then Freud uses another
quotation from Faust to cement his interpretation: he quotes the lines 'For
in the bloated rat he sees/ A living likeness of himself'. Yet it is Freud
himself, almost like a new Mephistopheles, who conjures up a rat association
in order to break through into the hidden areas of the young man's mind. He
uses his magic language to open up the dark cellar there. Freud's creation has
another Mephistophelean aspect. The Rat Man he creates is a creature which
ought to be destroyed: 'But rats cannot be sharp-toothed, greedy and dirty
with impunity: they are cruelly persecuted and mercilessly put to death by
man, as the patient had often observed with horror' (Freud 1955: 96).

The young man is really a rat ('just such a nasty, dirty little wretch, who
was apt to bite people when he was in a rage' (ibid.: 96)), and Freud is a
man. The young man would seem to have some reason to be afraid of Freud,
if Freud associates him with a rat. What does the persecuted rat represent,
and why has Freud produced a figure the psychoanalytic institutions will
find so compelling that they will make the Rat Man and the Wolf Man as
important to their mythos as Raven and Coyote are to some Native
American mythologies?

The rattiness of the patient is masculine violence. Freud and psychoanalysis are so horrified by it that they make it totemic of the power of

psychoanalysis, which, they claim is able to trap this rat. Psychoanalysis is a successful rat catcher because it knows how to speak to such animals. Freud sets about understanding the causes of the two periods of intense obsessional neurosis by investigating a beating the young man received from his father when he was 3 or 4 (of which he has no memory – his mother recalls it for him during the course of the analysis). Freud thinks it might have been a punishment for masturbation, but the man's mother thinks it was for biting his nurse. The event is dated by the 'fatal illness of an elder sister' (ibid.: 85) but no attempt is made to link the boy's behaviour to any distress this might have caused. This beating had powerful consequences:

> The little boy had flown into a terrible rage and had hurled abuse at his father even while he was under his blows. But as he knew no bad language, he had called him all the names of common objects that he could think of, and had screamed: 'You lamp! You towel! You plate!' and so on. His father, shaken by such an outburst of elemental fury, had stopped beating him, and had declared: 'the child will either be a great man or a great criminal'.
>
> (ibid.: 86)

Freud then adds in a footnote: 'These alternatives did not exhaust the possibilities. His father overlooked the commonest outcome of such premature passions – a neurosis' (ibid.: 86).

The young man has a total amnesia about the events, no fantasies or screen memories, and only his evident hatred of his father gives a clue to the existence of the beating. In Freud's account the strangeness of this beating lies in the boy's rage. Is this because the father's rage is taken for granted? Freud himself seems unconscious of the father's anger, as if it were either too obvious to need comment, and too obviously justified by the moral code (fathers have the right, and should use it, to punish children who bite others), or as if there might well be no anger at all in the father, who might be merely carrying out his duty with a passionless violence. The boy denounces his father as if this passionless violence were the case, as if the father were no more than a thing, a piece of household furnishing for the use of others, and of course under the control of the woman of the household, his mother. The boy could be questioning whether the violence is actually being done at his mother's orders.

This forgotten incident calls forth a lengthy footnote, in which Freud is at some pains to insist that although there is corroboration of the event, which is unusual, even the mother's memories may have been repressed, and there may after all have been some sexual character to the behaviour that provoked his father. Freud stresses that even though there was an event, the real importance for the patient lay in his multiple fantasies about it:

> A deeper interpretation of the patient's dreams in relation to this

episode revealed the clearest traces of the presence in his mind of an imaginative production of a positively epic character. In this his sexual desires for his mother and sister and his sister's premature death were linked up with the young hero's chastisement at his father's hand.

(ibid.: 88)

The patient has written his own *Faust*, and Freud will transcribe it, but this leads immediately to a problem. After asserting that the beating can take its place in an Oedipal scenario, Freud's text at once becomes defensive, saying that the analysis had to be suspended for a while due to the demands of the patient's daily life, and so Freud is 'not to be blamed, therefore, for this gap in the analysis'. It is as if Freud imagines his readers giving him a beating for apparently having taken a bite out of the story, as if he were really the rat. His own narrative then enacts this beating. He tells us that it was only in the transference fantasies that the importance of the Rat Man's childhood trauma became evident, and these fantasies were violent attacks on Freud and his family:

> Things soon reached a point at which, in his dreams, his waking phantasies, and his associations, he began heaping the grossest and filthiest abuse upon me and my family, though in his deliberate actions he never treated me with anything but the greatest respect.

(ibid.: 89)

Freud has become the rat, and in addition, a transferential father (and Freud's family the young man's family), and we readers are made to feel both sympathy for Freud and merciless in our persecution of the rat in him, at the very point where his theory seems most in jeopardy, from real events and bites missing from his analysis. As Freud says, rats are 'mercilessly put to death by man' (ibid.: 96). We ourselves are also rats because we try to bite Freud for his unavoidable omissions, and all this transferential running to and fro occurs because of the narration of the mother's memory of the father's violent treatment of his son.

Freud describes the behaviour of his patient in one of the sessions from the period of the verbal abuse in such a way that we can see that to the young man, Freud himself appears to be a potentially violent man. The young man, remembering that 'his father had had a passionate temper, and sometimes in his violence had not known where to stop', cowers and hides during some of his sessions with Freud, as if from imminent attack. When he was a boy his father's passionate anger led to violence and an unconsciousness of what he was doing 'in his violence'. And what is he doing? He is physically attacking members of his family, but appears to be unconscious of it. The son is now unconscious of the beating his mother has often told him about (and Freud adds without further comment that his father had, according to his mother, also referred to it), and Freud is unconscious of his own countertransference, with its fantasies of persecuting the Rat Man and being persecuted by his readers. We could say that the rat is a frightening emblem of male violence instead of the totemic figure able to 'open . . . the gates of all the ways of error and glory'.

Freud's own text is caught up in similar transferential relations to the psychoanalytic world. In the 1909 edition of the essay, a footnote to the account of his first session with the young man begins 'My colleague Dr Alfred Adler', but after his disagreements with Adler, the note was changed to read 'Dr Alfred Adler, who was formerly an analyst'. The adverb 'formerly' makes him a non-person in terms of the psychoanalytic community. But this critic occupies a role in relation to Freud curiously parallel to that between the Rat Man and his father. The footnote is there to mention Adler's suggestion that the first things said by the new analysand can be very important. Those words let the rats loose at once. The young man's first words 'laid stress upon the influence exercised over him by men, that is to say, upon the part played in his life by homosexual object-choice' (ibid.: 41). The footnote is caught at the intersection of several sets of possibly homosexual relations, the Rat Man's relation to his father, the Rat Man's relation to Freud, and Freud's relation to Adler. If Adler is right, then homosexuality is the key to the case, and Freud's expulsion of him may well be suspect. Adler's own preoccupations with power add to the significance of this appearance in a footnote. In 1914 Adler was already saying that 'the psyche has as its objective the *goal of superiority*' (ibid.: 7), thus elevating masculine competitiveness into a psychic principle. Getting rid of Adler means getting rid of this masculine struggle for dominance, but the footnote actually enacts the very thing which Adler claims is true of the psyche.

Male violence is one of the features of masculinities which seems most in need of some intrapsychic understanding. The case study about the Rat Man is pervaded with violence, murder and militarism, real and fantasized. Mostly the violence is a horizon of ritual coded activities like the manoeuvres during which the rat fantasy emerges. The toy gun, for example, with which the young man enacts a ritual murder of his brother, is an especially obvious example. Even the transference relation is violent. Freud elsewhere (in the Wolf Man case) likened the analyst's progress to that of an advancing enemy army and specifically compared psychic resistance to the resistance presented by an enemy army as one's own army invades (ibid.: 238). The young man's father was a soldier for some years before his marriage and his son is himself a reservist. Patrick Mahony cites the young man's military record, a document which indicates what it meant to be a good soldier and thus a real, excellent man, in that culture. The record says that he shows 'reliable and smart behaviour on the front', and 'leads his section decisively and also independently both in fighting and in formation' (Mahony 1986: 8). A real man maintains all the outward display of masculinity even at the front, indeed it is at the front that masculinity really proves itself, especially its independence and the resulting power that gives to dominate others. Other men are to be killed, led or formed into good order. As a boy, the Rat Man shot his brother with a toy gun by tricking him. He told his brother that if he 'looked up the barrel he would see something' (Freud 1955: 65). This gaze was punished by the Rat Man. He pulled the trigger and shot him, hoping to hurt him. The toy gun did no damage, unlike the guns he uses now as a man. Freud tries to persuade the Rat Man that the persisting self-hatred of 'the quality of *cowardice* which was so particularly horrible to him' which such memories induce, is misplaced because 'these reprehensible impulses originated from his infancy' (ibid.: 66). This explanation avoids discussing the contemporary pressures to be a real man, a heroic man incapable of cowardice.

Freud tells us that the boy's father had a 'soldierly manner' (ibid.: 81), was good-natured except when angry, and had become a good companion to his son, to whom he was as much friend as father later in life. This combination of soldier and father/friend may well have been unconsciously confusing to his son. The young man grew up assuming that the best men were soldiers, men trained to kill other men and to expect violence from them. He himself was to die as the result (whether of war wounds or disease is not clear) of male violence, in the First World War (he died four days after his capture by the Russians, in a prisoner-of-war camp). He has many violent murderous fantasies, not only about the woman he loves and his father, but about other men too, like the man who was occupying the rooms he wanted in the hotel at a health resort (who died a fortnight later), and the man, Lieutenant A, who told him about the rat torture and sparked off a bout of obsession about repaying a small debt. Lieutenant A appears 'cruel' to the young man, and his rat story confirms it. Clearly the officer recalls his father, but he also represents the underlying ethos of militarism, its male violence, and does so openly: 'at the officer's mess he had repeatedly defended the introduction of corporal punishment' (ibid.: 47). The Rat Man's fiancée's stepfather was also in the regiment and as Mahony (1986: 12) points out, 'liked to say "I will shoot you", and it was in his presence that Lanzer saw a rat'. This menace of corporal punishment (adult forms of the male violence evident in the childhood beating) seems to have started off the whole series of rat fantasies.

Manhood depends on using guns correctly. The Rat Man's father told him how gambling debts nearly destroyed him, and how the man who saved him with a loan also said: 'a man who does a thing like this ought to shoot himself' (Freud 1955: 209) (Freud left this out of the published case). Freud considers that the young man's obsession about repaying the postage arose because of an identification with his father's experience at that time. It was a moment when his father ceased to be a man, because a man would have turned the symbol of organized male violence, the gun, on himself. Being a man would have meant ceasing to be one, a deadly paradox.

Freud repeatedly emphasizes the man's rage at his father. Although Freud reports the young man as saying that he was never beaten again, we are also told that the father sometimes lost control of himself, and the young man's behaviour certainly suggests that there were other beatings. His sisters were beaten. I believe that we can therefore say that the young man's obsessions were at the least amplified if not caused by male violence. For the patient the problem is to come to terms with this male violence, which he experiences at every level of his existence, in the intimate relation with his parents, in the social world he grows up in, in the toys and language he learns, and even in the safe therapeutic environment of the analyst's consulting room. Above all he has to find a way of accommodating male violence in his relation to the symbolic. It is a mystery which toy guns, army manoeuvres and rat fantasies all try to resolve. Even sexuality is drafted in. For the Rat Man, the relation between his father's uncontrolled anger, and the controlled murderousness of war, is a direct one. What he has to learn is to suppress the first and go along with the second. Freud gives voice to the desire to kill his father as a means of undoing its damaging repression, but the chain of social symbolic relations in which it occurs cannot be broken so easily because even its mere acknowledgement would seem to undo the very possibility of psycho-analysis. How can a reflexive understanding of the basis of communication withstand something which would destroy the reflexivity itself? Male violence negates the very process on which the peculiar relation between analyst and analysand is based, if that relation is one between men.

THE FRONTLINE OF MASCULINITY

In Chris Marker's film *Sans soleil* (1983) there is an opening scene of a night ferry on which everyone is strewn around the seats trying to sleep, looking, as the voice-over puts it, like war refugees. Such images, continues the interpretative voice, are 'small images of war enshrined in everyday life', and for the film maker everyday life has become an intolerable battlefield as a result. The refugees are really overnight travellers. It is the voice-over that turns the image of travellers into refugees, but the movie viewer remains suspended between the two alternatives, aware of the imaginative imposition but also aware of its possibility, since most movies are simulacra peopled with actors. The war is neither actual nor imaginary but a continual possibility provoked by the male gaze. The philosopher Emmanuel Levinas (1969: 22) believes that 'the peace of empires issued from war rests on war. It does not restore to the alienated beings their lost identity.' He blames it on a 'morality based on the pure subjectivism of the "I"' (ibid.: 25). In this chapter I am suggesting that the small fragments of war that are worshipped in everyday life are fragments of a masculine state of permanent battle-readiness. Its sources are not so easily identified with the Western commitment to egological subjectivity, however.

The Rat Man lives in a world of male violence, and the case study becomes complicit with it. He dies in the First World War, and Freud is so affected by the events of the war that in 1920 he proposes a new instinct or group of instincts, the death drives, for which he argues the theoretical necessity is overwhelming, even if specific case material is less forthcoming. The death drives help to provide a theoretical means to understanding destructiveness and violence, as well as the repetition compulsion, and come close to introducing a masculine principle of catabolism, although the death drive was said by Freud to be universal in all living things. Its introduction was contentious in the psychoanalytic community and remained so, providing a point of departure for many of the subsequent divisions and redirections of theory from Melanie Klein to Jacques Lacan. The persistent difficulty is to account for the relatively single-sex character of what ought to be uniformly distributed across genders if it is a universal instinct. Only some very strange vicissitudes could contain it in men, and those vicissitudes became a central issue for several generations of analysts. I will consider some of these vicissitudes as they reflect back on the Rat Man's relation to masculine violence.

Freud (1984) conceives his investigation of the death drive as a push 'beyond the pleasure principle'. The first section firmly establishes the pursuit of pleasure as a fundamental motival principle. In the second section Freud explains that 'investigation of the mental reaction to external danger' leads inexorably to the hypothesis of a second, equally fundamental principle. The specific 'external danger' making this hypothesis inevitable is war. 'Traumatic neurosis' is nothing new. What is new is that the war has 'put an end to the temptation to attribute the cause of the disorder to organic lesions of the nervous system brought about by mechanical force' (Freud 1984: 281). His ensuing discussion focuses intermittently on what he calls the 'traumatic neuroses of peace' as well as the war neuroses, so when he says that fright rather than anxiety is the salient condition of mind in a traumatic neurosis there is a strong hint that this is true of the war neurosis also. Freud worries away at the term 'fright', saying that it is not the same as fear or anxiety, because fright depends on surprise.

Freud then seems to drop the theme altogether, having emphasized that traumatic neuroses often produce dreams which repeat the trauma, seemingly in contradiction to the wish-fulfilment theory of dreams. Instead he turns to the story of a little boy, his grandson, whose game of 'fort-da' has become the most famous game in psychoanalysis. The boy throws a cotton reel out of his cot saying 'da', and pulls it back in saying 'fort'. Less often remarked is the sequel, a game in which the boy:

> used to take a toy, if he was angry with it, and throw it on the floor, exclaiming, 'Go to the fwont!' He had heard at that time that his absent father was 'at the front', and was far from regretting his absence; on the

contrary he made it quite clear that he had no desire to be disturbed in his sole possession of his mother.

(Freud 1984: 285)

'Fwont' is one of Freud's English translator Strachey's impressionistic versions of the German. Freud transcribes the boy's speech as 'Geh' in K(r)ieg!' (Freud 1940: 14), the bracket indicating an elided consonant. 'Go to war' is considerably more blunt than the Strachey translation, but, for readers in the 1920s, the 'front' was probably more evocative because of the recent memory of the First World War when the front was a terrible reality. Like the Rat Man, Freud's son-in-law's manhood depends on good performance at the front, and Freud's grandson has already learned something of this. Freud's reproduction of the boy's mispronunciation deserves comment, even if it is less obvious than Strachey's comic version. Such transcriptions of mispronunciation, used by the poet Ezra Pound widely in *The Cantos*, function as a way of undermining the authority of what is said by the mispronounced words. No doubt the boy did mispronounce the word 'Krieg', but he probably pronounced many other words awkwardly too. Freud's emphasis on the childishness of the boy's pronunciation hints at an unease about the whole subject. For Freud the aim of this series of examples, especially the 'fort-da' game, is to show that the compulsion to repeat can overcome the pleasure principle. This little 18-month-old boy, we are told, 'never cried when his mother left him for a few hours' (Freud 1984: 204). He was a 'good boy' (Freud puts it in scare quotes). So good was the boy that he didn't even show grief when his mother died a few years later. This is a strong masculine constellation – the good manliness, the lack of grief, the game of making things disappear, sending toys like fathers to war. The tears and the toys and the fathers are all gone, where being gone means having gone off to kill other men and possibly be killed by them. The 'fort-da' game has the war as its subtext; war in which fathers leave sons behind to kill other sons and possibly be killed by them, war which threatens little boys (every departure may bring a death), a threat they learn to master in play.

Men dominated the earliest stages of psychoanalysis but this soon began to change. Foremost among the innovators was Melanie Klein who took the death drive very seriously, and began to look much more closely at all those 'fort-da' games which children were playing, her own and then those of analyst friends, so that gradually she became the leading authority on the psychoanalysis of children. Klein found violent fantasies of evisceration, castration and murder evident in the children's games, fantasies which in turn produced guilt as well as fears of retaliation and loss. For Klein these processes are internal to the children's mental life. Her description can be read another way. The play and communications which Klein interprets as symptoms of murderous fantasies could, in addition, be thought of as a means whereby infants come to terms with the realization that they live in a world where adults kill one another. Consider the summary of her analysis of Peter in the late essay on play technique. She describes a game in which she believes he re-enacts his anger at the witnessed copulation of his parents at the age of 18 months:

> He laid a toy man on a brick which he called a 'bed', threw him down and said he was 'dead and done for'. He next re-enacted the same thing with two toy men, choosing figures he had already damaged. I interpreted that the first toy man stood for his father whom he wanted to throw out of his mother's bed and kill, and that one of the two toy men was again the father and the other represented himself to whom his father would do the same.
>
> (Klein 1986: 45)

Klein's interpretation is immediately spoken to Peter, and this seems to enable him to continue playing instead of going into stasis – destroying the figures and ceasing to play, as was his wont. This anecdote is narrated in the course of a discussion about whether children can actually follow such interpretations. Klein emphatically believes they can. If, however, the boy can follow such an interpretation, then he must already have some language for death. Indeed he uses a pleonasm for it, 'dead and done for', which carries overtones of doom as well as death. We could interpret his behaviour as a fusion of the angers and fears directed at his parents, and something else, a realization of the murderousness of adults. Klein's interpretation is a consoling ratification of what he fears. Her identification of the figures seems oddly arbitrary, as good an interpretation as any perhaps, but the figures are obviously overdetermined, and could be the parents, the brothers or even the boy himself. The fantasy ritual circulates anger and violence between all these possible figures just because of its inexplicitness.

Klein's interpretation enacts what she thinks children do; it uses the discourse of adult violence to express inner feelings. This process is most evident in the essay, 'Symbol Formation in Ego Development', exploring the early stages of the Oedipus conflict when 'sadism predominates'. She writes:

> In phantasy the excreta are transformed into dangerous weapons: wetting is regarded as cutting, stabbing, burning, drowning, while the faecal mass is equated with weapons and missiles. At a later stage of the phase which I have described, these violent modes of attack give place to hidden assaults by the most refined methods which sadism can devise, and the excreta are equated with poisonous substances.
>
> (Klein 1986: 96)

Klein provides the language of adult activities to name the symbolic play of the child: weapons and missiles. The danger of doing this had led Freud to cast doubt on the possibility of child analysis in the Wolf Man case history, saying 'too many words and thoughts have to be lent to the child' (Freud

1979b: 235), although this did not mean that he was not interested in the possibilities if communication could be sustained, as it was in the case of Little Hans. In that case the father, who apart from mother and nurse would know the boy's idiolect best, made the detailed reports on Hans's utterances. Since these were made by a parent, they must also have been coloured by the specific character of the father/son relationship, and lacked the first-hand quality of Klein's clinical analyses, which took place away from the parents.

In an essay defending Klein's analysis of Little Dick, Mary Jacobus draws attention to Lacan's dismissal of this feature of Klein's practice: 'She slams the symbolism on him with complete brutality, does Melanie Klein', says Lacan (1988: 68). Jacobus thinks that Lacan is the brutal one, not Klein. He is conscious of the empathy in Klein's work, an empathy his own theory and practice lack, and he fears 'to find [empathy] driving the machine of language' (Jacobus 1990: 173) in damaging contradiction to his own theoretical position. Yet Klein does seem to impose her interpretations, however empathically, on the situation. Consider her account of the early stages of the Oedipus conflict:

> The earliest defence set up by the ego is directed against the subject's own sadism and the object attacked, both of these being regarded as sources of danger. This defence is of a violent character, different from the mechanism of repression. In boys this violent defence is also directed against his penis as the executive organ of his sadism and it is one of the deepest sources of all disturbances of potency. . . . The first part of the phase when sadism is at its zenith is that in which the attacks are conceived of as being made by violence. This I have come to recognize as the fixation point in dementia praecox. In the second part of this phase the attacks are imagined as being made by poisoning, and the urethral and anal-sadistic impulses predominate.
>
> (Klein 1986: 110)

Where does this discourse of violence and, even more oddly, poisoning, come from? Or indeed of evisceration and the other forms of attack described elsewhere in her writings? Klein writes as if the discourses of the fantasies arose spontaneously in the children's minds. Lacan argues as if they were simply and arbitrarily hers, but the efficacy of her interpretations suggests otherwise. There is another alternative. They could come from the adult world around the children, mediated in a hundred ways, through toys, brothers, parents, other adults, books, observations, even analysts. Klein's remarkable skill lies in her ability to offer discourses for what are evidently only half-emergent forms of symbolization. She writes as if the need was entirely to negotiate inner impulses. The way she is able to provide the names, the poisoning for example, shows that she too is aware of the violent possibilities of human relations, which these children need to understand in relation to their own strong and confusing impulses. It is not that Klein is inventing these aggressive impulses, but nor are they the sole originators of the adult negations of symbolic relations.

When Klein discusses the psychotic position in manic-depressive states, she names the extreme rage felt by one patient as an attack on an 'internalized father with burning excreta' (ibid.: 139). Such attacks could lead to their own extinction: 'If he then kills his father inside him altogether, the dead father becomes a persecutor of a special kind' (ibid.: 139). This representation of the conflict between love and hate uses a discourse belonging to the register of male violence and war. Much of what Klein is doing here is redefining the Oedipus conflict in terms of a negotiation with the circumambient atmosphere of adult violence, the whole complex of imaginary fears, representations of violence, symbols and silences, which make up the obscure threat of humanly caused pain and death. Freud insisted in the Wolf Man case that 'a child, like an adult, can produce phantasies only from material which has been acquired from some source or other' (Freud 1979b: 285). Both he and Klein are reluctant to consider adult violence as a possible source, but she comes much closer, because she produces a discourse for the responses to infantile aggression that makes use of the discourse of violence itself.

W.R.D. Fairbairn, who helped develop the object-relations theory of psychoanalysis, takes this process even further. He worked with soldiers during the Second World War and consistently referred all adult psychic difficulties to pre-Oedipal disturbances: 'the chief predisposing factor in determining the breakdown of a soldier . . . is an infantile dependence upon his objects' (1952: 79). For a soldier who suffers from imperfect repression of his bad objects, army life can be hell: 'every word of command is equivalent to an assault by a malevolent father and every spoonful of "greasy" stew from the cookhouse is a drop of poison from the breast of a malevolent mother' (ibid.: 81). The disavowal of the brutality of war and militarism, which leads to the dismissal of any suggestion that the commands are violent, or the food unwholesome, can be understood both as a necessary defence against feelings that war is an expenditure of spirit, and a defence of the power of psychoanalytic explanations in the face of the claims of present-day traumas. This turning away from the immediate emotional disturbances of the war leads to a particularly striking conclusion in the case of a man who was given twenty-four hours' leave to visit his bombed shop. Looking at it he felt a 'schizoid state of detachment' but that night he lay in bed with his wife at home and 'felt as if he were being choked and experienced a powerful impulse to smash up his house and murder his wife and children. His bad objects had returned with a vengeance' (ibid.: 77). Perhaps most striking of all is that Fairbairn's definition of a bad object could be applied to the man's experience of seeing the bombed shop. Fairbairn wants to retain the infant psychogenesis of all psychic disturbance, and so he treats the incident not as if the man's reaction were misdirected rage, but as a reprise of some early childhood relation. There is an indirect parallel with what Patrick Mahony has described as 'the void of the transfer-ential interpretations' (1986: 127) in the Rat Man case. Freud sidesteps the active relations established within the analytic situation in his interpret-ations. Mahony suggests that this is due to the relatively early development of psychoanalysis and Freud's own lack of experience as an analysand. I would add another reason, similar to that which seems to have prevented Fairbairn from considering the relations between men at war as operative psychic factors. Freud avoided too much attention to the transference because it raised too many questions about men's relations with one another.

Both Klein and Fairbairn imply that although murderous aggression is universal (since everyone will have repressed some bad objects) there are initializing conditions which construct these bad objects. D.W. Winnicott took the view that aggression was a fundamental impulse, necessary for the new-born infant well before the emergence of an ego. The 'aggressive component' acts as the foundation of all subject–object relations, and com-pared to the erotic impulses 'more surely drives the individual to a need for a *Not-Me* or an object that is felt to be *external*' (Winnicott 1958: 215). Aggression precedes the more conscious emotions of anger and hate, so it would be a mistake to imagine that aggression is entirely the result of what Winnicott calls 'frustration', or in other words some outside causal relation. In a different style, this becomes the theme of Jacques Lacan's work in the late 1940s and 1950s. He argues in 'Aggressivity in Psychoanalysis' (1948) that the splitting of the mirror stage inaugurates 'aggressive competitiveness' (Lacan 1977: 19). The 'ego appears to be marked from its very origin by this aggressive relativity' (ibid.), but Lacan historicizes his remark by suggesting that modern society encourages this specific form of ego development, and invokes Hegel to support his claim:

> before Darwin, however, Hegel had provided the ultimate theory of the proper function of aggressivity in human ontology, seeming to prophesy the iron law of our time. From the conflict of Master and Slave, he deduced the entire subjective and objective progress of our history, revealing in these crises the syntheses to be found in the highest forms of the status of the person in the West, from the Stoic to the Christian, and even to the future citizen of the Universal State.
>
> (ibid.: 26)

Aggression and competition become the most salient features of modernity, rather than more particularly the features of men in modernity. Lacan's use of the Master and Slave section of Hegel's *Phenomenology* treats one section in a wider narrative as if it were the key description of modernity, although Hegel then goes on to discuss wider forms of community more characteristic of modern society. As Robert Pippin says: 'it thus ought to be kept separate from Hegel's explicit extension of his idealism into ethical or social-ontological or ego-identity areas' (1989: 155), although I shall argue later that even at this level of abstraction it is still trammelled by a masculine structure of feeling. It is a very partial reading of the *Phenomenology* to say that Hegel deduces the entirety of modern history from this one episode. John McCumber points out that the Master/Slave dialectic is 'one of the conditions for reason. Prior to it, there are no "rational animals", and appeal can only be to force' (1989: 39). The struggle arises from the need 'to find a content that will define an ego which is at first empty and abstract' (ibid.: 45). The violence arises not as an iron law of modernity but because at this stage of emergent rationality there is no relation other than complete negation between selves.

A more politically nuanced version of Lacan's iron law and Freud's hypotheses about the patricidal prehistory of mankind appeared in Juliet Mitchell's pathbreaking *Psychoanalysis and Feminism*, a study of the relations between gender and ideology which largely set the terms of debate for the decade after its publication. For many British readers this was their first introduction to Lacan, and a powerful reminder of the continuing importance of Freud's work, which at the time was better known through its subsequent interpreters, especially the later members of the object-relations school. R.D. Laing was probably the most widely read quasi-psychoanalytic thinker, because his work seemed to offer a political dimension to psychological analysis. This too was initially Juliet Mitchell's ambition but she was wary of any attempt to downplay the importance of the unconscious. Instead she argued that the unconscious was indeed the place where ideology operated, and in doing so laid the foundations of a decade of syncretic theorizing in feminist theory and cultural politics. Psychoanalysis is important for feminist politics because biological and sociological solutions alone cannot end women's subordination:

> It is the specific feature of patriarchy – the law of the hypothesized prehistoric murdered father – that defines the relative places of men and women in human history. This 'father' and his representatives – all fathers – are the crucial expression of patriarchal society. It is *fathers* not *men* who have the determinate power.
>
> (Mitchell 1974: 408–9)

The law of the father is the problem, not the actual power of men. Men's power is only significant thanks to patriarchy. As a result there is a conflict in the modern world between the Oedipus complex ('the universal law by which men and women learn their place in the world') and the 'specifically capitalist ideology of a supposedly natural nuclear family' (ibid.: 409). A transformation of capitalism would probably leave the ideology unchanged, because ideology and economics are to a considerable extent independent:

The patriarchal law speaks to and through each person in his unconscious; the reproduction of the ideology of human society is thus assured in the acquisition of the law by each individual. The unconscious that Freud analysed could thus be described as the domain of the reproduction of culture or ideology.

(ibid.: 413)

Patriarchal law is now 'redundant' in a modern capitalist society. It sustains kinship patterns and incest taboos now largely irrelevant.

Juliet Mitchell's brilliant synthesis of ideas from Marxism, anthropology and psychoanalysis unfortunately hides a contradiction with far-reaching consequences for any extension of gender politics to include men. The viability of her structure of concepts as a general theory of gender and society is undermined by a circularity in her assumptions about ideology. Mitchell's 'specifically capitalist ideology of a supposedly natural nuclear family' (ibid.: 409) uses the term 'ideology' in the traditional Marxist sense to mean the process whereby the exploited are mentally persuaded to comply with their exploitation. To construct her theory she also has to use the concept of 'ideology' in a quite different sense. She needs to define patriarchy as a 'universal culture' (ibid.: 409) as well as an ideology (ideology provides the 'conditions of human culture' (ibid.: 411)). Ideology in this sense is independent of capitalist society, indeed: 'Patriarchy describes the universal culture – however, each specific economic mode of production must express this in different ideological forms' (ibid.: 409).

In this sense the universal culture of patriarchy finds expression in a specific mode of production, like capitalism. This form of ideology determines the mode of production rather than the reverse. Ideology produces ideology in this circular argument, knotted together by asserting that ideology is produced in the unconscious. Patriarchy suddenly disappears beyond reach of political challenge by men, not only because it is produced in the unconscious but because of the circularity of this structure which allows no place for intervention. Mitchell is hopeful because she thinks women are in a parallel position to the working class, ready to seize the potentially revolutionary contradictions of patriarchy under capitalism, where the nuclear family has lost its structural role. For men trying to challenge patriarchy there is simply no position to occupy other than that of the upholder of the law.

MALE DESIRE, DRIVES AND EMOTIONS

The search for a death instinct, or a patriarchal unconscious, results in circular arguments. A less universalistic, but sometimes similarly reductive, line of enquiry into masculinity characterizes all men's affectionate, intimate relations with one another as homosexual, without questioning the normative judgements implicit in such a categorization. (Jonathan Dollimore discusses the consequences for psychoanalysis of categorizing homosexuality as a perversion, in *Sexual Dissidence* (1991)). In the Rat Man case it would be hard to argue on the evidence that the young man had such strong attachments to women as he did to men, although Freud does not explicitly say this. We are offered no evidence of homosexual activity, but the young men's intense emotional relations are all with men, his father, his supportive friend, the frightening captain and Freud himself. Women are for sex, or they are manipulators of his emotions, trying to marry him off like his mother, or to constrain his affections like his woman friend (Strachey uses the word 'lady'). His rat fantasy is a highly overdetermined fantasy of anal rape, and Freud insists that he has a repressed wish to inflict this rat torture on his father and his woman friend. In the Wolf Man case a homosexual current is much more evident. According to Freud, the Wolf Man was dominated by fear of his father (something he shares with the Rat Man) and exhibited recurrent rages towards him. These rages were a means to an end other than simply catharsis or communication. They were attempts to 'force punishments and beatings out of his father' and obtain a masochistic sexual satisfaction (Freud 1979b: 257). Indeed what he most wanted was to be his father's passive sexual partner (ibid.: 266). Freud's methodological reversal of the fear into a wish is especially evident in this instance. How much then does the complex fear of male violence translate into homosexuality and the defence of homophobia against it? The Wolf Man apparently sublimates his homosexuality. As an older boy he 'developed an enthusiasm for military affairs' and came under the beneficial influence of a German tutor: 'Thus under a man's influence, he had got free from his passive attitudes, and found himself for the time being on fairly normal lines' (ibid.: 305). Then Freud goes on to say that the aim of treatment was to redirect his homosexuality:

> The repression of his over-powerful homosexuality, which was accomplished during the anxiety-dream, reserved that important impulse for the unconscious, kept it directed towards its original aim, and withdrew it from all the sublimations to which it is susceptible in other circumstances. For this reason the patient was without all those social interests which give a content to life. It was only when, during the analytic treatment, it became possible to liberate his shackled homosexuality that this state of affairs showed any improvement; and it was a most remarkable experience to see how (without any direct advice from the physician) each piece of homosexual libido which was set free sought out some application in life and some attachment to the great common concerns of mankind.
>
> (ibid.: 307)

This could easily be read as saying that the aim is to cure, by dispelling it, the Wolf Man's homosexuality, but Freud is saying that the aim is to allow this homosexual libido to participate in the social fabric, to become sublime in the symbolic. This evokes D.H. Lawrence's description of Will Brangwen's response to the later sexual activity with Anna that finally freed him from his inner self-absorption. Male violence, which the Wolf Man and the Rat Man learn to negotiate, is renamed homosexual libido. The successful integration of the young men's retaliatory aggressions, for example into militarism, is then named the sublimation of homosexual libido. What this does is to elide the possibility that men's relations with one another might be more than either violent or sexual. Possibilities of friendly affection are discounted, and so homosexuality itself is made to appear dangerous. The rattiness of man is stigmatized by a homophobia that wants to hunt it down and destroy it.

Freud praised the German tutor's influence because he drew the Wolf Man away from passivity. The passivity was women's influence, the women who had seduced him as a young child. In both case histories, homophobia is intertwined with another sexual disturbance, child sexual abuse, and in both cases, despite his theoretical insistence that his patients' memories of childhood seduction were fantasies, Freud accepts that sexual activities between an adult and the child actually occurred. The Rat Man's first obsessions began when, as a young boy of 6, he was the subject of considerable sexual attentions from a governess. Such attentions amount to sexual abuse, although the gender reversal is allowed to make it anodyne in Freud's account, as if a boy, unlike a girl, can never be too young to begin his heterosexual experience. The issue is not one of the real event versus the fantasy here, since there is an interdependence of the one with the other.

The Wolf Man was seduced by his sister, who also told him about his nurse's sexual activities with men on the estate as she did so. As a result of this seduction the Wolf Man became what Freud calls 'passive', and his 'masculine self-esteem' was damaged (p. 248). The sister also tried to seduce an older man by playing with his penis, and eventually committed suicide in her twenties after claiming that her female companion was tormenting her. It is hard to avoid the suspicion that the children were the victims, direct or indirect, of a sexually abusive male adult, but that must remain speculative. The Rat Man is not so victimized, although he too lives in a violent world where a child of either sex can be a casual sexual plaything. Violence and sexual violence are everywhere. Prostitution, syphilis and actual physical violence (the Rat Man's attack on his sister and servant for example) are further extensions of it.

In his verdict on the Rat Man case, Patrick Mahony emphasizes the limitations of Freud's handling of the transference:

> Understandably, because of his lack of experience, his own complexes, and those of society in some instances, Freud could not yet see a whole series of issues that we grasp and contend with more readily today: narcissism, early parenting, body schema, sibling relationships,

unresolved mourning, the transference in the here and now, including its maternal and negative varieties, and the resolution of transference neurosis.

(Mahony 1986: 215)

So far I have suggested that one reason for the difficulties was that the transference was caught up in aspects of masculinity, its 'rattiness', which neither Freud, nor his society, was ready to acknowledge. There is another aspect of the theorizing of the transference in this case history which I want to question, because of what I shall allege is a complicity with a pathological masculinity. Yeats presented a mismirroring in 'A Dialogue of Self and Soul' which was the result of a countertransference. The transference is a specular relation, a reflexive relation, and it is this reflexivity which I want to explore in connection with the Rat Man case. If a relation between two people were all transference and countertransference would they have any relation at all? Would it not all be mirrors? The authors of an essay on the Dora case describe this as a search for difference:

> In any relationship the only escape from the hall of mirrors is through a constant attempt to make contact with that in the other which is in excess of the transferences, even though the unknown quality in the other, to the extent that it is in excess of the transferences, cannot be recognised, cannot be known. Knowledge beyond the transferences is a knowledge of difference.
>
> (Collins *et al.* 1985: 252)

What, we may ask, is this unknown quality? So far it might appear as if it were something which linked men together, but could find no articulation, no place in the mirrors. Something in the psyche does not submit to the laws of representation.

Mary Jacobus tentatively argues in her article on Klein and Little Dick that the limitations made evident in Lacan's theory by the comparison with Klein can be understood by considering Julia Kristeva's discussion of 'Einfühlung' (empathy – I discuss the term later), or 'the assimilation of other people's feelings' (Jacobus 1990: 173):

> Probing beyond Lacan's question ('how does the imaginary give rise to the symbolic'), Kristeva asks instead: 'what are the conditions for the emergence of the imaginary?' [and so] she insists on the pre-existence of a symbolic function and on 'various dispositions giving access to that function'
>
> (Jacobus 1990: 173, citing Kristeva 1987: 44)

Kristeva's aim in asking this question is to alter the way the transference is understood:

> The object of love is a metaphor for the subject – its constitutive

metaphor, its 'unary feature', which, by having it choose an adored part of the loved one, already locates it within the symbolic code of which this feature is a part. Nevertheless, situating this unifying guide-line within an objectality in the process of being established rather than in the absolute of the reference to the Phallus as such has several advantages. It makes the transference relation dynamic, involves to the utmost the interpretative intervention of the analyst, and calls attention to countertransference as identification, this time of the analyst with the patient, along with the entire aura of imaginary formations ger-mane to the analyst that all this entails.

(Kristeva 1987: 30)

The strategy she adopts, like Klein's, is to posit developmental stages prior to the Oedipus and the entry into the symbolic, which are nevertheless engaged in identification and emergent symbol-making.

Why does Lacan's theory seem to call for this revision? One possibility is that Lacan's theory is based on a limiting theory of subjectivity as purely self-reflection or self-mirroring (Frank 1989: 316). According to Manfred Frank, Lacan 'did not really grasp the function of the notion of a pre-reflective or nonthetic cogito' (ibid.: 310). For Lacan, the ego is the result of a misapprehended reflected image of the self in the field of the Other. This presupposes that there is also a prior self, but Lacan assumes that this self is unconscious and yet grounded in language. If it is unconscious, then 'it is hard to see by what criterion the specular I (moi) can identify with itself at all' (ibid.: 309). The mirror-stage theory that the ego forms itself when the self misapprehends itself as a unity in the field of reflection provided by the Other, depends on the questionable assumption that the self is already capable of knowing how to know itself as a self.

One possible conclusion from these discussions of reflexivity is that there is something left over, an unknown quality, a prior stage, which is not included in this specular model of consciousness. The Rat Man case suggests that what is left over is something about masculinity that is unspeakable within the existing framework. Kristeva and Jacobus suggest that that quality is in part empathy or more generally emotion. To understand further what that might mean we need to turn to Freud's treatment of emotion in the Rat Man case. What is it that is hard to drag into the light of masculine specular consciousness?

At one point in the case history Freud says that 'like other obsessional neurotics, our patient was compelled to over-estimate the effects of his hostile feelings upon the external world, because a large part of their internal, mental effects escaped his conscious knowledge' (1979a: 112). This strik-ingly close to the argument of the men's movement about men and emotion. They would surely agree with the idea that most men allow the internal effects of feeling to escape conscious knowledge, and over- or underestimate the effect of their feelings on those around them. Freud's analysis of the conflict between the Rat Man's love and hatred for both his father and his fiancée, emphasizes the importance of such conflicts in all obsessional neuroses, and would also find support in the men's movement outlook. The primary difference arises in Freud's scientific account of the causal structure of emotion. I will trace the development of Freud's argument in the Rat Man to show how he suppresses the relational character of emotion in favour of a more mechanistic and autonomous model. This emphasis on drives has led one recent author of an account of psychoanalysis, Stephen Mitchell, to say that there are two paradigms in the history of psychoanalysis, the drive model and the relational model. Different schools of psychoanalysis usually emphasize one at the expense of the other, but always keep the other paradigm on somewhere in the background of their theories. Empathy is an example of a concept used to introduce relational structures into a drive model of the psyche.

A look at Freud's ambivalence about the discourse of emotion in the Rat Man case will show why a concept like empathy could become important to later psychoanalysts. After observing that the Rat Man suffered extremes of love and hate for his father, Freud argues that:

> We should have expected that the passionate love would long ago have conquered the hatred or been devoured by it. And in fact such a protracted survival of two opposites is only possible under quite peculiar psychological conditions and with the co-operation of the state of affairs in the unconscious. The love has not succeeded in extinguishing the hatred but only in driving it down into the unconscious; and in the unconscious the hatred, safe from the danger of being destroyed by the operations of consciousness, is able to persist and even to grow.
>
> (Freud 1979a: 118)

Freud then traces the development of obsessional states. As he does so, his language imperceptibly moves from the discussion of emotions to the discussion of energies and systems. This move is justified by focusing on what is described as the 'energy dammed up' in the intentions arising from the conflicting feelings. His final description drops all reference to feelings in favour of impulses:

> A thought-process is obsessive or compulsive when, in consequence of an inhibition (due to a conflict of opposing impulses) at the motor end of the psychical system, it is undertaken with an expenditure of energy which (as regards both quality and quantity) is normally reserved for actions alone; or, in other words, *an obsessive or compulsive thought is one whose function it is to represent an act regressively*. No one, I think, will question my assumption that processes of thought are

ordinarily conducted (on grounds of economy) with smaller displacements of energy, probably at a higher level [of cathexis], than are acts
intended to bring about discharge or to modify the external world.

(ibid.: 125)

Freud's analysis moves away from questions of relation to questions of
internal dynamics. At a couple of points in this passage Freud seems aware
of possible objections. He says that compulsions tend to take the form of
'infantile sexual acts of a masturbatory character' which are then entirely
self-directed, 'for such acts no longer relate to another person, the object of
love and hatred' (ibid.: 124).

Freud's commitment to drives and instincts is most evident in his concept
of the death drive, which might seem at first sight to offer a means of
theorizing many of the features of masculinity we have been concerned with
here. In *Beyond the Pleasure Principle* Freud ponders the repetition compulsion at length, replays the 'fort-da' game, and then finally, almost reluctantly, brings out into the open his speculations about the death drive as the
drive behind repetition compulsions. Death instincts would be the counterpart to those of self-preservation, 'component instincts whose function it is
to assume that the organism shall follow its own path to death' (Freud 1984:
311). Freud has difficulty in producing an example of such a drive, and when
he does finally offer one, the sadistic impulse, his description is heavily
coloured with masculine assumptions.

> During the oral stage of the reorganisation of the libido, the act of
> obtaining erotic mastery over an object coincides with that object's
> destruction; later, the sadistic instinct separates off, and finally, at the
> stage of genital primacy, it takes on, for the purposes of reproduction,
> the function of overpowering the sexual object to the extent necessary
> for carrying out the sexual act.
>
> (ibid.: 327)

This covert biologism naturalizes male violence by making it necessary for
copulation (in the *The New Introductory Lectures on Psychoanalysis* Freud
says that one cannot talk of feminine libido because 'the accomplishment of
the aim of biology has been entrusted to the aggressiveness of men and has
been made to some extent independent of women's consent' (Freud 1973:
166)). The masculine ideology of the passage from *Beyond the Pleasure
Principle* is echoed in his strange image of the psyche as an organism whose
surface layer is always in danger of letting in too many stimuli and being
destroyed. To guard against total destruction, the surface of the psyche
becomes a shield made out of a half-dead outer layer, analogous to skin. The
beleaguered psyche dies at the surface of its relation to the world to protect
its inner softness. This is a very masculine image, indeed one which turns up
commonly in romances as much as in men's self-representations. In

103

romances, as Janice Radway (1984) shows, the hero is only vicious on the outside. His inner self is gentle, and his brutal behaviour needs to be interpreted with that in mind.

A great deal in *Beyond the Pleasure Principle* depends on what Freud means by instincts. He is at pains to stress that all instincts except the sexual ones are wholly regressive:

> Is it really the case that, *apart from the sexual instincts*, there are no instincts that do not seek to restore an earlier state of things? that there are none that aim at a state of things which has never yet been attained? I know of no certain example from the organic world that would contradict the characterization I have thus proposed. There is unquestionably no universal instinct towards higher development observable in the animal or plant world, even though it is undeniable that development does in fact occur in that direction.
>
> (Freud 1984: 314)

What we call the development of human civilization is simply the delaying tactics of erotic suppression. At best, social development is the 'result of the instinctual repression upon which is based all that is most precious in human civilization' (ibid.: 315), the repression of erotic desire. This is one of the clearest instances of Freud's assumption that all motivation ultimately derives from instinct rather than from feelings, morality, God, language or society.

Many contemporary analysts have been unhappy with this. Some analysts have gone so far as to argue that psychoanalysis is really what Heinz Kohut (1978: 450) calls a science of empathy. A contemporary psychoanalyst, Herbert S. Strean, introducing a popularized account of an analyst's work, begins by saying what I suspect many analysts actually believe about their work:

> For many years I have felt that unless I could permit myself to free associate to my patient's unexpressed thoughts and words and constantly explore what I was feeling in the analytic process, I could not really be of much help to the patient. If the analyst cannot put himself in the patient's shoes and feel the patient's anger, dependency, and sexual fantasies, he becomes, in my opinion, a mere mechanic rather than a feeling human being trying to help another human being who is suffering deep psychic pain. The analyst has to be constantly aware of the feelings of the patient, react silently to what the patient is feeling and saying, and, out of this morass of emotions and words, offer a few ideas to help the patient.
>
> (Strean 1988: 6)

Later he warns of the danger of both over-identifying and under-identifying with a patient (ibid.: 121), but his basic assumption is clear. Analysis depends on the negotiations of a non-verbal emotional rapport for its effectiveness, as much as on intellectual analysis and the transference. Emotion can be shared, even caught like a cold, without words. Empathy is not the same as the transference. The transference is a triggered regression to early libidinal cathexes. Empathy is a broader process which might well include archaic emotional responses but is also an interaction based on contemporary circumstance. Heinz Kohut devoted much of his career to explaining its significance. In this extract from a lecture on his work and its relations to other sciences, he offers a useful summary of his conclusions:

> (1) Empathy, the recognition of the self in the other, is an indispens-able tool of observation, without which vast areas of human life, including man's behaviour in the social field, remain unintelligible. (2) Empathy, the expansion of the self to include the other, constitutes a powerful psychological bond between individuals, which – more per-haps even than love, the expression and sublimation of the sexual drive – counteracts men's destructiveness against his fellows. And (3), empathy, the accepting, confirming, and understanding human echo evoked by the self, is a psychological nutriment without which human life as we know and cherish it could not be sustained.
>
> (Kohut 1978: 704)

Empathy is a means of objectively studying subjectivity:

> Through empathy we aim at discerning, in one single act of certain recognition, complex psychological configurations which we could either define only through the laborious presentation of a host of details or which it may even be beyond our ability to define.
>
> (ibid.: 450–1)

It makes psychoanalysis different from other sciences. It is clear in this quotation that Kohut thinks of empathy as something different from narcis-sistic projection, although he also says that empathy is 'cognition via the narcissistic investment of the other' (ibid.: 701), making cognition do the work of saving narcissism from using the other as a mere mirror for its gaze. Empathy has an earlier connection with art which makes it an especially loaded term for literary and cultural studies. It was first systematically used to translate the German word 'Einfuhlung', employed in the aesthetics of Theodore Lipps to describe the moment when the perceiving subject merges with the object of perception (Reed 1984). Later it became an indispensable psychoanalytic term. Its origin in an aesthetic theory of relations between a subject and an object is a reminder that it carries a baggage of assumptions about intersubjectivity which might hinder our understanding. Empathy is a term used to avoid the more difficult question of emotion, because psycho-analysis has had difficulty in attributing a non-regressive and cognitive component to emotions.

105

Julia Kristeva's difference with Lacan has something to do with her interest in this process of empathy. Lacan is extremely dismissive of any great emphasis on emotion and empathy. In his essay on treatment he ridicules the idea that psychoanalysis might be called the 'emotional re-education of the patient' (Lacan 1977: 226), as one contemporary of his had called it (whereas Kristeva, for example, says that in clinical psychoanalysis 'constructive interpretation re-establishes signification and allows meaning to rediscover affect' (quoted in Smith 1989: 46)). Yet even Lacan cannot do without the term 'feeling'. Listen to his address to his students in the seminar where he discusses Melanie Klein:

> I have taught you to identify the symbolic with language. On the other hand when Melanie Klein tells us that the objects are constituted by the interplay of projections, introjections, expulsions, reintrojections of bad objects, and that the subject, having projected his sadism, sees it coming back from these objects, and by this very fact finds himself jammed up by an anxious fear, don't you have the feeling [*ne sentez-vous pas*] that we are in the domain of the imaginary?
>
> (Lacan 1988: 74)

Lacan's casual use of the verb 'sentir' when talking about the relation of affect and identification in Klein is a hint that he too works with empathy, but the dismissive tone, and the use of the word to mean something not quite articulated, are symptomatic of his suspicion of everything that is not linguistic. As Mary Jacobus (1990: 69) says, his suspicion of Klein's 'animal instinct' is a suspicion of this salience given to empathy. Kristeva (1987: 29) says in contrast to Lacan: 'Einfühlung gives the language signifier exchanged during treatment a heterogenous, drive affected dimension. It loads it with something preverbal, or even nonrepresentable that needs to be deciphered while taking into account the articulations.' She now recognizes, like an earlier revisionist, André Green, that affects are a more salient and complex element of mental life than the terminology of drives and desire can acknowledge.

In the second half of this book I shall take up the enquiry into the relations between masculinity and emotion, drives, affects and subjectivity. I will conclude the discussion of Freud with a glance at the way Paul Ricoeur revises Freud's psychological theory of desire to take account of the emotional relations necessary for a society to continue. In *Freud and Philosophy* Ricoeur develops parallels between Freud and Hegel, partly in order to clarify similar parallels already deeply embedded in Lacan's work. For Lacan the parallels are direct. In the essay on treatment he writes as if Freud had assimilated Hegel's position directly:

> Freud's discovery is confirmed first by regarding as certain that the real is rational – which, in itself, was enough to knock our exegete off

balance – and then by affirming that the rational is real. As a result, Freud can articulate the fact that what presents itself as unreasonable in desire is an effect of the passage of the rational in so far as it is real – that is to say, the passage of language – into the real, in so far as the rational has already traced its circumvallation there.

(Lacan 1977: 272)

Lacan uses Hegel's formulation about the real and the rational ('the real is the rational') as a direct paradigm for understanding the interplay of desire, language and reality. Ricoeur is more circumspect. He sees differences, where Lacan sees similarities: 'Whereas Hegel links an explicit theology of mind or spirit to an implicit archeology of life and desire, Freud links a thematized archeology of the unconscious to an unthematized teleology of the process of becoming conscious' (Ricoeur 1970: 461).

In Hegel's *Phenomenology of Spirit*, as I shall show later (pp. 213–16), emotion plays a role that is never made explicit. In Freud's work the activities of reason, its logic, cognitive range and continuing development from birth (possibly throughout a lifetime), are similarly disregarded. Reason as a logical process is never touched by all the goings-on in the unconscious, just as most nineteenth-century scientists assumed that Newton's laws were absolutely valid whatever the circumstances of their instantiation. As Ricoeur puts it, 'Freud's theory of the ego is at once very liberating with respect to the illusions of consciousness and very disappointing in its inability to give the *I* of the *I think* some sort of meaning' (1970: 428). Ricoeur's answer to the problem is to reiterate the main claim of his study of Freud that Freudian theory is a hermeneutics which considers only regressive libidinal cathexes and then to offer a tentative addition to Freudian theory, a hermeneutics of innovation. Explaining our love of money as a love of excrement still leaves untouched another dimension of economics in which new feelings develop, feelings which do not originate in the sexual domain. These are feelings aimed at what we call variously ownership, possession and having:

> What is important to note, however, is that the areas in which these feelings, passions, and alienations multiply are new objects, values of exchange, monetary signs, structures, and institutions. We may say, then, that man becomes self-consciousness insofar as he experiences this economic objectivity as a new modality of his subjectivity and thus attains specifically human 'feelings' relative to the availability of things as things that have been worked upon and appropriated.

(ibid.: 508)

Power is another sphere in which 'specifically human feelings, such as intrigue, ambition, submission, responsibility' as well as 'specifically human alienations' (ibid.: 509) develop. Indeed 'man becomes human insofar as he can enter into the political problematic of power, adopt the feelings that center around power' (ibid.: 509). Ricoeur accepts that Freud's metapsychological analysis of crowds in *The Ego and the Id*, for example, which derives social structures from the cathexis of libido, is persuasive up to a point, but limited. Freud himself acknowledges that:

> there is some difficulty in giving a description of such a diversity of aim which will conform to the requirements of metapsychology . . . if we choose we may recognize in this diversion of aim a beginning of the *sublimation* of the sexual instincts, or on the other hand we may fix the limits of sublimation at some more distant point.
>
> (Ricoeur 1970: 514)

Ricoeur claims that sublimation is a more complex process than Freud acknowledges, because it requires not only the regressive reference to libido but another, 'innovative' reference, if it is to comprehend the 'diversity of aim' found in the social world. New meanings as well as old are knotted into the workings of power in the social sphere.

I want to conclude with a speculation about the attractiveness of the regressive theory of libido as Ricoeur calls it. In *The Origins of Love and Hate* Ian Suttie explains the prevalence of mock abuse amongst men as a kind of psychic scar of the painful process of psychic weaning from 'the pre-Oedipal emotional and fondling relationship' (1988: 86). This weaning produces a 'psychic blindness to pathos of any kind' (ibid.: 88). Psychic blindness sounds very like some of the liminal states we have traced in the modernist writers and will find later (pp. 197–9) in descriptions of the sublime in postmodernist writing. As I said earlier, I don't think we can attribute such phenomena solely to early mothering. Suttie gives us a means of understanding the obsession with early mothering when he says that in masculine cultures: 'the taboo upon regressive longings extends to all manifestations of affection until we can neither offer nor tolerate overt affection' (ibid.: 89). The fear of regressive longings for mother love has been noted by many commentators. Suttie's formulation suggests that the psychoanalytic theory of emotion as solely regressive libido might be a mirror image of this fear. If masculine cultures widely believed what Suttie claims, then a psychoanalytic culture itself might share that initial fear and convert it into a manageable knowledge. If all emotion is not regressive and if there are existing taboos on the representation of emotion in everyday life, especially amongst men, it helps to be able to stigmatize them as regressive. Theory would help sustain and be sustained by a prevailing masculine ideology. Men whose masculine self-image is at stake may strongly resist the recognition that some emotions are actually present-time social phenomena. Mothers may play a more active role in men's theories of subjectivity than is generally admitted. Fear of the memory of their shaping influence may, like Kryptonite, Stephen Dedalus's mother or the Rat Man's mother, be responsible for much of the defensive structure of men's theories of adult life in ways unadmitted by the regressive scenario.

The Rat Man case study gives us a brilliant portrait not only of the formation of a normative masculinity, but also of masculinities in action, as Freud narrates his encounters with the neurotic young man. Freud's relative neglect of the present state of emotional relationships in the transferences, and his ordinary masculine habituation to male violence, are part of the social structure of masculinity. The unexplored horizon of male violence looming in the background suggests that the wider social implications of emotional disturbances for men's subjectivity need more research.

Part II

Part II

5

THEORIES OF MODERN MASCULINITIES

MEN'S DIVIDED SUBJECTIVITY

In 1962 the novelist Doris Lessing published *The Golden Notebook*, a complex novel about the difficulties of being a woman writer that anticipated many of the issues central to the women's movement a decade later. Gender, class and postcolonialism are represented in realism, fantasy, autobiography and even a proleptic postmodernism. It's a novel that ought to speak directly to the contemporary theorist of culture. Yet the novel's reputation doesn't quite corroborate my description. Widely acknowledged to have been one of the key books along with *The Second Sex* (first published in 1949) for the early women's movement, it now stirs up ambivalent reactions. Elizabeth Wilson for example tells us how she once admired Anna Wulf, the woman writer at the centre of the novel, and her fictional creation, Ella:

> *Then* I looked up to Anna/Ella as an experienced 'older woman'. Now I judge her, looking back at her from a further, perhaps more cynical, possibly more stoical, landmark of experience, as one of *those* women – the ones who cry 'freedom' while hugging their chains.
>
> (Wilson 1982: 71)

These chains are men, and the problem with the novel is its treatment of the forgers of those chains, masculinities. At once real and false, masculinity is presented by the novel as a problem of disturbed inwardness. By giving too much attention to men's inwardness and women's emotional dependence on this psychological labyrinth, and not enough attention to men's power and women's capacity for autonomous development, the novel seems compromised. Feminists have had much to say about men, their power, their violence against women, and their oppression of women, but comprehending men's inner selves, the driving forces of their masculinities, has been understandably left up to men. Until recently men mostly ignored the task. Few bothered to reflect on how and why they themselves might be part of the chain of oppression and how this affected their subjectivities.

Because of its attention to the desires and languages men's subjectivities generate, *The Golden Notebook* can help us map out the difficulties of representing masculine subjectivities both for men and feminism. Anna Wulf, whose notebooks and novel 'Free Women' comprise *The Golden Notebook*, is a writer with a writer's block that only lifts after a traumatic sexual relationship with an American film maker, Saul Green. Saul appears schizophrenic to Anna. He can behave in contradictory ways simultaneously and be unaware of it. He treats her as the sexual object of his gaze: 'I have never in my life been subjected to as brutal a sexual inspection as that one' Anna recalls (Lessing 1973: 532). Then he talks with great insight about a mutual woman friend: 'I could not remember any other man talking with this simplicity, frankness and comradeship about the sort of life, I, and women like me, live' (ibid.: 534). This split in Saul's character outrages Anna. Saul stands in her kitchen talking sensitively about cold-war politics while posing like:

> a caricature of that young American we see in the films – sexy he-man, all balls and strenuous erection. . . . It was unconscious but it was directed at me, and it was so crude I began to be annoyed. These were two different languages being spoken to me at the same time. . . . I nearly challenged him in his turn, saying something like: 'What the hell do you mean by using that grown-up language to me, and then standing there like a heroic cowboy with invisible revolvers stuck all over your hips?'
>
> (ibid.: 536)

Saul becomes Anna's lover, but continues to see other women, turns his affections on and off unpredictably, and is frequently unreliable. He often appears unconscious of what he is doing. In other words, he is Anna's chains. At the end of the novel Anna has a measure of revenge on him in the fictional portrait of Saul which she puts into 'Free Women'. Saul is transformed into Milt, a mocking reduction from Old Testament patriarch to fishy sperm.

The problem with Saul is that he uses two languages. This early male feminist is simultaneously capable of an aggressively sexual assertion of manhood, and a highly rational understanding of others, especially women. What Freud said about the 'Rat Man', might also be said of Saul:

> I cannot take leave of my patient without putting on paper that he had, as it were, disintegrated into three personalities: into one unconscious personality, that is to say, and into two pre-conscious ones between which his consciousness could oscillate. His unconscious comprised those of his impulses which had been suppressed at an early age and which might be described as passionate and evil impulses. In his normal state he was kind, cheerful, and sensible – an enlightened and superior kind of person – while in his third psychological organization he paid homage to superstition and asceticism. Thus he was able to

have two different creeds and two different outlooks upon life.

(Freud 1979a: 128)

Freud's explanation uses the opposed terms enlightenment and passion which I will show later have a special significance for the discussion of masculinity. His phrase 'psychological organization' suggests that we could perhaps talk of psychological organizations which produce the schizoid personality of a Saul, and thereby recognize that these result from the disposition of drives, affects and their representations, rather than a fixed psychic essence. To do so would be to treat Saul as a case, to reduce the social and political implications of his behaviour to psychic, libidinal deter-minations. Most commentators are wary of this, especially if it sidesteps the problem of men's power. Lynne Segal, for example, the author of *Slow Motion: Changing Masculinities, Changing Men* 1990), in an article sum-marizing her views on masculinity, argues against Klaus Theweleit's (1985) thesis that the roots of fascism lie in murderous fantasies like those of the men of the German Freikorps. She cites evidence from Claudia Koonz (1988) that the men who organized the daily extermination in the camps of Auschwitz, Treblinka and Dachau were men with good, loving relations to their families: 'men who could separate off "doing their duty" from their love for their wives and children' (Segal 1989: 18). The duties of power would seem to be the motivation, not some lust to kill. Segal also cites the instance of David Morgan, a fighter pilot, who shot down more planes in the Falklands war than any one else. When interviewed by Yvonne Roberts he turned out to be a man

> completely without bravado, who was modest, above all simply pleased to be back home again and able to spend as much time as possible with his wife and children. . . . 'Death doesn't bother me. . . . I've no qualms now at all [about bombing and killing people].'
>
> (Segal 1989: 18)

Segal explains Morgan's responses as the result of a 'lack of imagination' (ibid.). I think it is insufficient to say that the character of a fighter pilot results from a lack of imagination, or even an ability to compartmentalize one's life. A much greater degree of numbness or carefully cathected mur-derous rage than such an explanation suggests is surely necessary to par-ticipate in the killing of other men. The conclusion Segal draws from these various examples is that 'this is exactly what we should expect if mascu-linity is . . . not any single or fixed type of thing, but an aspect of power created in and through social relationships' (ibid.). We need to note, how-ever, that masculinity could be the result of psychological developments and still not be a unitary disposition. Only if the psychological expla-nation were to attribute masculinity to the outcome of a fixed mental function might that be the case, and even then it is arguable whether

115

other intervening factors might not result in wide variations.

Yvonne Roberts's account of David Morgan gives a more troubled picture than Segal acknowledges. The interview is one of a collection investigating why men seem strangely unconscious

> not only of their own motivations and the roots of their prejudices, but also of the range and variety of attitudes within their own sex. As long as they remain unaware, I believe, they are equally oblivious of the force of their united pressure on women.
>
> (Roberts 1984: 2)

These masculine unconsciousnesses are politically significant because they help make men oblivious of their power as a sex over women. The interview with David Morgan offers a notable example of a masculine unconscious at work. He uses bland clichés to talk about his life, especially his feelings about his family, as Segal notes, but he also hints at much more disturbing thoughts and feelings. He says he talks 'too much' (Roberts 1984: 182) about the Falklands. His account of what happened when he achieved four 'kills' in one sortie is animated, but unemotional. Only when the fight is over is an emotive word used, and then unobtrusively: 'we were desperately short of fuel' (ibid.: 183). The emotion is almost attributed to the aircraft. Roberts prompts him, asking whether he was angry watching the bombing of a British ship, and he says, 'oh yes, blazing anger' (ibid.: 183). The naming of this anger has to be drawn out of him. Moreover, when she asks him if the proximity to death worried him he says no, denying at a conscious level that events have left an emotional mark. It is when she asks him if he has been changed by events that he admits that:

> The first thing I noticed is that I lose my temper a lot quicker. I got back and was absolute hell to live with. I found it very difficult and it annoyed me intensely if anyone asked me to make a decision on anything that wasn't a matter of life or death. . . . I was absolute hell and I still have to be very careful to control the temper.
>
> (ibid.: 185)

This is a picture of a deeply divided man who in his own words is 'absolute hell', yet unconscious of how much this is inside his life. He describes the hell in the alienated form of himself as the object of someone else's judgement. The anger arising from deadly combat is compulsively repeating itself in the ordinary life of a modest, quiet man.

In *The Golden Notebook*, Saul's masculinity is a symptom of the problem which has caused Anna's block, a problem she needs to overcome if she is to be capable again of writing a novel; that is, capable of writing for others and not just the private world of her notebooks. But how much does the transformation of patriarch into sperm help Anna? The novel she writes is demonstrably limited by comparison with her notebooks, as if to show that reducing power to male sexuality may not be sufficient. What can be done about these chains other than refusing to be involved with them? Is masculinity simply male power or male sexuality at all, or is it this whole cinematic display of empathy, power and sexuality unpredictably darkened by an unconscious for which there is as yet no name?

Anna's problem with Saul, and feminist problems with Anna, help illustrate the problem of masculinities with which I am concerned here. How is it these two languages of masculinity can co-exist? Is it thanks to their apparently mutual unconsciousness of one another? How is it that masculine rationality can stand alongside oppressive forms of masculine sexuality and violence? Are they simply unconnected or are they secretly forms of the one rationality differently embodied, analogous to the fundamentally oppressive character of enlightenment rationality, as some critics of the enlightenment have argued? *The Golden Notebook* seems to say that Anna's block results from her refusal to make connections between different areas of her life, but her merger of those areas takes place through a relation with a man who embodies such separations in a stark form. She learns to love her chains. The novel suggests that the result is not only an end of the writer's block, but also a loss of scope and understanding. 'Free Women' is a pale shadow of the notebooks.

One response to this might be to consider masculine subjectivity as something fairly readily described, and agree with Dorothy Richardson (albeit reluctantly perhaps) that when considering 'a man's consciousness . . . one could know exactly how it would behave' (1979: II, 27). On the other hand Saul's behaviour might be attributed to something other than his gender, to his nationality, or his work in the movie industry, despite the way Anna perceives him. Many thinkers would deny that masculine subjectivity exists at all. They would probably argue that Saul's behaviour is due to his power, the 'chains' in which he can place women because of the power modern society reserves for men, not to some form of inner psychic structuration resulting from his contemporary or childhood environments. Such an argument is related to a more general argument against the very term subjectivity. Poststructuralism has presented a decentred subject, a kind of subjectivity-less subject: interpellated by ideology, constructed by discourses, constituted by the desire of the other. Talk of consciousness, intention or agency is alleged to be a return to a humanist, bourgeois fiction, a dangerous, oppressive fiction. One man's experience is another man's discursive practice. Power, ideology, sign systems, difference and discourses are the spaces where subjectivities are produced and determined.

Poststructuralism is a critique of older ideas of subjectivity, especially the idea that there is a unified subject, a kind of all-seeing central ego in command of conscious mental life. These older ideas are themselves far from unified. Understanding of what constitutes subjectivity has changed radically over centuries, and has always produced dissent, dissent becoming ever more intense as the study of mind as the supposed ground of reason, knowledge and reality became the core of philosophy. A central difficulty in assessing this history is that although the concept of the subject and its subjectivity is intended as a logical move necessary to generalize from human diversity and spatial and temporal differences, this logical move is used to explain mental phenomena which are themselves not necessarily fixed. Some features of mental life may vary over time and space rather than forming an unchanging background reality. Theories of the subject are not full, exhaustive descriptions of psychological phenomena as many interpreters have wanted to believe. Add to this the obvious fact that the theories of subjectivity which have dominated Western thought in the modern period were developed by men, and there are further grounds for uncertainty. They may have masculine biases built into them. These theories may omit features of subjectivity which men were unfamiliar with or even unaware of, due to anything from men's psychological organizations to the specific limitations of men's everyday worlds. As Genevieve Lloyd says: 'maleness, as we have inherited it, enacts no less, the impoverishment and vulnerability of "public" reason' (1984: 107). She specifically mentions the exclusion from the responsibilities of the nurturing tasks of the private domain as a formative influence on such masculine public rationalities. Recent philosophical arguments by Manfred Frank and others that we cannot wholly identify self-reflection with self-consciousness or language lend further weight to a growing awareness that many familiar theoretical terms – rationality, emotion, consciousness, the unconscious, intention, ego, the self, desire – are shifting, unstable sands on which to build theories of gender.

MEN'S MOVEMENT THEORIES OF EMOTION AND EXPERIENCE

Men theorists have produced two influential theories of masculine subjectivities over the past decade. Both rely on psychoanalysis, but they differ widely in their choice of psychoanalytic authorities. One is the theory that separation from the mother and the absence of the father in early childhood lead to an impoverished emotional development in men, who consequently lack the skills necessary for intimacy. Various forms of this theory have been widely promulgated within men's movements and the humanistic psychologies of the past two decades. The other theory appears more sophisticated because it emerges from the complex arguments of poststructuralism. This theory presents masculinity as the effect of the way the relations of language, the unconscious and the patriarchal order as symbolized by the phallus, are structured. The poststructuralist theory of sexual difference probably has more credibility with feminists than the humanist account, although the exponents of the sexual difference theory have mostly been academics, whereas the other account has been adopted by men from a much wider range of backgrounds.

This division into two theories is a simplification of a range of debates, but it usefully highlights the different sources and political sites of negotiation with which these theories are concerned. The affective theory has its roots in a humanist aesthetics which is reactionary according to poststructuralist theories of the subject in language. This theory continues to enjoy support because of the influence of a range of humanistic psychologies from Gestalt to Re-evaluation Co-counselling. Poststructuralist theory is now the dominant theory in cultural studies, even if it takes extremely heterogenous and sometimes irreconcilable forms.

The men's movement, even more than the women's movement, is a decentralized, heterogeneous network of magazines, small consciousness-raising groups, gay men's organizations, and alliances within psychotherapeutic movements. There is no general theory, political structure or social background which unites these men. My own involvement is probably typical. At different times I have been to co-counselling workshops on men, open workshops on sexual politics, conference sessions on sexual politics and masculinity, and also planned a collection of essays on the changes in men's lives since feminism, and belonged to a men's group. I want to stress this heterogeneous activity because in what follows I may seem to treat the men's movement as if it were homogenous and had certain orthodoxies. I do think that certain ideas about men are widely shared, and certain intellectual influences are fairly common, but there are still sections of the men's movement to whom these generalizations would not apply. My aim is not to provide an objective history of the men's movement but to discuss the importance of some of its most prevalent ideas about men. Not all of my sources for the quotations that follow would identify themselves as a part of any men's movement, but they share a sense that men need to change, both in response to feminism and for their own sakes as well.

Many men in the men's movement believe that emotional conflicts are the most important issue for men. What do they understand by this? Steve Mason in an article about the work of a Bristol-based group of men tackling male violence, published in a typical men's movement magazine, the *Men's Antisexist Newsletter* (1986), summarizes generally held beliefs:

As men we are very out of touch with our feelings – we have had the language of feeling beaten out of us, often literally, during childhood. Those feelings we are left with have acquired connotations which makes us shun or misapply them. So – love and warmth imply shame; joy and delight imply immaturity; anger and frustration imply physical violence. We need to reclaim our feelings and shed the connotations – to learn that feeling is good for us. Our dissociation from feeling

119

allows us to be violent more easily, as it dissociates us from the consequences. Anger and violence need not be synonymous and learning to feel more deeply will help us find a path away from violence.

(Mason 1986: 17)

Violence against men, especially boys and young men, has destroyed their ability to use emotion as a language as well as their ability to articulate their feelings. Mason assumes that feelings have been both eliminated and reconfigured – love turned into shame. Steven Dedalus's humiliation at the hands of his fellow schoolboy Heron or the beating Dan Dare gives Tremloc would be examples of Mason's claim. A schizophrenic dissociation like Saul's behaviour can result. Mason's answer is to train men to feel more deeply, and thus allow emotion more psychic space both as a stimulus to consciousness and as a psychic event of its own. Emotion should be a valued part of our subjectivity. Not surprisingly there are now many self-help therapy books for men that try to teach how and why to feel more deeply. If the problem is a lack of psychological development, then men ought to be able to retrain themselves individually. Men can be encouraged by a rhetoric that stresses sexual difference to the advantage of women, and therefore fosters a new awareness of men's deprivation. *Iron John* (Bly 1990) uses this strategy extensively. Michael E. McGill in his book on 'male intimacy' gives a clear summary of the assumptions behind these works:

> We know that love, intimacy, and being close mean very different things to men and women. For men, sex seems to be the supreme intimacy, the context in which all issues of relational closeness are considered. Other dimensions of emotional bonding – time together, variety of exchanges, value of exchanges, exclusivity, and collective concern – are unknown to most men; their loving is limited to their narrow knowledge of what love is. By contrast, women are aware of the richness of loving relationships in all their dimensions.
>
> (McGill 1985: 31)

Men are effectively defined as a social group for whom only a limited range of forms of interaction are valid within public space. Steven Naifeh and Gregory White Smith think that this situation results from the conditions of employment:

> Many men are still imprisoned in emotional isolation, living out repressive masculine roles. Even though many men today have a clearer awareness of their need for emotional fulfilment, the essence of what it means to 'be a man' has changed surprisingly little. The pillars of maleness continue to be strength, invulnerability, and maintaining a competitive edge. Many men continue to feel that they must prove themselves every day. For many men, even after years of changing

120

stereotypes, emotional honesty and openness are still among the sacrifices they must make to manhood.

(Naifeh and Smith 1987: 3–4)

Strength and invulnerability are already familiar as components of the fantasy figure of Superman. The risk of this kind of argument is that it can develop into special pleading for men. McGill is well aware of the temptation to find exonerating excuses: 'the absence of intimacy thus serves two purposes for a man: it gives him the power he associates with success in life, and it protects him from feedback that might reveal his inadequacies' (1985: 233). Men's lack of intimacy is a strategic secrecy. Men hide feelings in order to withhold information which might give others power over them.

These writers believe that the suppression of feeling is a key element in the construction of masculinities. McGill goes so far as to say that 'there is no intimacy in most male friendships and none of what intimacy offers: solace and support' (ibid.: 184), and gives a particularly poignant example of the consequences. A man whose close friend Steve has recently died describes how, despite the close ties between himself and two other friends of Steve, they didn't quite know what to do, whereas his wife and Steve's wife:

> were really emotional in a way a man could never be. In the midst of it all, I had a sense that they were really helping each other. . . . As for me, I just had Tom and Jim. I knew that they were really hurt by Steve's death, too, but for some reason we couldn't really share what we were feeling. While the women were together with each other, we men were together by ourselves, drinking, staring off into space, each of us full of grief. But for whatever reason, we chose to deal with it inside, each in his own way, instead of talking about what we were feeling.
>
> (ibid.: 174)

How like Superman they are, staring off into space rather than gazing at one another face to face, responsively. Yvette Walczak's fifty-one 'Men in the Eighties' (a cross-section of British men interviewed as a sample of current masculinities) concur in such views. The 37-year-old lecturer says: 'Women can have close, longer-lasting friendships with other women much more easily than men do.' The 54-year-old scientist says: 'Men recognise each other's qualities, women work harder at friendships' (Walczak 1988: 81). The men's explanations for this range from the plausible (men are too competitive), to the implausible (women have more time), but there is wide agreement amongst these 'ordinary' men. It might be truer to say that male bonding, which can be a powerful means of excluding women, has certain limits and depends on a lack of self-exposure. In a men's movement anthology, Don Sabo recalls what it was like as a young athlete: 'I can see in retrospect that as boys we lacked a vocabulary of intimacy which would

121

have enabled us to share sexual experiences with others' (1990: 18). Locker-room boasting took its place: 'their minds lead them toward eroticism while their hearts pull them toward emotional intimacy' (ibid.: 20). Without doubting its applicability to his experiences, we should note that Sabo writes in retrospect, with the benefit of the kind of thinking the men's movement promotes. The way current ideas can infiltrate even the most powerful personal statements is very clearly demonstrated in a short piece by Sy Safransky on his own heterosexuality. He reflects on the intensity of sexual desires which have led him into three marriages:

> Is it the women I haven't understood, or myself? The need to love and be loved – how much of it really had to do with them, their individual temperaments, charms, braininess, magic, their faces so ordinary and so adored? What have I looked for in their eyes but a truer reflection of myself? How passionate I've been, in pursuit of life through these other lives. What a devotee of desire! But not merely of the honey breasts and milky thighs, not merely of tastes tasted, the stuttering tongue appeased – but desirous, most of all, for desire itself. I've been hungry for hunger. I've come before my women like a starving man to a banquet table . . . with undying devotion to my hunger, my awful hunger. . . . We reenact the old hurts, we summon forth the ghosts of Mom and Dad and resurrect for them a new body, a new face, a voice with just a hint of the old, and we bid them to sit down beside us, here at the banquet table, and beg them once again to feed us, please, and please, this time, with a little love.
>
> (Safransky 1990: 122)

This powerful evocation of the neediness of desire is both very personal and curiously impersonal when it reproduces the Lacanian observation that we desire the desire of the other, thus universalizing itself by making this masculine behaviour exemplify a supposedly general psychic structure, and the commonplace idea of the transference. The move into theory acts as an immediate guard against too much self-exposure, because it legitimates what is being said by making it both normative and intelligible. Behind the explanations is some other process, one which is more violent (the devouring of women) and less metaphorical than the rhetoric of starvation and frozen emotional need might suggest. Behind the comments on emotional intimacy, openness, sharing and so forth lies a body of unexamined ideas about emotion and masculinities.

For one thing, as Philip Hodson reminds us, 'it is actually only two thirds of his emotions that a man is enjoined to conceal since the rules of the game permit him to express violent anger and rage' (1984: 9). Stuart Miller notes that even when he warms to a potential male friendship doubts arise: 'But so many people I have interviewed lately have told me that fear of homosexuality is what keeps men apart that I find myself suddenly wondering if my rosy good feeling doesn't have some erotic flavour to it' (1983: 139).

Anthony Astrachan emphasizes the importance of the feelings men have about women during a period when women have instigated many changes in their relations with men: 'most men tend to have more and stronger painful feelings than pleasurable ones about these changes' (1986: 15). The suppression of emotion may have a more direct connection to men's power over women than some arguments about men and emotion admit to. Samuel Osherson emphasizes that to 'understand men's feelings about love and work we need to understand our unfinished business with our fathers' (1986: 4). These and other studies of men from within this general perspective complicate the idea that to be masculine means that emotions are suppressed, but the basic premiss remains. Tim Beneke, who has made extensive studies of male sexual violence, suggests that emotional repression may be one major cause of rape. His transcription of a young man's comments on women shows just how dangerous emotional suppression can be. The young man says that sometimes the sight of an unavailable, pretty woman can make him feel very bad:

> A lot of times a woman knows that she's looking really good and she'll use that and flaunt it, and it makes me feel like she's laughing at me, and I feel degraded. I also feel dehumanised, because when I'm being teased I just turn off, I cease to be human. Because if I go with my human emotions I'm going to want to put my arms around her and kiss her, and to do that would be unacceptable. I don't like the feeling that I'm supposed to stand there and take it, and not be able to hug her or kiss her; so I just turn off my emotions. It's a feeling of humiliation, because the woman has forced me to turn off my feelings and react in a way that I really don't want to.
>
> (Beneke 1989: 404)

Beneke's point is made very forcefully by the fact that this is just an 'ordinary' 23-year-old American man, not a rapist, yet quite capable of saying without reservation, 'if I were going to rape a girl, I wouldn't hurt her' (ibid.: 405). The contradictions inherent in that mistaken belief are painfully obvious and only emotional blankness could hide them from the speaker.

In Britain these ideas about men's alleged difficulties with emotion have found widespread acceptance. They have been promulgated within the more humanistic psychotherapies, and in the men's movement, most notably in *Achilles Heel*, a kind of men's counterpart to *Spare Rib*, although much less successful. The play on names tells us something about this. The women's magazine title is an ironic play on the idea that women are no more than the outgrowth of a superfluous part of men, and perhaps merely, like spare ribs, there to be consumed by others. The men's magazine title refers to one of the greatest warrior heroes of all time, whose mother, Peleus, had given him invulnerability except on the ankle where she had held him as she applied the magic treatment. This point on his body where she held him is Achilles' only connection with his mother, because his father reared him. Hence his name, which means 'no lips', chosen by his mother because he had never sucked at her breast (Graves 1955: 272). Achilles' only weakness is his ankle which symbolizes this lost connection with his mother. Colloquially an Achilles heel is the weakness by which an enemy can destroy its possessor. The men's magazine title presupposes both men's fear of other men, and their desire for invulnerability, to which it responds with a curiously flattering admission of weakness – 'we are all just Achilles heels' it seems to say. These elements were very evident in a collection of essays compiled by many of the contributors to *Achilles Heel*, a collection called *The Sexuality of Men* (Metcalf and Humphries 1985). The editors set the tone for the remaining essays by somewhat disowning sexuality:

> Heaven forbid the notion that we might actually question whether we want all of this sex we are urged to consume. The most pernicious aspect of all this is that men, dodging behind the banner of women's sexual pleasure, have allowed their own complex and emotional needs to be unacknowledged and even to remain unknown to themselves.
>
> (ibid.: 6)

The book asks how and why men have let this happen. Have they encouraged it, or has it been thrust upon them? Tony Eardley argues that 'emotional illiteracy . . . is part and parcel of male socialization' (ibid.: 101). Richard Dyer talks about the way popular culture encourages men to 'identify with heterosexual feelings' (ibid.: 40). Many of the contributors trace the process of emotional suppression back to early childhood, leaning on a popular version of the ideas of Nancy Chodorow and other earlier object-relations psychoanalytic theorists. Tom Ryan writes:

> Masculinity, then, can be viewed as a defensive construction developed over the early years out of a need to emphasise a difference, a separateness from the mother. In the extreme this is manifested by machismo behaviour with its emphasis on competitiveness, strength, aggressiveness, contempt for women and emotional shallowness, all serving to keep the male secure in his separate identity.
>
> (Metcalf and Humphries 1985: 26)

There is a danger that this kind of argument can then provide a kind of Achilles heel explanation for the adult man's behaviour, in which it seems as if it were the mother who is to blame somehow for messing up the making of her heroic son. Victor Seidler's essay 'Fear and Intimacy' runs this risk, despite its attractive attempts to mingle autobiography with theory. When he says that 'since we can so easily discount our own emotional needs and wants it can be difficult to respond to the needs and wants of others' and that 'a fear of intimacy has held men in terrible isolation and loneliness, though this is rarely acknowledged' (ibid.: 159), these claims can sound like an attempt at dishonourable exoneration. Men do suffer, but this suffering cannot justify their treatment of others. There is also a risk that the only political action that results will be wholly personal. Jeff Hearn (himself a long-term men's movement activist) says in *The Gender of Oppression* that 'the most drastic action that men can take politically, personally, or academically is not to try and solve the problems of women for women, but to recognise our love and responsibility for each other, to change our relationship with each other' (1987: 180). In the context of his book this sentiment is not an avoidance of politics, but it echoes a very common sentiment widespread in the men's movement, especially the earlier men's movement, which has led some recent commentators to take issue with the whole emphasis on emotion.

Kobena Mercer, a writer active in black cultural politics, has two objections to *The Sexuality of Men*. One is that 'the emphasis on inner feelings and the "person centred" stress on identity at the expense of environment is a limited way of addressing the issues' (Mercer 1988: 118). This approach only works amongst people for whom individuality is the most important feature of their lives. A more collectivist culture would find the use of psychotherapeutic language unhelpful, and even for the white middle-class men whom he believes are most likely to use these theories of emotional suppression, there is a danger that political action will go by the board. *The Sexuality of Men* also universalizes a local problem and so unconsciously reproduces a colonialist discourse. Discussing Tom Ryan's contribution to the book he says:

> Ryan's psychoanalytic discourse assumes that it has universal relevance and applicability. This conceals a dangerously Eurocentric assumption which demonstrates gross insensitivity to the different ways in which emotions are expressed in different cultures. How could you say that black men like Miles Davis or Michael Jackson, James Brown or John Coltrane are 'emotionally illiterate'? It is often said that black people are more emotionally expressive. Whether or not this has any validity as a generalisation, there is a grain of truth here as the expressive qualities of black music, from blues and jazz in the past to reggae and soul today, bear witness to a culture in which the open expression of deep structures of feeling is valued as an end in itself.
>
> (Mercer 1988: 122–3)

Mercer uses Raymond Williams's term 'structure of feeling' to signal that emotion is a social form and not just an aggregate of individual expressions. Jennifer Somerville, a feminist sociologist, cites evidence in her review of *The Sexuality of Men* that difficulties with emotional expression can certainly be found across American social classes, if not, as Mercer claims, across different ethnic groups. *The Hite Report*, she says, has shown that:

> the contradiction between outer machismo and inner insecurity, emotional deprivation and identity anxiety revealed by the participants of men's groups could not be discounted as a peculiarity of neurotic, intellectually over-developed, self-indulgent, middle-class professional and academic men, but was generalisable to a broad cross-section of American males. The problem was no longer to prove that such a contradiction lay at the heart of masculinity, but how to explain it.
>
> (Somerville 1989: 278)

Cultural and class differences are hard to assess. Emotion, subjectivity and identity are not simply universal concepts understood in the same way across cultural and class differences. Somerville, however, is highly critical of the way emotion is used as an explanation in *The Sexuality of Men*. She takes Victor Seidler to task for saying that men use 'sexual contact as a way of fulfiling our needs for dependency', saying that 'research evidence on the meaning of sexual contact for women suggests that it consists of the same confusion of desires, demands and needs also often unsatisfied' (Somerville 1989: 299–300). She thinks that 'in the treatment of the erotic [that] the text smacks of hair-shirt penitence'. Instead of considering the pleasures of the erotic for men, and their development as sexual beings, there is a tone of 'piety' which she finds exasperating. Somerville's reaction is one which has been widespread amongst feminists who have been sympathetic to the aims of the men's movement in general, but felt that the emphasis on emotional expression and development was sidestepping the important issues, and was potentially self-indulgent and self-exonerating. Men's deafening silence about their own sexuality as opposed to the objects of their desire continues. I believe, however, that this is not a silence easily replaced with articulation (my experience in writing this book confirms this), because there is not some pre-existent sexuality, easily described in ready-made psychoanalytic terms waiting for expression, and only held back by self-consciousness or fear of humiliation by other men. The silence is the silence of an undeveloped or lost language. No one individual can simply invent a language, it has to emerge out of a social process in which many men begin to become aware of their own self-representations of sexual consciousness and sexual desire within their social interactions.

As if to counter the objections of feminists like Somerville, Victor Seidler published a book, *Rediscovering Masculinity: Reason, Language and Sexuality* (1989), subsequent to *The Sexuality of Men*, which attempts to ground the men's movement arguments in a wider philosophical context, especially that of poststructuralism. For example, Seidler praises Derrida for showing that there is no one absolute form of reason, but only 'a proliferation of discourses, each representing the reality and experience of a different group' (ibid.: 184). In praising him Seidler uses the very term, 'representation', which his commitment to emotion might seem to exclude. He is also critical of Derrida because deconstruction is wholly 'intellectualist':

> Derrida leaves little space for the contradictions men feel in relation to their masculinity. . . . Not only does this emphasis on discourse threaten to continue to denigrate our emotions and feelings, but it also organizes our experience in definite ways. It cripples our emotional lives as we become incapable of connecting to these parts of ourselves. It leaves our emotions and feelings, needs and desires unrecognised, and it forms them in particular ways.
>
> (ibid.: 184)

In arguing that deconstruction is limited because it does not recognize the claims of emotion, Seidler shows that he still accepts the basic premises of the men's movement position. He believes that the false claims of reason evident in the philosophical tradition can best be explained in terms of a masculine denial of the claims of feeling: 'for men who have been brought up to identify so directly with our minds, it can be equally important to stress the independent existence of feelings and emotions as sources of knowledge and understanding' (ibid.: 186). Elsewhere in the book Seidler also argues that emotion is a social relation. This ambitious attempt to give legitimacy to the theory of emotional suppression shows some of the ways forward for rethinking the dominant claims of reason, but his account of Derrida and poststructuralism needs to be supplemented by an analysis of emotion and its conceptual implications, in order for the criticisms to address the complexity of Derrida's position, and further clarify the misleading claims to inner authenticity made on behalf of emotion.

In *Rediscovering Masculinity*, Seidler cautiously alludes to one of the most influential sources of men's movement thinking about the formation of masculinity, object-relations psychoanalysis, tacitly acknowledging that it has been criticized widely by feminists for its lack of attention to social and psychic complexities. Feminists like Somerville argue that object-relations psychoanalysis replaces desire (a concept which goes back to Hegel's description of self-consciousness, and plays a major role in Lacan's linguistification of psychoanalysis) with need (a literal fact rather than a representation). It often fails to recognize the importance of fantasy and the unconscious in psychic life and so conflates psychic and social life too readily. The poststructuralist theory of sexual difference avoids such pitfalls because it is a theory of representation.

Several of the contributors to *The Sexuality of Men* rely on object-relations psychoanalysis, and in particular one version of it, that of Nancy Chodorow in *The Reproduction of Mothering* (1978). Her work occupies a unique status in the men's movement because it provides the only widely accepted theoretical framework that seems to fit the idea that men grow up emotionally suppressed. Feminists have been more sceptical. Critics like Somerville say that it shows an 'unwillingness to confront the psychical dimension in its own terms and not as a product of the social' and treats psychoanalytic processes as 'mere psychic mechanisms through which socially appropriate gender characteristics are transmitted' (Somerville 1989: 302). Many feminists fear that Chodorow's theory is a recurrence of the ideological use of psychoanalytic theory to pressurize women back into motherhood, by blaming mothers for creating the psychic structures of masculinity. Chodorow's own summary of her theory definitely gives some grounds for her critics to reach such conclusions:

> Masculinity becomes an issue as a direct result of a boy's experience of himself in his family – as a result of his being parented by a woman. For children of both genders, mothers represent regression and lack of autonomy. A boy associates these issues with his gender identification as well. Dependence on his mother, attachment to her, and identification with her represent that which is not masculine; a boy must reject dependence and deny attachment and identification. Masculine gender role training becomes much more rigid than feminine. A boy represses those qualities he takes to be feminine inside himself, and rejects and devalues women and whatever he considers to be feminine in the social world.
>
> (1978: 181)

This description makes everything sound very conscious – the boy represses 'what he takes to be' the qualities he doesn't want, and 'associates' them with mother. There is some confusion of theoretical systems. Role theory is not readily compatible with psychoanalytic theories of the unconscious. Yet its strengths lie in just this summary of a structure of expectations, intentions and feelings. It is the structure and unconscious processes which generate masculinity as much or more than any intentional act.

Lynne Segal's suspicion that the appeal of Nancy Chodorow's version of object-relations theory for the men's movement lies in its emphasis on mothering, and on its avoidance of the uncomfortable issue of power is convincing (Segal 1987: 141–5), but Chodorow's theory has another source of appeal, its emphasis on emotion. This of course makes cultural theorists even more suspicious, because so many ambiguities surround the concept of emotion. Summarizing her aims, Chodorow says:

> The psychoanalytic account shows not only how men come to grow away from their families and to participate in the public sphere. It shows also how women grow up to have both the generalized relational capacities and needs and how women and men come to create the kinds of interpersonal relationships which make it likely that women

will remain in the domestic sphere – in the sphere of reproduction – and will in turn mother the next generation.

(Chodorow 1978: 38)

What are 'relational capacities'? Her use of psychoanalytic sources gives her no conceptual help for analysing the role of emotion in the processes she is describing. Chodorow begins with an orthodox reading of object-relations theory and then adds on her own interpretation of certain features of it which entails this new reference to emotional and relational capacities. She argues:

A child both takes into itself conflictual relationships as it experiences them, and organizes these experiences of self-in-relationship internally. What is internalized from an ongoing relationship becomes unconscious and persists more or less independent of that original relationship. It may be generalized as a feeling of self-in-relationship and set up as a permanent feature of psychic structure and the experience of self.

Internalization does not mean direct transmission of what is objectively in the child's social world into the unconscious experience of self-in-relationship. Social experiences take on varied psychological meanings depending on the child's feelings of ease, helplessness, dependence, overwhelming love, conflict and fear.

(ibid.: 50)

The primary difference between this account and that of her critics is not a denial of the unconscious or a confusion of psychic and social, but the introduction of feelings into the account. Her emphasis on 'relational potential' is strongly revisionary. It enables her to spot Freud differentiating male and female super-ego in terms of a relation to emotion in his essay 'Some Psychical Consequences of the Anatomical Distinction Between the Sexes' (1925):

I cannot evade the notion (though I hesitate to give it expression) that for women the level of what is ethically normal is different from what it is in men. Their super-ego is never so inexorable, so impersonal, so independent of its emotional origins as we require it to be in men.

(Chodorow 1978: 143)

Chodorow's rejoinder to Freud's misogyny is a celebration of women's capacity for greater psychic subtlety than men's. She asserts that: 'there is greater complexity in the feminine endopsychic object-world than in the masculine' because they have a greater relational capacity: 'girls emerge with a stronger basis for experiencing another's needs or feelings as one's own' (ibid.: 167). She also refers less persuasively to the Oedipus complex as the basis for 'relational development' (ibid.: 166). This relational capacity is not simply an ability to 'relate' to others, nor is it, as Parveen Adams reads it, a fixed disposition towards certain kinds of relations which may well be largely oppressive. Adams (1983: 49) also thinks that Chodorow believes that a child has a 'fundamental sociality'. Chodorow certainly believes that a child lives socially as well as psychically, and in believing that is in good company. The philosopher Emmanuel Levinas argues that a fundamental sociality or 'face to face' relation is more fundamental than the ontological or subject/object relation: 'man's ethical relation to the other is ultimately prior to his ontological relation to himself (egology) or to the totality of things which we call the world (cosmology)' (Kearney 1984: 57). The idea of a fundamental sociality also evokes Paul Ricoeur's claim that some emotions are fundamentally social, not regressively libidinal (Ricoeur 1970: 507). It all depends on what is meant by emotion. For Adams (1983: 50), the idea of 'relational potential' would lead to an illusory 'androgyny of the emotions'. These differences between psychoanalytic feminists hang on unexamined differences in their theories of feeling.

Feelings and emotions are usually understood to be primary expressions of the given fixed self of the individual. Chodorow's account then appears to be another version of liberalism in which society is no more than the sum total of individual wishes, and open to the kind of criticisms Segal and Adams make. As a limited hypothesis about the effects of parental asymmetry I believe that it remains important because it draws attention to the way young male children in Western societies commonly experience a different relation to the adult world from that of female children. Men, whom boys will one day join, are largely absent, non-nurturing and powerful. An account of masculinity which only stressed the external aspects of this power would leave unexplored much that is puzzling. Masculine subjectivities will not be understandable if we entirely neglect the 'relational potential' constructed by all their relations with men and women.

The idea that 'as men we are very out of touch with our feelings' has some support from feminists and widespread support from men in the men's movement. Men, they believe, must learn to be emotionally literate. The politics of this are far from obvious. Few men have been able to use this insight as the basis of an active political intervention, especially one which supports the struggles of the oppressed, whether gay men, women or Third World countries. The theoretical implications are also far from clear. It is unconvincing to say that deconstruction leaves out emotions and feelings, because emotion is a term which deconstruction only recognizes as part of the phallologocentric structure of Western thought. Emotion is referred to in many different, possibly incompatible, ways by men who argue for its importance in men's lives. Nor is the attempt to ground these convictions in object-relations psychoanalysis entirely convincing. The psychoanalytic tradition sidelines emotion, largely ignores adult interaction (or what Wendy Hollway calls 'the recursive reproduction of gender difference in adult social relations' (Hollway 1989: 5)), and has been closely tied to political demands for full-time good mothering. These reservations can be answered, but they would need to be seriously addressed by men who write about masculinity, if object-relations psychoanalysis is going to be a valid method for such projects.

Other doubts about the men's movement trust in emotion remain. Can we be sure that 'feeling is good for us'? Aren't some feelings demonstrably dangerous, misleading and oppressive? The men's movement theory of men's subjectivities relies on a concept of emotion in need of further investigation. Emotional expression may not always be good, authentic and natural.

THE POSTSTRUCTURALIST THEORY OF MASCULINITY

The ideas about men and masculinity promulgated by the men's movement have found little support outside it, especially from feminists, because it is widely believed that men have largely failed to tackle their collusion with power and oppression. In a sympathetic but often critical account of the American men's movement, Anthony Astrachan seems to confirm this. He says that:

> after a decade of local, regional and national meetings, most of the men in the movement worry about three things, singly or in combination: relationships with other men, the male sex role, and 'the way women keep changing the rules of the game'.
>
> (Astrachan 1986: 290)

Men's power has proved extremely resistant to self-analysis within the movement. If, as writers on masculinity like Lynne Segal argue, men's power is the primary determinant of masculinities, then this is a serious failure. Like many other feminist theorists, and some men theorists, Segal looks to theories of power as a theoretical resource for understanding masculinities. The most prominent of those is Foucault's theory of power, which has been linked to other poststructuralist theories, especially Lacanian psychoanalysis, because, as Lynne Segal puts it, 'desire . . . plays a central role in constructing "masculinity" and affirming or subverting men's power and authority' (Segal 1990: 101). Desire replaces emotion in what has become known as the theory of sexual difference.

The theory of sexual difference, often referred to simply as sexual differ-ence (omitting any reference to its hypothetical status now that it appears to be firmly established), is the most widely held academic account of masculi-nities. One reason for this is indicated unconsciously by Paul Smith, the co-editor of *Men in Feminism*: 'Feminist theory broadly speaking sees ("through" phallocentric theory) that male-centred social and psychical structures place biological men as enforcing agents for those structures'

131

(Jardine and Smith 1987: 35). He then asks whether men ('male theorists') can understand and 'be of any political use to feminist theory' and decides that they can, because 'the intellectual task of understanding feminist theory is not a problem since feminist theory is situated within the array of poststructuralist discourses with which many of us are now perhaps over-familiar.' Although many feminists have queried the validity of this link between feminist theory and poststructuralism, such connections have been historically important, especially in the academic world. Paul Smith, how-ever, simply assumes that the two are identical, and that therefore a man with access to semiological theory has automatic access to feminist theory. The masculine imperialism of that assumption was immediately challenged by other contributors to the collection, but it accurately represents a wide-spread academic position. Masculinity can only be understood by using poststructuralist theory, because feminism has already been situated within this radical space. Any other account of masculinity would be conservative and so potentially supportive of men's power.

Freudian psychoanalysis has only recently had much political respectabi-lity in Britain. In the United States its widespread adoption led to feminist attacks on it from the late 1960s on. Ample evidence of Freud's patriarchal contempt for women could be cited. Penis envy was only the most salient example. There was plenty of other material for a demolition job. In France psychoanalysis offered much more assistance to feminism than in the English-speaking world. Lacan's school created a kind of alternative to the dominant institution, and recruited many women into it. Juliet Mitchell made available to English-language readers their ideas in her substantial study *Psychoanalysis and Feminism* (1974), which argued that despite the excrescences of male chauvinism in Freud, the basic theory could be used as a radical political critique, if the importance of the unconscious was properly understood. From her work, and the development of a Lacanian film theory in the pages of *Screen*, emerged a substantial body of initially feminist, sexual difference theory, which, as Paul Smith's remarks show, has enjoyed a renewed authority in recent work on masculinity. According to sexual difference theory, gender is constructed within discourses and their work of representation, on the basis of the sexual difference that is only achieved through the Oedipal process and the entry into language.

Psychoanalysis was attractive to cultural theory because it seemed to promise the possibility of a theory with practical transformative power. Interpretation becomes a political act. Psychoanalysis is a theory of psychic formation which emphasizes the plasticity and instability of sexual identity, as well as the slow and complex formation it requires. The centrality of the unconscious for this process seems to provide an alibi, and an explanation, for oppressive social structures which function without the conscious intent of individuals. It is only a short step then to identifying ideology with the unconscious, if one can find a common mechanism at work in both, and this in turn can lead to the appropriation of a whole range of recent poststructuralist theories. Foucault's theory of discourse is used as the basis of the idea that knowledge and therefore gender are effects of discourses. The Kantian concept of representation recycled by structuralism is used to indicate that what are produced are not real objects in themselves but cognitive models of them. Lacan's rereading of the Oedipal transmutation of desire as the process whereby the subject enters language (and by extension the symbolic, the whole array of culture understood as a series of sign systems) is used to produce an equation between the semiological concept of language as a system of differences, and sexuality. The system of sexual differences can then be assimilated to Derrida's narratives of 'différance'.

The difficulty with this conjunction for understanding masculine subjectivities arises from its reliance on a selective version of psychoanalysis, and the latent idealism of poststructuralism. First, psychoanalysis itself is not treated as a developing field of enquiry in which newer scientific papers and theories are understood to replace or challenge earlier ones. For most cultural theorists, psychoanalysis is a theoretical framework which provides materials for theories whose coherence is tested by reasoned argument, not by some empirical testing procedure. More case studies won't help. Psychoanalysis provides founding texts. Secondly, psychoanalysis is an institution deeply complicit with men's authority and power. Any appropriation of psychoanalysis to theorize masculinity would have to begin by challenging its evidential, structural, institutional and ideological formations. None of the recent attempts to extend psychoanalysis into the critical analysis of masculinity has done that. Feminism offers a misleading ease in its use of psychoanalysis, because it is able to work oppositionally through the already constituted marginality of women to the discipline. Feminism provides a critique of psychoanalysis not dissimilar to Marx's critique of the classical economists. The language of psychoanalysis has also provided a place for feminists to develop an articulation of silenced experience, because of its richness in terminologies for desire which women historically have been unable to articulate publicly. This language provides the opportunity for oppositional emancipatory dialogue, not an authoritative theory of the psyche. To develop such a theory would require theoretical critique of the whole range of modern psychologies and their social foundations.

Psychoanalysis operates as a kind of immanent critique of the analysand's speech. It also has a normative dimension. The shared rationality which forms the communicative relation between analyst and analysand is contrasted with the actuality of the analysand's life, the fantasies and frustrations that it evidences. These conflicts are then interpreted by the analyst's theorization of the case in such a way that some of the painful contradictions can be healed. A feminist appropriation of psychoanalysis can question the processes of this resolution by reinterpreting the divisions as the result of social processes of gender-based domination, and therefore relocate the therapy as politics. The latent emancipatory project of psychoanalysis, its aim to understand self-division in order to heal it (a healing that at its most extreme may be simply a tragic reconciliation with inevitable division, as it is in some of Lacan's work), is made explicit but then transferred from the domain of categorical reason to social history. Instead of the restoration of functioning reflexivity, feminist psychoanalysis offers a transformation of such restorations which is revolutionary in scope. A project that would link psychoanalysis to an analysis of masculinity aimed specifically at transform-ation would have to bring to psychoanalysis a politics which could similarly reconfigure its latent moral imperative into a social, political process. Psychoanalysis cannot do that itself. Nor can feminism as such because its appropriation places masculinity as that very process of conservation. Masculinity is the name given to the refusal of a politics that is the positivist and therapeutic horizon of psychoanalytic institutions. What would be needed would be what Seyla Benhabib calls a 'utopian' form of critique (I discuss her ideas at the end of this chapter), if masculinity were to be transformed in psychoanalytic terms.

Sexual difference theory is a shaky basis for a politics of masculinity because of the idealist effect of its semiological appropriation of psycho-analysis. This idealism lies behind the apparent success of the theory in challenging widespread fallacies that derive gender difference from either biology or a universal idea of sexual division like right- and left-handedness. Sexual difference theory explains both the biological fallacy and the univer-salist fallacy (whose structure does not need further elucidation because of its more familiar form) in semiological terms, as examples of a metaphysics of the referent. Both fallacies are alleged to be what Parveen Adams, writing in *m/f*, called the result of assuming that there is 'a prior and given state of social being', prior, that is, to the work of representation. Only what is represented for us is real, in this essentially phenomenological account. 'The work of representation produces differences that cannot be known in ad-vance' (52). Michele Barrett seized on this assertion in *Women's Oppression Today* where she pointed out that such a position would make a historical materialism impossible:

> Without denying that representation plays an important constitutive role in this process we can still insist that at any given time we can have a knowledge of these categories prior to any particular representation in which they may be reproduced or subverted.
>
> (Barrett 1980: 93)

Knowledge of class and the social relations of production would be incon-ceivable. Yet despite her critical stance, Barrett still uses the Kantian termi-nology of categories, knowledge and the *a priori*.

Sexual diference is contrasted by Parveen Adams with sexual division, which is her label for the biological and universalist fallacies. Sexual division depends on an absolutely prior reality which wholly determines it, just as the metaphysical idea of the sign depends on the prior, given reality of a referent outside discourse. 'Prior' is a term which merges temporal precedence and absolute logical precedence, and therefore makes temporal precedence or history appear to be a claim to transcendental priority. 'Given' imbricates material determinism and logical priority.

A child is only slowly able to grow into or through the process of positioning that sexual difference effectuates. To say sexual division is 'prior' in this context would mean that the child was born already wholly constituted as a masculine or feminine individual, whose traits simply had to emerge like the plant out of a seed. Contrary to that, sexual difference theory argues that the desire of the child confronted by the differentiation of the mother and father positions will, during the process of development, result in the child taking up a position in the system of sexual difference not determined by internal factors. If 'prior' did only imply such an assumption about the emergence at birth of a fully gendered individual, then this critique would be very effective but 'prior' can be interpreted in more ordinary, historical terms. There surely is a sexual division prior to the emergence of the child, if we mean that gender already has a history. The child is not born into a world without sexual division and could not take up a position outside it. Sexual division is prior to the child in the very persons of the parents, but not in the form of an absolute fixed pair of identities. This division always has a history and is as varied as our class and multi-racial society can be.

The term 'prior' is an abstraction of history. 'Given', on the other hand, is an abstraction of material causation. It implies that any appeal to a material determination (for example to physiology or chromosomes) also makes a logical claim. If epistemological positivism were the only form that reference to an outside world could take, this might be valid. The pre-existent category of an objective reality in the character of an externality considered as permanent and universal is not the only theoretical implication of 'given', if we step outside the scientistic framework. Material differences may be given but may not therefore be necessary determinants of gender in social relations. The meaning assigned to what is given is dependent on the history of both material differences and human meanings. Neither is logically determinant on its own.

Physiology is part of the material that the social relations of gender work with but it does not determine them. Sexual difference theory is far more Kantian. It argues that it is the way physiology is constructed and represented within a society's discourses which forms the social relations of gender. The problem with this is that it is a resolutely dualist model which fails to grasp that there is no biology to be represented. Biology is already a theory. This need not, however, mean that biology is only a representation in an idealist sense. Sexual difference theory ignores the role of history in the formation of gender. By focusing on the synchronic sign and the *ab initio*

135

development of the child it can lose sight of the way we all begin with existing sexual differences as we think, speak, mature and ourselves reproduce what we have learnt.

Sexual difference theory replaces the theories of material determinism (or essentialism as it is often called), which it explicitly challenges, with an idealism that maintains that very Kantian problematic in an inverse form. Its success in exposing essentialist errors is paid for by the inability of the theory to conceptualize determination. Odd circularities result from this. Consider the phrase 'sexual difference' itself. The meaning of the sexual is the very thing difference is supposed to make possible. Its inclusion in the phrase suggests that sexual difference has to smuggle in a socially determined meaning for the sexual in order to give meaning to the process of difference in the first place. Otherwise we would not know what the word 'sexual' meant in this context. For these reasons sexual difference theory is not transferable directly to a men's sexual politics. Feminism is able to use psychoanalysis from points of both internal and external opposition, so that its very use becomes a powerful political strategy and a useful analytic method. For feminist politics, sexual difference theory does not need to be an authoritative general theory of the psyche. We can't transfer sexual difference theory to an emancipatory political discourse of men's gender on the grounds that sexual difference is such a general theory, and therefore applies across the board. The asymmetries of power and knowledge make it impossible simply to extend or reverse that critical strategy to consider men and masculinity without reinstating the very authoritarianism which feminism was challenging. Sexual difference theory needs considerable rethinking first.

Paul Smith's alliance conceals other problems besides the uncertain status of psychoanalysis. Just as object-relations psychoanalysis entails unhelpful assumptions for the arguments the men's movement wishes to make, so too some features of poststructuralism bring assumptions which hinder the development of a radical men's politics, and obscure the valuable insights about emotion we want to explore. Poststructuralism is commonly presented in the English-speaking world as a radical theory; even those Marxists who have criticized its influence use much of its terminology. For that reason the resistances it places in front of a possibly radical political practice are not always easy to see.

Paul Smith, like other contributors to *Men in Feminism*, believes theory is radical because men and women can be united by their common grounding in theory:

> there are academic men for whom feminism has been as integrally a part of their theoretical education as any other discourse, and who have both a lived and a theoretical sense of their own difference which has been instituted and inspissated by their 'understanding' of feminist theory.
>
> (Jardine and Smith 1987: 39)

136

Unfortunately theory is also a bulwark of the academic establishment and so only 'when poststructuralist feminist theory turns to construct its public sphere' will there really be working alliances between men and feminists. In theory men and feminists are united, in that theoretical education, but the practice is very different. For a man like Paul Smith, feminist theory is an impossible language to speak. He can feel that he will never use it correctly:

> There is always the probability of being incriminated, the continual likelihood of appearing provocative, offensive, and troublesome to the very people who have taught me to ask the questions, even at the very moment when I begin to grapple with the only theoretical language available. These feelings, these fears, are in a large part the result of having to engage with a discourse whose laws I can never quite obey.
>
> (ibid.: 38)

Feminists appear to have the only theoretical language going. Men seem to have none. What significance do these 'feelings', which have made an appearance in a discussion of theory and the subject, have for his argument? *Men in Feminism* concludes with a dialogue between the editors, in which Alice Jardine laments that 'many of the students now learn it [feminist theory] just for pleasure without living it in its emotional complexity' (ibid.: 262). What are these feelings? What does it mean to live a theory in its emotional complexity? Presumably one thing it means is to experience the solidarity which both male feminists and what Paul Smith calls 'women feminists' hope for. The vocabulary of emotion as the truest sign of the inner man reappears at the point where the hoped-for solidarity of theory meets the actual historical and political divisions, and the emotions, in both Jardine's remark and Smith's confession, have the effect of suturing the material self and the 'theoretical sense'. A similar division is also apparent in a passage from Stephen Heath's paper for the same panel. The scrupulous care for the complexity of the questions facing men who support feminism makes it exemplary:

> Do I write male? What does that mean? We have learnt – from semiotics, psychoanalysis, deconstruction, the whole modern textual theory – not to confuse the sex of the author with the sexuality and sexual positioning inscribed in a text. There is no simple relation of direct expression between myself as male or myself as female and the discourse, writing, text I produce, this production involving me in the whole mesh of discursive orders of language, all the available forms and constructions with their particular positions, their particular terms of representation, all the defined senses of 'masculine' and 'feminine'

(and in which I am anyway caught up from the start, given as 'man' or 'woman').

(Heath 1987: 26)

This passage demonstrates very clearly the difficulties a man has in writing about gender from outside any acknowledged oppositional position (the available languages of opposition). Its awkwardness about the relation between the self and language derives from an ethical uncertainty about the self's responsibility for the actions of its gender. The passage constantly shifts its pronominal position, from 'I' to 'we' to a kind of neutrality, and back again: 'Do I write' – 'We have learnt' – 'myself as male or myself as female'. The collective pronoun introduces not only an appeal to the reader ('we have learnt'), which implies that the learning of theory unites men and women, but an appeal to the authority and modernity of this theory. Ostensibly the sentence is saying that the 'myself' which has a sex doesn't just issue itself forth in writing, but saying 'myself as male or myself as female' severs the material self (and hence 'the body') from self-consciousness, the 'I', in the phrase 'text I produce'. At the time these papers were written, Smith and Heath disagreed about men's relation to theory, and Heath responded to Smith's paper by saying that feminist theory was not just theory, but practical, political and ethical as well; yet they shared a commitment to poststructuralist theory that sits uneasily with their recognition of the complex issues feminism raises for men. Their scrupulous attention to these difficulties makes visible a splitting symptomatic of postmodern representations of masculine subjectivities. Only Smith talks directly of feelings, but both men theorists find themselves gesturing at inner subjectivities not produced by discourse in the way theory would propose. Those central, deeper subjectivities are hard to represent because they seem to undermine the possibilities of alliance held out by the comradeship of theoretical rigour.

In *What a Man's Gotta Do* (1986), Antony Easthope presents one of the few explicitly poststructuralist accounts of masculinity prepared to work with specific cultural texts. Dominant masculinity is a myth in Roland Barthes's sense:

At present in the dominant myth the masculine ego is imagined as closing itself off completely, maintaining total defence. To be unified it must be masculine all the way through and so the feminine will always appear as something other or different and so a security risk. When it is in the external world outside the self the feminine will be a lovely enemy for whom desire triumphs over narcissistic anxiety. But when the feminine seems to have infiltrated within, as it must do because of the bisexual nature of every individual, it threatens the whole castle and must be savagely suppressed. Either way, since defence is attack,

138

the more the 'I' strives to be total master, the more aggression it releases.

(Easthope 1986: 42–3)

To make this picture work the ego must be able to 'close itself off'. If the ego is constituted by its relations with others, this closing off, which is apparently under the ego's control, is hard to understand. By what agency does it occur? This is a process which sounds very similar to Tim Beneke's young man, who 'switches off' his emotions (see p. 123). As a whole, the picture is very similar to that offered by the men's movement, of men cut off from both their inner emotional lives and those of the people around them. Emotion still plays a role as the motivation of the savagery of the reactions, albeit an unacknowledged one. Aggressivity is tacitly assumed to be an inevitable part of the process without quite allowing us to see from where it arises.

Easthope's terminology derives from British appropriations of Lacan:

At every point this system turns on what is seen as the male symbol. Sexual difference is represented by having or not having the phallus. . . . But the phallus, however deeply wrought by the traditions of patriarchal culture, is nevertheless merely a symbol.

(Easthope 1986: 170)

Easthope refers this point to Juliet Mitchell's introduction to *Feminine Sexuality* (1982: co-edited with Jacqueline Rose), one of the most influential syntheses of Lacan and feminist theory, confirming Paul Smith's observation that this way of theorizing masculinity derives directly from feminism.

Feminine Sexuality provided powerful analytic methods for the feminist study of subjectivity, but has been much less useful to men reflecting upon men's subjectivities, for reasons I shall now explore. The problems arise when this feminist critique is turned into a new theory of subjectivity. The argument can be taken that way, and has certainly been widely read in that manner, because it offers itself as a general theory of subjectivity through its use of the generalizing terms of structuralist theory, especially the terms 'language', 'discourse' and 'reality'. The conflation of the technical meanings of these terms with their everyday meanings makes possible an extrapolation not warranted by the theory itself. The problem doesn't lie in the arguments of Rose and Mitchell. It lies in the political contexts in which these essays have been read. The contradictions to be found in the arguments result from extrapolation out of the oppositional position of feminist critique.

Towards the end of her introductory essay Rose makes the key epistemological claim that there can be no 'pre-discursive reality', a formulation alluding to both language and discourse. This assertion is based on a remark from Jacques Lacan's *Séminaire XX: Encore*, which she translates as 'How return, other than by means of a special discourse, to a pre-discursive reality'

139

(Mitchell and Rose 1982: 55). His comment occurs in a discussion of ontology, where he says that philosophies of being tend to imagine that there could be a state of being which knew itself without language, rather like Hegel's state of 'sense-certainty' in his *Phenomenology of Spirit* (Lacan 1975: 33). To conclude that reality in its entirety is discursive would be an extrapolation of Lacan's point, especially given that Lacan uses the term 'real' elsewhere to mean psychic reality. Lacan's argument would seem to be close to Wittgenstein's theme that there can be no thought without language. In both cases the argument is not that non-discursive fields of subjectivity don't exist, but that the rationality of what we mean by the terms 'reality', 'being' or 'thought' is only intelligible if we recognize that they are forms of articulation. Lacan is also careful to use the term discourse rather than language, because discourse is a communicative social relation. Reality is what we speak.

Rose's conflation of language, discourse and 'reality' creates a potential paradox which does not affect its value for feminist challenges to the masculine hegemony of psychoanalysis, but, if applied to the analysis of masculinity, would result in contradictions whose roots lie in the structuralist model of the (effectively) transcendental relation of *langue* to *parole*. She writes:

> In so far as it is the order of language which constructs sexuality around the male term, or the privileging of that term which shows sexuality to be constructed within language, so this raises the issue of women's relationship to that language and that sexuality simultaneously.
>
> (Mitchell and Rose 1982: 53–4)

The English word 'language' is used here to refer to *langue* as a univeral set of rules and structures (an 'order') which logically precedes any specific social practice. Therefore sexuality is constructed at the level of a structure that transcends discursive practice. The word 'language' is used three times in the sentence, twice without any article at all, implying universality, and the third time with the deictic 'that' ('the issue of women's relationship to that language and that sexuality'). This third appearance produces a distance between women and language. It can therefore be read as implying that 'the order of language which constructs sexuality around the male term' is not the only possible language. The acknowledgement that language is a practice, not a logically necessary condition of all experience, then empowers women because their practice somehow dislodges the transcendental structure that preserves men's power. This reading implies that the transcendental structure is a masculine illusion, an ideology maintaining men's hegemony. Women are historically locatable individuals whose categorization is historically determined and changing. If, however, language as the condition of subjectivity really does structure 'sexuality around the male term', then the terms 'male' and 'female' are *a priori* since they are co-existent with this unified ahistorical structure, language, at the moment of its becoming itself. The terms are then empty, universal linguistic structures with no logical connection to behaviour, context, practice or any actual human beings. This form of idealism, which has been widespread in the past decade, is especially obstructive of any attempt to consider the construction of masculinity, because it leads to the conclusion that masculinity is co-extensive with language itself, and therefore fixed and unchanging. The assumption that language is a knowable system (I discussed the problems this gives rise to in recent theory in my essay 'Linguistic Turns' (Middleton 1989a)) creates a model of sexual difference which illegitimately merges *a priori* concepts and historical practice. Masculinity would then incidentally be theorized as the inevitable condition of the symbolic. The valuable feminist emphasis on the instability of subjectivity and sexual difference gets partially obscured by the use of 'masculine' and 'feminine' as structural terms at the level of *langue*.

During the past decade a variant of sexual difference theory based on the concept of 'discourse' has become extremely influential. One of the attractions of using the concept of 'discourse' to analyse the social structures of representation is that it claims to recognize the importance of social life for the study of gender without recourse to either sociological functionalism or the unexaminable totalizations produced by Althusserian theories of ideology. The theory of discourses (which should be distinguished from discourse theory, the linguistic study of spoken interaction) has been used primarily to explain social structures rather than simply to describe patterns of linguistic usage. It is common to hear people talk of sexist discourse and discourses of masculinity as if the existence of such recurrent usages was an index of a social formation. In ordinary use the word 'discourse' means 'speech' or 'argument'. Discourse theory uses the term both metonymically and metaphorically, but not literally. Metonymically it indicates the variety of verbal forms a historical institution can take. Metaphorically it suggests the conditions of actual practice as opposed to structural paradigms (which structuralists had set in opposition to *parole* or discourse, as the proper foci of cultural enquiry). The theory of discourses was developed by Michel Foucault as a means of analysing the history of specific knowledges, especially legal and medical ones. The well-defined uses by Foucault and others give little support for unjustified reference to discourses of masculinity.

Foucault's theory of discourses is a pragmatics: 'This field is made up of the totality of all effective statements (whether spoken or written) in their dispersion as events and in the occurrence that is proper to them' (1972: 26–7). Analysis of intention or *langue* is irrelevant. Nor does discourse analysis examine the logical coherences in these events. The nearest thing to a logic which could be analysed that Foucault can offer is the idea of a recognizable relation between a 'system of dispersion' and a 'number of statements' (ibid.: 37): 'Whenever, between objects, types of statement,

concepts, or thematic choices, one can define a regularity (an order, corre-
lations, positions and functionings, transformations), we will say, for the
sake of convenience, that we are dealing with a *discursive formation*' (ibid.:
38). This summary is made in the specific context of an attempt to formulate
general principles for the study of economics, medicine and grammar.
Therefore a legitimate extension of Foucault's discourse theory to gender
politics would have to observe several conditions:

1 It could not make statements about intention, whether individual or
collective. We cannot talk about the intentions behind a sexist discourse
for example.
2 It must identify both statements and a '*system* of dispersion'. The existence of statements doesn't prove the existence of a system.
3 This would be a pragmatics. Analysis would have to study in detail the
structures of social relations in order to assign significance to the statements. The statements cannot be treated as self-evidently meaningful in
the absence of such an analysis of contexts.

Much of the attractiveness of what has been used as an aestheticizing
linguistification of politics by the left, especially in cultural theory, dimi-
nishes if these conditions are observed. The need for a political and historical
account of masculinities cannot be sidestepped by projecting those relations
from the analysis of statements (or representation in general) into a determinate structure of social relations.

To speak legitimately of a discourse of masculinity it would be necessary
to show that a particular set of usages was located structurally within a
clearly defined institution with its own methods, objects and practices.
Otherwise the reference to discourses of masculinity is simply a reference to
repeated patterns of linguistic usage, which may be significant, but cannot be
theorized in the way some legal and medical discourses can. Masculinity is
produced within some discourses in the stricter theoretical sense, but most
examples of 'masculine' utterance are not discourses. They are not organized
around specific knowledges. The presentation of men in popular cultural
forms or the recurrent use of specific languages to describe men are very
significant but we cannot simply call them discourses and assume we have
established a link with histories of power and knowledge.

In a series of papers distributed at the Southampton University Sexual
Difference Conference in 1985, the Representations of Masculinity Study
Group from the Centre for Contemporary Cultural Studies (Birmingham
University) argued explicitly for a Foucaldian version of the theory of sexual
difference. Masculinities are 'produced in and by different discourses of
representation' (Brown *et al.* 1985: 1) and 'male discourse' can be a 'strategy'
when adopted by a woman who 'speak[s] with its codes but as a biological
female . . . run[s] rings round its assumptions and prejudices' (ibid.: 3). This
appealing form of subversion depends on the tacit assumption that there is a

self outside the discourse which can choose to adopt some of its features. Discourse is said to produce gender, and then through an appeal to experience a position outside it is embraced in order to allow the possibility of resistance. That resistance masks the way masculinity is then made into the fixed product of discourse.

The attempt to spot-weld subject and discourse together often leads to the appeal to various forms of traditional subjectivity, especially emotion, in discourse theory. A striking example occurs in an essay by Wendy Hollway and the commentary it elicited from Teresa de Lauretis. Wendy Hollway's essay 'Gender Difference and the Production of Subjectivity' (1984) uses Michel Foucault's theory of discourses to analyse the relations between gender and subjectivity, and particularly 'the recurrent splitting between women and men of gender-specified characteristics' (Hollway 1984: 228). She offers long, transcribed quotations from heterosexual men and women talking about their relationships, and then comments on the quotations in the manner of a literary critic. Wendy Hollway treats these quotations as if they were wholly authentic statements of what the interviewees feel, the facts that theory must account for. Despite the insistence that subjectivity is constructed by discourse, the essay talks of emotion as if it were a given, pre-linguistic, entirely private phenomenon. The consequences of this necessity for a theory of discourse to find a way of describing the link between self and discourse can be seen very clearly in Teresa de Lauretis's study of the *Technologies of Gender* (1987), where theories of representation and desire replace humanist discussions of realism and affect. She asserts that 'gender is (a) representation' and that 'the representation of gender *is* its construction' (de Lauretis 1987: 3). This process of construction is maintained by what she calls 'technologies of gender' (ibid.: 2), a term which she deliberately uses to include the usual institutions of ideology as well as those usually exempt fields of theory and politics. Thus when she discusses Wendy Hollway's account of the way gender positions are produced by discourses she summarizes it in this manner:

> If at any one time there are several competing, even contradictory, discourses on sexuality – rather than a single, all-encompassing or monolithic, ideology – then what makes one take up a position in a certain discourse rather than another is an 'investment' (this translates the German *Besetzung*, a word used by Freud and rendered in English as *cathexis*), something between an emotional commitment and a vested interest, in the relative power (satisfaction, reward, payoff) which that position promises (but does not necessarily fulfill).
>
> (ibid.: 16)

This description of Hollway's work supposes that there is a subject, the 'one' which will take up a position because of an investment or 'emotional commitment'. To make discourse theory work it is necessary to posit a prior emotional vector, the origin of which cannot be examined. This theory that gender is representation appears to discard any such humanist appeal but then tacitly assumes a similar affective core to the subject, in order to explain the otherwise unmotivated adoption of one discourse rather than another (the argument is very similar to Hume's about salience (Hume 1969: 460–5)). I should add here that in her more recent work Hollway recognizes that in 'human relations discourse . . . feelings have been privileged with representing the "real" person' (Hollway 1989: 69). She makes explicit the importance of the 'relational dynamic' for understanding subjectivity and its articulations, although she doesn't theorize the significance of emotion for this dynamic.

The people quoted by Wendy Hollway, whose statements are treated as fixed points of reference, are not nearly so sure of themselves as the article that surrounds them. One woman admits that her partner is emotionally dependent on her, but adds, 'I still don't know how to know it' (ibid.: 249). Knowing how to know emotions is the problem. Or as Sam, another of the interviewees, says: 'I'll tell you something – which I don't know what it means but I'll say it anyway' (ibid.: 245). The 'I' doesn't know what it knows, but saying is the only way to find out, and meaning isn't easily available. The speakers present a split between saying and knowing, which we might suspect is both created and negotiated by emotion. If you get out of practice in 'doing the feelings' as that man did, you have problems, as Jim, another of Wendy Hollway's interviewees, explains:

> In a relationship for me, this 'frozenness' of certain feelings is really terrible. Much more of the time than I would like, we're doing this specialization job. There's maybe a split second in which I feel in touch with the set of feelings that I'm not normally responsible for, and that I don't particularly avow. And I don't even know if I feel them. And I think, 'Shit I actually felt that'. For two or three weeks I don't feel anything about it again, and I have to say, 'Well, at the moment I don't feel anything, but I do remember'.
>
> (ibid.: 254)

The power of these utterances comes through clearly because Wendy Hollway has transcribed them with great fidelity to their complex, unofficial syntaxes. These carefully transcribed utterances adumbrate a cognitive social structure of feeling, whose disturbances (not knowing how to know it, or the infrequency of feeling) could be a constitutive feature of most social formations as well as sexual politics. Restricting gender to representation leaves affectivity out of consideration and the old terms for it – emotion, feeling and desire – re-emerge unchanged and unexamined to do the work they did in humanist critique, and therefore perpetuate a Cartesian split of body and self. Emotion is used as the all-purpose glue between subjectivity and society (much as some extrapolations of Foucault use power) when no other connection can be found.

As long as the analysis of gender begins with the political project of feminism, concepts like discourse form a network whose analytic power is still unsurpassed. Once they are moved sideways to try and ground an analysis of the entire social process that also founds them, a social process deeply collusive with modern masculinities, these unresolved connections prove obstacles to a viable political analysis for men. Poststructuralist theory shows that gender is fluid, unstable, constantly reconstructed and embedded in the symbolic realm. Most of all, poststructuralist theory emphasizes the way subjectivity is, in part, an effect of various processes which always require the interaction of a self, language and their others. At times this flexibility is lost when some 'supersubject' (Smith 1989: 88) is made the sole determinant of gender. The apparently unnoticed reintroduction of emotion in many actual versions of this theory and the utopian models for relations between men that theory is supposed to provide, suggest that certain areas of masculinity remain unconscious within the linguistic projects of poststructuralism.

OPPRESSION AND POWER

At a London conference on 'Changing Identities' in 1989, the speakers always identified themselves by an oppression. A black speaker was black and not First World. A middle-class man was gay, not middle class. A middle-class white southerner would probably say he was a socialist. And so forth. No one was prepared to speak even in part from components of their identity with oppressor connotations. The effect of this was to obscure the inevitability of internal divisions within subjectivity. Such internal divisions are constitutive of identity. No one was trying to con the audience. The speakers clearly felt that there was no other position from which to speak an emancipatory discourse than from one of their determinate oppressions. To do otherwise, and either speak from the position of being a member of a First World country, a man, an academic, white, a southerner, or some other potentially hegemonic formation, would render their political discourse inauthentic and therefore ungrounded. This dilemma depends on a wide-spread belief in multiple oppressions, a good discussion of which can be found in Sue O'Sullivan and Susan Ardill's essay, 'Upsetting an Applecart: Difference, Desire and Lesbian Sadomasochism':

> As we see it, there are two key ingredients: an analysis of the world as made up of a fixed hierarchy of oppressions (or a select collection of oppressions) around gender, sexuality, age and ability; and notions of the 'authenticity' of subjective experience – experience which can be understood only with reference to the hierarchy. . . . Within these

politics there's little room for distinguishing between politics and those who speak them. . . . .To speak experiences, to claim identities, is to be tied into positions, and everything is assumed to follow on from them. A lesbian mother, then, will automatically have certain positions on men, women, money, sex.

(O'Sullivan and Ardill 1986: 33)

In the past ten years the women's movement has been faced by a parallel dilemma to that of politically conscious men who wish to support feminism, a dilemma that has developed around the idea of multiple oppression. Black women have confronted white feminists with their complicity in racism. As a result white women have had to acknowledge that, despite their feminism, they might still be supporting the oppression of women of colour, and would certainly be benefiting from the general racism of our society. Women could not automatically assume sisterhood on the basis of gender. The theory of multiple oppressions explains such conflicts by concluding that an individual can be oppressed in a cumulative way. Someone with several oppressions could claim a kind of political priority and existential authority over someone with only one oppression. The tendency to do this, and also to asume the right to speak for an oppressed group purely on the basis of one's identity as a member of this oppressed group (and not one's activities, allegiances or conscious principles), has been criticized by some feminists, but its influence in political debate remains strong. To claim oppression gives one an identity and an understanding of one's own history. The difficulty arises when some members of a political grouping to which one belongs are claimed as oppressors by another group with which one is identified. Multiple oppressions mean multiple schisms.

Oppression confers an identity. For members of an oppressed group to recognize that they are oppressed is crucial, because that is the moment when they perceive that their experience is not the result of their own specific nature or the nature of the world, but the result of an alterable state of things (however difficult change might be in practical terms). It is the recognition of injustice, of the fact that their oppression is the result of a systematic treatment of the group with which they are identified by others, whether or not they identify with it themselves (Countee Cullen's poem 'Incident' gives a sharp picture of this. When he was 8 and living in Baltimore he smiled at another similar, but white, little boy who: 'poked out/ His tongue, and called me, "Nigger". . . . Of all the things that happened there/ That's all I remember' (Carruth 1970: 241)). This treatment has physical, emotional, intellectual, economic and political consequences for the individual. Recognition of the oppression is the first move towards organized resistance because it is the moment of recognizing the possibility of change. As an organized group the oppressed can begin to act politically and at the same time identify the group(s) causing their oppression.

Feminism arose because men oppress women. Since the early 1970s it has made the concept of oppression central to its sexual politics. Men who want to challenge dominant masculinities and support feminism have to accept that they appear to be at best tacit supporters of this oppression. For men this presents an immediate problem. If they are oppressors how can they challenge oppression without wishing themselves out of existence? I believe it can be shown that an apparently insurmountable paradox results from a widespread tendency to use the term 'oppression' as a causal explanation for social phenomena rather than a description of their governing conditions. This tendency derives from current assumptions about the relation between singular and collective subjects, in this case the assumption that one man represents and is represented by all men. This conflation of different forms of subject is closely related to the theoretical difficulties in conceptualizing both intrapsychic and interactive relations which we have been looking at in terms of emotion, phallogocentrism and discourse.

Unlike many other key concepts in feminist debate, such as sexual politics itself, or the male gaze, the concept of oppression seems not to have emerged in the work of one theorist, but to have developed in the heat of public debate. There is no founding text where the concept is extensively analysed and demonstrated. Oppression has never been well defined in the way that other feminist concepts have. Its primary roots lie in the long tradition, going back to essays like Mill and Taylor's *On the Subjection of Women*, which analyses women's position in terms of political inequality, and associates women's lack of rights to slavery. In the late 1960s and 1970s when parallels between liberation politics in the feminist and black movements were politically useful, this concept helped to sustain the connections. Such parallels helped articulate the new forms of political action and analysis which feminists were developing. For feminism the term 'oppression' did not need to be analytically exact because it operated as a basic evocation of the conditions which require a politics, rather than an analytic concept. Its universal use gave it the clarity of the obvious. The *Webster* dictionary definition of oppression bears out the link to black politics and its roots in anti-slavery and civil rights campaigns. The entry for the 1971 edition, which can be taken roughly as the standard meaning from which American feminism began its extension of the term, reads:

1a: unjust or cruel exercise of authority or power esp. by the imposition of burdens; *esp*: the unlawful, excessive or corrupt exercise of power other than by extortion by any public officer so as to harm anyone in his rights, person, or property while purporting to act under color of governmental authority.

(Webster 1971: 1584)

Oppression is defined not simply as the exercise of power, but its misuse. The term is therefore a natural heir to nineteenth-century feminist arguments about the exclusion of women from the legal rights enjoyed by men. In the 1970s the term was extended to mean not just the misuse of power but the possession of power itself. 'Men have power over women' is a common formulation. The traditional use of the term 'oppression' was based on the acceptance that there were rules which applied to everyone. The extension of the concept has meant that in some cases the rules themselves have been assumed to be at fault, and the implication would then be that the oppressors had constructed some of the rules purely to suit themselves. Justice is partial. This position might seem unexceptionable from a Marxist standpoint, because it could be reformulated in the more familiar concepts of recent theories of ideology.

The Marxist concept of ideology assumes that a legal system is a direct extension of the existing forms of social power and so there can be no generally valid laws which everyone would accept as just (once they were free of the unconscious influence of ideology), unless all forms of domination ceased. The dictionary definition of oppression implies a consciousness of the reality of the rules that are broken. Oppression depends on both a standard which has been violated, and an intention to do so. Ideology does not. Ideology is the delusory form which consciousness of those rules will take amongst those who benefit from them.

In its earlier form oppression meant that an appeal could be made to the rules which bound both oppressors and oppressed, however much such an appeal was likely to fail. The oppressors could be condemned as intentional violators of rules that everyone should observe. Oppressors who were convinced by this appeal that they had indeed broken the rules could in theory facilitate political change by returning to a proper adherence to those rules, because their own will, which had been the cause of the breach, was equally sufficient for its remedy. The extension of the concept of oppression keeps the form of the judgement implied by the earlier definition but extends its scope far beyond the constitutive legal rules of a society, to include many other forms of behaviour. This concept of oppression holds that the rules themselves are the problem, and the power they confer illegitimate, so the only option for the oppressor who wishes to reform is to abdicate altogether, relinquishing the power conferred by the rules which themselves somehow disappear at the same moment. The difficulty with this account is that there is now apparently no set of rules or standards to appeal to. We cannot say to the oppressors that they have misused their power by breaking a rule which we can specify, but simply that their power is an abuse, without any qualification. Keeping the old structure of the concept means, in the case of men and women, that when Jeff Hearn says that men 'are the gender which routinely engages in the oppression of others, women, children and indeed animals' (1987: xiv) he thereby makes oppression definitional of men, despite his gesture at contingency with the word 'routinely' (his title names men as 'the gender of oppression'). The result is that a judgement, which attributes an intention and implies the possibility of change, based on an appeal to universally accepted norms which have been allegedly violated, is retained in a new context, so that it appears that the oppressors intend the oppression they institute, and could therefore end it if they wished. They appear to be violators of accepted norms, but at the same time no such norms are specified. The oppressors appear to be refusing change which they are capable of, and to be accepting the violation of basic rights, yet at the same time no such rights are acknowledged by both sides.

From the early 1970s there have been protests from men about the widespread use of the term 'oppression' to define axiomatically the relations between men and women. Such protests usually take the form either of a denial that men oppress women, or of an argument that men too are oppressed. That latter argument was often used in the men's movement in the 1970s and can still occasionally be heard. Most recent books by men writing on masculinity have rejected both arguments and insisted, like Hearn, that men do oppress women. R.W. Connell, in the Preface to his comprehensive study *Gender and Power*, insists that the men's movement was wrong to say

> that men are equally oppressed. This claim is demonstrably false. Some of the relevant evidence is set out below . . . as an introduction to the facts of gender inequality for those not already familiar with the issue.
>
> (1987: xi)

For Connell the facts can speak for themselves. Men are 'beneficiaries of an oppressive system' (ibid.: xiii). Like Hearn, Connell effectively defines oppression in terms of the 'facts' of inequality. These men writers on masculinities have gone a long way towards meeting the challenge of feminism for men. Denying the existence of women's oppression won't do. Nevertheless the claim that men are oppressed deserves more attention. Mark Cousins in his essay 'Material Arguments and Feminism' (1978) in *m/f*, one of the few feminist journals that published men theorists, argues that the concept of oppression is problematic, saying that the 'concept of the oppression of women often results in an algebra where one man's power is another woman's oppression', in a way that epitomizes the common frustration amongst men at the use of the term, and his answer to the problem seems promising. He goes on using the term 'oppression' while he argues that its 'referents' cannot be assumed to be 'an unproblematic totality of women as concrete individuals' (ibid.: 70) The concept of oppression creates a double-bind because it makes the individual subject co-extensive with a collective singular subject.

According to Seyla Benhabib, who has analysed the conceptual difficulties of collective singular subjects in detail, 'the claim that there is a *subject* of history to whom we can ascribe an interest rests on a confusion of empirical and normative categories' (1986: 130). Marx does this because he inherits two different concepts of humanity from German philosophy and tends to conflate them. Humanity can be the aim of social progress or it can be the empirical collection of individuals in history. Only in historical struggle can the character of humanity emerge. For Marx there is a collective singular subject of history: humanity. Benhabib argues that 'the subjects of history, in the sense of *agents* of history, are human beings in the *plural*, not humanity in the singular as such' (ibid.: 131). I think that the relations between men and women cannot be adequately described in terms of the tug-of-war of two collective singular subjects, men and women, without confusing the normative and the empirical. Ideal norms of masculinity are confused with the behaviours of individual male agents, who are then assumed to be acting out those very norms, because they are men.

Oppression operates only in terms of collectivities. An individual is oppressed as a part of a group. You could not be oppressed if you were the only member of your group. Oppression is a theory of collective singular subjects. It may be mediated through individuals but oppression implies that the individual is acting as a member of the oppressor group. Therefore the individual may act in an unpleasant or even cruel way and still not be acting oppressively, if his or her behaviour is not determined by membership of the oppressor group. We cannot assume all behaviour, of whatever kind, that takes place between members of the two groups, is determined by that one general group relation. If there are more than two groups in relation the situation is even more complex. The idea of an individual oppressor has little meaning, because the individual's action, however horrifying, is only oppression within the framework of the relation of collectivities. This recognition severely limits the range of the concept. Arthur Brittan and Mary Maynard (1985), for example, balk at this conclusion and ridicule what they call 'reductionist theories'. Such theories

> treat those who oppress as though they are clockwork oppressors, wound up by some inexorable determining mechanism which resides in the 'system'. . . . Clockwork oppression thus assumes a world without agency or purpose, where both oppressors and oppressed are engaged in a continuous round of stimulus-response relationships in which sexism and racism are seen as simple reflexes or preprogrammed responses to objective situations.
>
> (Brittan and Maynard 1985: 212)

But against this they have to insist that 'human actors in specific social contexts can and do oppress each other, not roles, genes, or modes of production' (ibid.: 213). They want to retain individual agency and intention, and can only imagine interaction on a mechanical stimulus-response model. Unfortunately it is meaningless to talk of an individual's *intention* to act oppressively because oppression is a systematic determination (and in-

150

terpretation) of individual behaviours. The concept is fundamentally interpretative of the relations between collectivities and is not a valid description of specific instances or intentions. Oppression is a term that
refers to a general structure, and in that way is very close to the concept of
power which has gained wide currency in theories of sexual politics. For
Connell (1987: 130), the 'oppressive system' of patriarchy is a 'reverberat-
ing set of power relations and political processes'. Many theorists believe
that men's power is the root of the problem of men. Lynne Segal argues
that power rather than psychological formation is the engine of gendered
oppression.

Power is an elusive concept shadowed by Aristotelian ideas of potential,
transcendental ideas of necessary preconditions, and Marxist theories of
class struggle, now given a new configuration by Michel Foucault as a
practice in which we are all inscribed. Power is a 'virtual' force, not an action
or a history, but a potential for either. The concept of power answers
questions about the conditions necessary for events to occur. It is a catch-all
concept for an originating dynamic of historical change. Its widespread use
today is the result of the disappearance of agency in poststructuralist theories of the subject, a disappearance which has left a conceptual vacuum. Social
groups were formerly theorized as singular subjects and so the poststructuralist deconstruction of the subject has made it extremely difficult to sustain a
coherent analysis of the functions of such collectivities as long as they
continue to be understood as collective singular subjects. A semiological
critique of the philosophy of the subject leaves them without any potential
for interaction. Power substitutes for this potential but the resulting model
of society cannot account for instances of action in history without taking
the concept of power out of its legitimate field and misusing it as a means of
explaining historical events. Power, however, cannot act. In its current form
the concept of power hides the irreducible heterogeneity of social process
necessary for different forms of power. Power is the possibility of affecting
others, effects that can be bodily, emotional or cognitive. The mode of effect
differentiates powers. Power is a network of possibilities into which any
individual may be able to place him or herself, but the entry restrictions are
complex and exclusive. The weakness of the general concept of power is that
it assumes that the possession of power is equivalent to the intention to
abuse it. Yet power need not corrupt despite Lord Acton. Adults have
power over children but this does not mean that children are directly
oppressed by adults (although there is a case for arguing that some oppression does result). The use of the term 'power' as a general analytic hides the
necessary intra- and inter-psychic processes, such as intention and effect,
necessary for abuse to occcur. It results from a tautologous logic which says
that if abuse and violence occur, then power is being used by an oppressor.
The tendency to misuse the concept of power occurs for the same reason
that oppression, another virtual concept, is taken as identifiable through

individual experience. We tend to think of groups as singular subjects; man and men are seen as conforming to the same analytic and theoretic constraints. What we need to recognize is that groups are not united, singular subjects. Oppression and power are perfectly valid concepts within a restricted sphere of analysis. They explain the potential of groups to act in certain ways in relation to one another. They give answers to questions about experience by specifying not causes, but limiting conditions. The relations between men and women are and have been oppressive. The deprivations, cruelties, exploitations and misrepresentations that social and psychological structures enable men to perpetrate on women are pervasive and sometimes appalling. Nevertheless the concepts of power and oppression cannot be used to axiomatize relations between the sexes. Instead, the importance of understanding the damaging results of oppression and power is such that much more investigation of the subjectivities caught up in them is needed. Emotion is one way people affect one another and so must be part of the instantiation of both oppression and power.

The concepts of oppression and power are hindrances to the development of a men's politics not because men don't want to face these realities but because when treated as analytic tools they prevent an understanding of the interactions on which both oppression and power depend. We need to go outside the implicitly transcendental model of the collective subject and the conditions of possible action, to consider the *means* of action and to open up the collective singular subjects of gender to view. To do that we need to rethink the role of affectivity in social relations as the men's movement suggests, and to recognize the force of the poststructuralist argument that there is no authentic fixed self from which emotion could originate.

MASCULINITY AND MODERNITY

Anna Wulf in *The Golden Notebook* often doesn't know what to make of Saul. He sometimes seems tall and then on closer examination just ordinary height. He has lost weight during an illness and so his clothes are too large for him. He is hard to see for what he is. Masculinity is similarly hard to grasp. Is it a discourse, a power structure, a psychic economy, a history, an ideology, an identity, a behaviour, a value system, an aesthetic even? Or is it all these and also their mutual separation, the magnetic force of repulsion which keeps them apart? I believe modern masculinities are misrepresented when they are described solely in terms of sexuality, power or identity. Masculinity is a centrifugal dispersal of what are maintained as discrete fields of psychic and social structure. In a formula: modern masculinities depend on the maintenance of discrete islands of subjectivity unconscious of one another.

The term 'masculinity' is almost as elusive as 'subjectivity' but whereas subjectivity has been in the glare of intellectual attention for centuries, masculinity has been left behind the scenes, writing the scripts, directing the action and operating the cameras, taken for granted and almost never defined. Its relation to other nouns like male, man, manhood, manliness and virility is far from obvious. As adjective, the term 'masculine' moves between the identification of a person's sex as male and socially validated norms of acceptable behaviour for males. As noun, its referent will depend on what assumptions about subjectivity and society determine its context. For some sociologists masculinity is a role, for some poststructuralists it is a form of representation. Central to all the usages seems to be an element of acculturation. Masculinity is socially constructed, but how and why will depend on the theory we use, as well as the significance given to the idea of social construction.

The fullest account of masculinity as a system is that in R.W. Connell's wide-ranging sociological study *Gender and Power* (1987). Connell argues that we should refer to masculinities in the plural rather than as a singular definable entity because different institutions produce different masculinities. This does not mean that masculinities are roles in the way that sociological role theory has argued. A soldier, businessman or teacher is not following a script. (In fairness to advocates of role theory it should be said that they no longer defend it in this form. Joseph Pleck, author of several works in the field, now argues that the standard paradigm of the 'Male Sex Role Identity' needs to be replaced with a more flexible paradigm, the 'Sex Role Stereotype'. His detailed commentary on the latter shows that he now conceives it less in terms of the theatrical metaphor of a script and more in terms of the interpretations made of male behaviours. These interpretations have the force of ideology.) Nor is there one primary determinant of masculinities; there is no first cause like original sin, the economic base or the death drive. The sexual division of labour, the hierarchy of power, and the social organization of cathexis ('emotionally charged social relations' (Connell 1987: 112)) are relatively autonomous structures whose interaction produces the continuities and stabilities of everyday gender. Connell identifies a hierarchy of masculinities that result: 'hegemonic masculinity, conservative masculinities (complicit in the collective project but not its shock troops) and subordinated masculinities' (ibid.: 110). As an example, he describes how an army is actually an alliance of different masculinities. Not everyone is a warrior. His guiding insight is similar to Raymond Williams's argument that social structures are constantly in the process of constitution. Structures identified by analysis, such as ideology, language, power, the state, the relations of production, sexuality and so forth, exist only in solution, they are not absolutely prior to the subject but themselves always in process of formation. Social and personal life are practices. In the final section of this book I shall discuss in detail the third of Connell's structures, the 'construction of emotionally charged social relations' as a component of modern masculinities, in relation to the range of theories about emotion developed by philosophy, psychoanalysis and modern literature.

Connell gives credit for his basic premisses to Juliet Mitchell's proposal in *Woman's Estate* (1971) that we should think of women's lives as determined within four different, and partially independent, structures. She writes:

> The key structures of women's situation can be listed as follows: Production, Reproduction, Sexuality and the Socialization of Children. The concrete combination of these produce the 'complex unity' of her position; but each separate structure may have reached a different 'moment' at any given historical time.
>
> (Mitchell 1971: 101)

He takes issue with her over the specific identification of the structures, saying that her proposed structures are not really structures at all, but 'types of practice' which overlap one another (Connell 1987: 96). Instead he proposes the tripartite division into labour, power and cathexis (ibid.: 91ff.), but since he admits that these too overlap, and doesn't explain in any detail why Mitchell's structures are really practices, his objections are not wholly clear. For one thing her field of attention is different. She is explicit that her analysis is focused specifically on women's situation, while Connell is discussing gendered social relations. Mitchell's analysis is certainly uneven, particularly because she has awkwardly amalgamated incompatible theoretical paradigms like role theory and the Marxist dialectic, but she does emphasize the importance of childbirth, child care and sexuality, all assimilated into the background by Connell's different division of structures. There is also another reason for Connell's preference for the tripartite division, a preference that reveals how easily masculine assumptions can intrude into theory. To explain it I will first have to outline current theories of modernity.

Saul is a Hollywood film-maker in exile. His is a thoroughly modern masculinity. In a way the concept of masculinity itself is a modern invention, a somewhat mysterious one, a new invention that remains a black box to most men, however attractive its workings. Modernity is a description usually applied not just to the twentieth century but the great period of modernization and social change since the industrial and political revolutions of the eighteenth century. The impact of this social transformation on men's lives is obvious. If men have largely dominated the means of production and the public sphere, they have in turn been changed by that involvement. Men have been affected by universal conscription and total war, by the technologization of their work, the almost complete division of work and home, and their mass organization in work, culture and politics. Men's dominance has also been challenged, and at times diminished, as women have gained the vote, entered the workplace in large numbers, gained access to education, and slowly improved their legal status.

What were the subjective consequences of such changes? Jurgen Habermas describes the process this way. Max Weber, he writes:

> characterized cultural modernity as the separation of the substantive reason expressed in religion and metaphysics into three autonomous spheres. They are: science, morality and art. These came to be differentiated because the unified world-views of religion and metaphysics fell apart. Since the 18th century, the problems inherited from these older world-views could be arranged so as to fall under specific aspects of validity: truth, normative rightness, authenticity and beauty. They could then be handled as questions of knowledge, or of justice and morality, or of taste. Scientific discourse, theories of morality, jurisprudence, and the production and criticism of art could in turn be institutionalized. Each domain of culture could be made to correspond to cultural professions in which problems could be dealt with as the concern of special experts. This professionalized treatment of the cultural tradition brings to the fore the intrinsic structures of each of the three dimensions of culture. There appear the structures of cognitive-instrumental, of moral-practical and of aesthetic-expressive rationality, each of these under the control of specialists who seem more adept at being logical in these particular ways than other people are.
>
> (Habermas 1983: 8–9)

The resulting fragmentation of everyday life, and the loss of control over many aspects of our lives, could only be resolved by a reintegration of the mutually opposing spheres of specialized practice (an aim common to many of the modern avant-gardes): 'A reified everyday praxis can be cured only by creating unconstrained interaction of the cognitive with the moral-practical and the aesthetic-expressive elements' (ibid.: 11–12). There are dangers in this, however. Terrorism as well as fascism can result when attempts are made to aestheticize politics, or to replace politics with moral extremism. Habermas does not want to abandon the project of modernity, despite these risks, because, as Martin Jay puts it, to do so 'would mean a loss of hope in the creative reappropriation of aesthetic rationality into an increasingly rationalized everyday life' (Jay 1985: 137).

In *The Philosophical Discourse of Modernity* (1987), Habermas traces the sources of the discourse of divided subjectivity in detail in the work of the German Idealists. For Hegel modernity was equivalent to the triumph of subjectivity, a triumph most clearly signalled in Kant's philosophy where the tribunal of reason subjects all dogmas to judgement. On the basis of this genealogy Habermas then argues that the typical modern stance towards the world is reflexivity. This reflexivity operates in each of the three spheres:

There is a reflexive medium not only for the cognitive-instrumental

and moral-practical domain, but for evaluative and expressive manifestations as well. We call a person rational who interprets the nature of
his desires and feelings [*Bedürfnisnatur*] in the light of culturally
established standards of value, but especially if he can adopt a reflective
attitude to the very value standard through which desires and feelings
are interpreted.

(Habermas 1987: 20)

Rationality depends not on the quality of reason itself but the quality of its
relation to emotion. A rational person is someone in whom reason can
interpret emotion, not necessarily someone who has no feelings, suppresses
them or dictates to them with logic. Interpretation may do no more than
lend emotions a helping hand as they try to achieve their aims. Habermas
asks even more of reason than this. A truly rational person is the one who is
capable of turning the interpretative process reflexively on itself to check its
validity and effectiveness. The relation between reason and emotion should
be able to reflect upon itself, to be self-aware, self-conscious, so that the
relation is a matter of choice, whether individual or collective.

Habermas further generalizes this relation between reflexivity and modernity in other recent writings, arguing that reflexivity leads to the modern
concept of the distance between actuality and our models of it, models
which we can choose to adopt and which are independent of that actuality.
Recent studies of modernity have taken Habermas's ideas further, and
looked in more detail at the contributions of Hegel and Heidegger to the
picture of modernity, showing that many of the very terms in which
modernity understands itself are themselves modern. One concept familiar
to anyone concerned with gender politics, 'identity', has been explored by
David Kolb in one of the most interesting of these studies, *The Critique of
Pure Modernity*:

> Hegel and Heidegger would agree that the most obvious phenomenon
> distinguishing modernity is empty subjectivity. The self affirms itself
> over against the content of its life, confirming its freedom by trans-
> cending any given objects or ways of life. Context is fixed, represented,
> manipulated, and dominated for whatever goals the subject has chosen.
> Both thinkers would agree that this search for self-certitude through
> distance and manipulation ignores the basic conditions that make
> modern subjectivity possible at all.

(Kolb 1986: 203)

Kolb calls this modernity's 'self-description', a description of a person as
someone whose 'human identity is defined without reference to history, set
values or God; let alone race, creed, or national origin. A person is defined in
a way that separates the process of choice from the content chosen' (ibid.: 6).
Identity comes to mean the process of choosing clothes for the self (as

156

Stephen Dedalus became himself by dressing as a man), rather than a self necessarily made the way it is, and so, despite claims to the contrary, is still very much bound up with the idea of 'role'. Identity and role are something external to the self which occupies them. To discuss gender in such terms is to become trapped in a vicious circle because doing so assumes what Kolb calls the 'modern self-image'. Much recent theory denies the relevance of the concept of choice itself, but the sense of division remains, and gender is made to depend upon it. Kolb's analysis shows how necessary it is to re-examine the relations between identity, gender and reflexivity, remembering that these will remain hard to articulate in the general absence of sustained, self-conscious political and theoretical discourses of men and masculinities. Gender remains complex and to an extent mysterious because it is an unfinished project. We don't yet know, and can't know, what men and women are. Too many possibilities are yet unrealized, too many confusions have been built into our thinking from birth, to make it possible to produce some immediate complete clarification.

Cultural modernity has found many different forms during the period from Romanticism to postmodernism. Critics of modernism remind us that reflexivity has been a source of uncertainty for many of these cultural projects. Georg Lukacs's rejection of modernist experiment as a superficial-mirroring of the subjective fragmentation produced by capitalist development compared to the insight offered in the great realist novels into the social processes which produce such effects, or Paul de Man's scepticism about all claims to be modern (de Man 1983), should be borne in mind. The self-image of the modernists is not all it seems, and too dependent on the assumption that self-awareness depends on simple self-reflection. As Perry Meisel puts it: 'If our received notion of the modern tends to equate modernism as a structure with the will to modernity that is only one of its symptoms, then it is largely mythical, insufficiently ironic to account for the objects of its veneration' (Meisel 1987: 5). The will to modernity is a will to escape cultural determination, to find a human nature, conscious or unconscious, outside culture. Meisel uses Harold Bloom's model of literary influence and belatedness to define modernism as an attempt at self-grounding reflexivity that necessarily fails: 'Hardly the flight toward immediate vision that we think it is, then, modernism is instead a structure of compensation, a way of adjusting to the paradox of belatedness that is its precondition' (ibid.: 5). Bloom's theory of belatedness is an Oedipal reading of the relations between authors, so it would be possible to interpret Meisel's theory of literary modernism as a literary version of the Rat Man's struggle to accommodate the negations figured by his father's masculine violence. Or we could take the line of some feminists and interpret men's literary modernism as a strategy for representing the obstacle to such reflexivity as woman.

Alice Jardine, in *Gynesis: Configurations of Women and Modernity* (1985), uses the term 'modernity' to indicate the continuities between modernism and poststructuralist postmodernism. This enables her to argue that modernity is marked by a 'new kind of discursivity on, about, as woman, a valorization and speaking of woman' (Jardine 1985: 26). Postmodern thinkers have 'coded as *feminine*, as woman' (ibid.: 25) the silences in what Lyotard and others have called the grand narratives of modern thought. Both postmodernism and modernism could be read as crises for certain forms of masculinity, masculinities questioning the completeness of their self-understanding. Even men's high postmodernist theory can be read as a reflection on the uncertainties of men's relations with themselves and others.

In a synoptic account of the phenomenon, David Harvey argues that the postmodern 'emphasis upon ephemerality, collage, fragmentation, and dispersal in philosophical and social thought mimics the conditions of flexible accumulation' (Harvey 1989: 302). His description of the effects of the speeding up of the economic process, its 'time-space compression', for example, are indebted to Fredric Jameson's (1984) theory that the 'cultural logic of late capitalism' is the cause of postmodernism. Many of these phenomena are not new, as Harvey notes, but what does seem to have changed is the way postmodernism responds to discontinuity, fragmentation and change. 'Postmodernism swims, even wallows, in the fragmentary and the chaotic currents of changes as if that is all there is' (Harvey 1989: 44). Take away the pejorative tone of 'wallow' and you have something similar to Habermas, with one significant difference. Fragmentation may well have gone much further than tripartition. Implicit in the idea of swimming in fragmentation (itself a fragmenting metaphor) is the assumption of deliberate, self-conscious choice, a choice whose self-awareness could constitute a form of self-understanding for postmodern masculine subjectivities. Postmodernity produces a particular form of self-awareness, a 'schizophrenic way of experiencing, interpreting and being in the world' (Harvey 1989: 53). Jameson describes this in terms of loss – loss of depth and historical continuity. A new self-consciousness of the limitations of men's subjectivity brings the discomfort of lost illusions to men, while opening out possibilities to those previously marginalized and unrepresented in the cultural sphere. Hence that characteristic tension so obvious in postmodernist art between the creative richness of work from hitherto marginalized peoples, and the intense, decreative self-questioning of men's high postmodernist productions.

We are now in a position to see why Connell insists on the division into labour, power and cathexis. These correspond to the three spheres of modernity. Labour belongs to the cognitive-instrumental, power to the moral-practical, and cathexis to the aesthetic-expressive sphere of rationality. Connell's division shows how readily masculinity can be understood in terms of modernity's self-image, but instead of simply improving on Mitchell's paradigm it also conceals features of social and historical life to which women have made primary contributions, despite its apparently greater conceptual rigour. Mitchell's four structures complicate his model if we consider the importance of what she calls 'socialization' (Mitchell 1971: 117), or the emotional and intellectual nurture of children. We can use the tripartition of human life as a useful heuristic for understanding masculinities only if we recognize the deep complicity between the model and the masculinities it would explain. Andrew Bowie, in a study of *Aesthetics and Subjectivity* (1990), argues that there is a philosophical tradition going back to Schelling which is critical of the tripartite division of subjectivity and for which aesthetic phenomena like music suggest that there are 'aspects of subjectivity that are not reducible to the cognitive, the ethical or the emotive' (Bowie 1990: 10). The deconstructionist philosopher Rodolphe Gasché argues in a surprisingly similar vein that 'the non-cognitive and non-reflexive state, of which self-knowledge is an alienated product, cannot simply be conceptualized in terms of the irrational, emotional and intuitive' (Gasché 1986: 81). Some forms of understanding are based neither on self-reflection nor feeling. These other areas of subjectivity might have correspondent social spheres also. Despite what Connell argues, Mitchell's four spheres may well indicate structures of subjectivity given little or no house room by men theorists and philosophers. Given also the tendency to assume that emotion is non-cognitive, these structures of subjectivity may have closer relations to emotion than Bowie and Gasché suggest.

THE POLITICS OF MALE FEMINISM

Male feminism occurs sporadically in Lyotard, Derrida, Eagleton, Harvey, Jameson and many others, but there is still no attempt to connect these issues with men and masculine subjectivities in the work of our leading theorists. Indeed there has been remarkably little work on men in literary and cultural theory by any heterosexual men critics. Gay men have produced by far the most important work by men on gender issues, but even gay critics have so far not turned their attention much to literary and cultural texts, although there are signs that this is changing. For heterosexual men to develop an emancipatory politics has been difficult because once made the subject of reflection on itself, gender deconstructs almost all the founding concepts on which theories of language, culture and self are based. Gender is a much more radically destabilizing concept than men theorists have recognized. It is not enough to add on women's struggles to other forms of political struggle, or to expose the workings of sexual difference, or to expose male power, because the very terms in which the analyses are made were formed either when the category 'men' did not have its modern meanings, and only biologically male educated people (to use a clumsy paraphrase) were able to forge an intellectual culture, or have been part of this crisis itself. That is why all the analytic concepts used in sexual politics need to be re-examined before men can use them effectively to understand how modern men came into being.

To say 'we men' itself raises problems. As Denise Riley has shown, the category 'women' is not a fixed one to which appeal can be made as the basis of a politics without the risk of misrepresentation: 'There is, as we have repeatedly learned, no fluent trajectory from feminism to a truly sexually democratic humanism' (Riley 1988: 17). She tentatively proposes that feminists restrict their use of the category 'women' as much as possible, and when they use it, do so flexibly. Such caution is not intellectual fussiness; it empowers self-awareness:

> So an active scepticism about the integrity of the sacred category 'women' would be no merely philosophical doubt to be stifled in the name of effective political action in the world. On the contrary, it would be a condition *for* the latter.
>
> (ibid.: 113)

The same is true of the category 'men'. Far from being used as a means of subjection as the designation 'women' has, the term 'men' has been either used as a form of inclusion in the world of subjects, or more recently in modernist work as a form of special pleading on behalf of a sex that was less and less certain of its position. An appeal to 'men' might have a radical political potential because it could enable a recognition of responsibility and common ground where such has not been recognized, but that will depend on the kinds and quality of self-reflection by men. This reminds us again of the degree to which men's self-consciousness of their gender itself becomes a theoretical issue of great importance for any emancipatory politics. The category 'men' needs to be exposed as a modern invention which nonetheless draws its legitimacy from appeals to a historical continuity supposedly guaranteeing its universality. The aim is to recognize that we are, sometimes, men, in all the ways which that recognition can be understood.

Even from those sympathetic to such a project as this there are likely to be doubts. Isn't an attention to gender a turning away from class and economic oppression? Isn't there a likelihood that a critique of men will become a covert celebration of male power in some new form? And isn't this project a highly localized one pretending to a spurious universality? Cultural difference is vital to an emancipatory politics. Can such a new men's studies be a form of emancipatory politics at all? Many theorists probably share something like Stephen Heath's view expressed in his paper on 'Male Feminism' for a Modern Language Association conference panel on male feminism in 1984 that:

> The truth about men and their bodies *for the moment* is merely repetitive (this has to be put without any suggestion of some inverse romanticization of women and their bodies): the régime of the same,

the eternal problem of the phallus, etc. (with its celebrants Lawrence on, through Miller and Mailer on into the present day). Taking men's bodies away from the existing representation and its oppressive effects will have to follow women's writing anew of themselves: for today, telling the truth about the male body as freeing subject is utopia, about the female body, *actuality*.

(Heath 1987: 26)

Not all the speakers agreed with this. Another contributor, Alice Jardine, actually called for just such a male discourse:

there's men's relationship *after feminism*, to death, scopophilia, fetishism . . . the penis and balls, erection, ejaculation (not to mention the phallus), madness, paranoia, homosexuality, blood, tactile pleasure, pleasure in general, *desire* (but, please, not with an anonymously universal capital D), voyeurism, etc. Now this *would* be talking your body, not talking *about* it. It is not essentialism; it is not metaphysics, and it is not/would not be representation.

(Jardine and Smith 1987: 61)

Joseph Allen Boone cites this passage as a good starting point for a new cultural critique of masculinity by men (Kauffman 1989: 176). Jardine is writing in response partly to Heath's paper, so her insistence that this kind of men's writing would *not* be essentialist or ideological representation is directly aimed at such assumptions as his that it would be. For Heath the issue is clear:

For men, though, exactly because of the fundamental asymmetry that holds between them and women (their domination), there can be no equivalent: men's writing, male discourse, will simply be the same again; there is no politically progressive project that can work through that idea (unless perhaps in and from areas of gay men's experience, in a literature for that).

(Heath 1987: 25)

'There is no politically progressive project': that sums up the problem nicely for many men who support feminism, have a good grasp of cultural and feminist theory, and are engaged in some form of radical politics. There is simply no politically progressive project. Jardine's exhortation to 'take on – as men *after* feminism – some of the symbolic fields most addressed by feminist theory' doesn't really help them. It appears too much like special permission, a lifting of the theoretical and political barriers in order to facilitate work feminism could find useful. It is not so easy for men to accept that such work is neither essentialist nor metaphysical nor ideological. Part of the problem of finding a politically progressive project for men is a problem of *theory*.

161

Feminist theorists have occasionally taxed their male colleagues with the failure to reflect on their masculinity, refusing to accept that silence is the most progressive stance of all. One of the most trenchant of all such public statements (private ones are more common) was Elaine Showalter's essay 'Critical Cross Dressing: Male Feminists and the Woman of the Year' (Jardine and Smith 1987), a review of recent books of literary theory written by men engaged with feminism. This essay became notorious because it sharply questioned the validity of recent male critical appropriation of feminist theory. One of its targets was *The Rape of Clarissa*, Terry Eagleton's book on Richardson's *Clarissa*. A harsh judgement on male feminism was expressed in her subheading for the section of Eagleton's book: 'Writing as a Woman: Terry Eagleton and the Rape of Feminist Theory'. The interpretation of Clarissa's anxiety about writing results from

> the male gender anxiety of the character, the novelist, and ultimately the Marxist critic, who fears that his writing will be effeminate (compared to revolutionary action). By possessing feminist criticism, so to speak, Eagleton effectively seizes for himself its 'phallic' signifying power.
>
> (Jardine and Smith 1987: 128)

I think this goes to the heart of the issue. Men are being accused of using feminist theory to restore the power they have lost because of feminism. She concludes: 'What I chiefly miss in *The Rape of Clarissa* is any sign from Eagleton that there is something equivocal and personal in his own polemic, some anxiety of authorship that is related to his own cultural position' (ibid.: 130). The male critic fails to be progressive to the extent that he writes as if gender were outside himself and fails to reflect inwardly on his gender and sexuality.

Showalter is harsh because of Eagleton's status as a critic. Invited to reply to these criticisms, Eagleton chose instead to write a very short autobiographical piece about the experience of class, not gender at all, implying that there is a direct parallel but not trying to say what it is. The personal memories of Cambridge in this piece are probably immediately recognizable to most readers familiar with the stylistic and behavioural extremes of the British class system:

> The group we *really* couldn't stand, however, were the English public school socialists. With Conservatives you knew where you were; what really spooked us was to discover a minority of chinless braying Jeremies who actually spoke our own political language, quoted *Capital* in languid tones and ran the university Labour club.
>
> (Jardine and Smith 1987: 133)

Yet these men scorned by the working-class socialists were often the same ones who stayed socialists in later life, while most of the working-class men left socialism behind as they became more affluent. Eagleton concludes that he and the other young working-class socialists were wrong 'to be that choosy' because radicals are too few to be spurned like that, but then his next paragraph seems to question this conclusion. Middle-class socialists were untrustworthy after all. Historically it has been such politicians who have repeatedly betrayed working people. The working class needs its sectarian prejudices because it can be so easily abandoned by those who don't understand the realities of class oppression at first hand.

Eagleton's analysis depends on masculine metaphors. The betraying characteristic of the upper middle-class socialists was their 'chinless' appearance (think of all those strong chins in the boys' comics). Like Pound's modern politicians in *Hugh Selwyn Mauberley*, they were not quite men. The allegorical response to Showalter is that yes, she is right to mistrust men who speak feminism, just as the young working-class socialists were right to mistrust the middle-class student socialists, but that feminists need allies just as the working-class radicals did. The failed men of middle-class socialism not only lack chins; they will betray others. A manly middle-class man would be a Conservative. The parallel between gender and class also implies an answer to the question about the possibility of male feminism. If the middle-class socialists are the ones to watch out for, then so are the male feminists, because they are the potential betrayers. Obliquely the piece seems to take up the same position as Stephen Heath. A radical gender politics from men is likely to prove a Trojan horse. An honest man will stay out of it.

In response to the demand that he display his own masculine anxiety of authorship, Eagleton reveals how the experience of class and political activism informing his work as a literary critic is symbolized in terms of successful and weak versions of masculinity. It is a way of saying that this socialist politics was a form of masculine discourse all along. Eagleton's response to Showalter shows how important masculine codes are, even to rigorous Marxist cultural analyses.

Literary theory itself is largely premised on an emancipatory critique. It is not always recognized that the reason why theory has emerged from an uneasy synthesis of psychoanalysis, semiotics, deconstruction, feminism and Marxism is that all of these areas of enquiry claim not just the status of explanatory method, but socially transformative power as well. Otherwise literary theory could appropriate many other areas of psychology, sociology or philosophy. The radicalism of literary and cultural theory has made it important far beyond the confines of the academic world but its definitions of politics and critique are narrower than is often recognized, and these limits are especially constraining for the analysis of masculinities. There is a tendency to assume that the only valid form of theory is immanent critique, and to fail to recognize the political dimension of many forms of art and culture. Literary and cultural studies badly need a greater awareness of other emancipatory political theories.

Seyla Benhabib claims that two different forms of critique need to be distinguished from one another within the tradition of social thought that runs from Hegel and Marx through the Frankfurt School to Habermas. Marxist critique begins as a form of immanent critique. It 'presupposes that its object of investigation is reflexive; it presupposes that what is investigated is already a social reality which has its own self-interpretation' (Benhabib 1986: 33). Such self-interpretation is unquestioning self-reflection. Immanent critique will then show that this self-interpretation is at odds with other identifiable features of that social reality: 'both content and form, the given and the "ought", are reflected to their ground and shown to be the products of a form of consciousness embedded in a form of life that is divided, bifurcated, and alienated' (ibid.: 42). The other form of critique she defines like this: 'defetishising critique: by defetishising critique is meant a procedure of analysis whereby the given is shown to be not a natural but a socially and historically constituted, and thus changeable reality' (ibid.: 47). Both forms of critique are to be found in recent cultural theory, and both forms of critique depend on a normative appeal: 'If an ideal of a *unified ethical and political life* underlies the method of immanent critique, behind defetishising critique lies the vision of a unified mankind collectively transforming the conditions of its existence and then reappropriating what it has externalised' (ibid.: 43). Both forms of critique aim at the same kind of emancipation, 'fulfilment': actualizing the implicit but frustrated potential of the present. Benhabib argues that the Marxist tradition also speaks of another kind of emancipation, which she names 'transfiguration'.

> The term 'transfiguration' by contrast, is intended to suggest that emancipation signifies a radical and qualitative break with some aspects of the present. In certain fundamental ways, the society of the future is viewed to be, not the culmination, but the radical negation of the present.
>
> (ibid.: 41)

This transfiguration would mean 'the *qualitative* transformation of needs and pleasures, and the re-education of our capacities' (ibid.: 113). Transfiguration remains outside the remit of the two kinds of critique because it is considered too utopian, and because it is dependent on the establishment of norms for which no consensus exists. Benhabib argues that transfigurative emancipation is not only a necessary part of the political project, it is also already implicit in Marxist thought as an ideal.

Benhabib helps us identify where the difficulty lies when we try to develop an emancipatory discourse for men and gender. Ordinary forms of critique insistently remain within present-day situations and interpretations. Such critiques can show that the present gender differentiation is socially constructed, and violates the ideals which men officially espouse, but the best consequence of such a critique would be a redistribution of existing possibilities according to the explicit ideals those arrangements violate. As many feminists have argued, such a development could merely perpetuate masculine ideals (for example, the differentiation of domestic and public spheres), however much men might be replaced by women in existing social practices and positions of power. Men might stay at home with children much more (no bad thing) and many more women might have careers, but the structure would remain the same. Such change is important, but the '*qualitative* transformation of needs and pleasures' would not be thinkable within such critiques. A politics of masculinity might require a seemingly utopian transformation of men's needs and pleasures. No obvious basis for that yet exists. To make it more possible we need to know much more about needs and pleasures, and one way to find out is to rethink what our culture means by emotion. How formative is emotion for social structures?

6

THE LOST LANGUAGE OF
EMOTION

Superman kept his diary in a lost language. The lost language of Krypton was once spoken by an entire planet but now it's a private language of family origins and the family romance because Superman is its only user. A truly private language in the philosophical sense ceases to be a language (Superman's private language could in theory be taught to others and so is strictly speaking not a philosophical private language), and so Superman's private language provides a convenient allegory for men's relation to emotion. Why might a man's language of the libidinal dramas of early childhood become private and therefore non-linguistic? One possibility according to some philosophers is that it was never a language in the first place, and therefore needed to be left behind. Hegel says in the *Encyclopedia* that a language of emotion could never be a real language, because emotion could never be articulate:

> Because *language* is the product of thought nothing can be said in it which is not general. What I only *mean* is *mine*, belongs to me as this particular individual; but if language only expresses the general I cannot say what I *mean*. And the *Unsayable* [*das Unsagbare*], emotion, feeling is not the most excellent, the most true but rather the most insignificant, most untrue.
>
> (Bowie 1990: 127)

Because this is a key passage I will also cite the Wallace translation:

> Now language is the work of thought: and hence all that is expressed in language must be universal. What I only mean or suppose is mine: it belongs to me, – this particular individual. But language expresses nothing but universality; and so I cannot say what I merely *mean*. And the unutterable, – feeling or sensation, – far from being the highest truth, is the most unimportant and untrue.
>
> (Hegel 1892: 32)

But if the language were utterly lost, and even its sole surviving speaker forgot it, the historical change represented by the destruction of Krypton and Superman's escape to Earth would become invisible. The absence of the

166

language of emotion would appear to be a logical necessity. Superman's historical explanation for what Hegel argues is logical necessity has a parallel in Alasdair MacIntyre's philosophical fable about the demise of ethical principles during the Enlightenment. MacIntyre thinks that the state of modern moral thought is similar to what might be the state of science after a disaster (a nuclear war perhaps) in which only incoherent fragments of thought survived. In this imaginary post-catastrophe world:

> Nonetheless all these fragments are reembodied in a set of practices which go under the revived names of physics, chemistry and biology. . . . Nobody, or almost nobody, realizes that what they are doing is not natural science in any proper sense at all. For everything that they do and say conforms to certain canons of consistency and coherence and those contexts which would be needed to make sense of what they are doing have been lost, perhaps irretrievably. What we possess, if this view is true, are the fragments of a conceptual scheme, parts which now lack those contexts from which their significance derived. We possess indeed simulacra of morality.
>
> (MacIntyre 1985: 1–2)

What was the catastrophe that caused this unrecognized fragmentation of moral discourse? According to MacIntyre, the failure of Enlightenment thinkers to provide an independent rational justification of morality in place of waning religious belief resulted in this early version of the postmodern condition. The moral scheme which these thinkers inherited:

> required three elements: untutored human nature, man-as-he-could-be-if-he-realized-his-*telos* and the moral precepts which enable him to pass from one state to the other. But the joint effect of the secular rejection of both Protestant and Catholic theology and the scientific and philosophical rejection of Aristotelianism was to eliminate any notion of man-as-he-could-be-if-he-realized-his-*telos*.
>
> (ibid.: 54)

To our modern ears the moral principles sound like the mediating factor between basic man and ideal man, but this is not the case. It is the image of virtue that provides the drive to develop basic human capabilities for goodness. Without this drive the only way to be virtuous is to follow a set of conscious principles, but the necessity to apply those principles has gone missing. MacIntyre's hyphenated man is not some inner potential, nor is it an abstract ideal. It is more like the potentiality of the entire social fabric's capacity to be a full community. I believe that this potentiality can be called emotion, and that we have lost a full understanding of the way emotion can act as a mediator between reason and desire.

The recognition that emotion is one form which human purposes take when understood as forms of intersubjective relation has largely disappeared.

In the opening of his book on *Politics and Culture*, Michael Ryan describes his response to the challenge from a 'Habermassian' that he has a 'soft spot' for Jacques Derrida's work: 'the thought, or is it a feeling?, well, let's just say the mental representation lingers that the distinction between hard ideas and soft spots could do well to be reconfigured' (Ryan 1989: 1). Ryan's ironic, self-conscious uncertainty about the term to use – thought, feeling, mental representation – points to the widespread indeterminacy caused by the lack of a cultural theory of emotion. The feminist philosopher Andrea Nye is clear about the problem. She argues that we don't have a linguistics to describe 'the language we all speak to each other, subtle, nuanced, already equipped with the means of interpersonal adjustment'. What's worse the special languages of theory 'conceal the hate, love, sympathy, and jealousy that motivate any speech' (Nye 1987: 685–6). The leaflet advertising the conference on 'Changing Identities' I discussed in the section on oppression and power (p. 145), said much the same about current British discourses of emancipation: 'the left is still looking for a way to engage with the subjective side of political life. It needs a new language.'

If the theoretical language for affectivity is lost, those who theorize men's subjectivity will face difficulties. Different theories of masculine subjectivities repeatedly converge on the emotions and, like Eliot's Shakespeare, find it hard to drag the stuff into view. Boys' comics showed men who lacked even a practical language, and needed to resort to cathartic neologisms, to put a face on inarticulate feelings of rage and grief. Some men's movement theorists have gone so far as to claim that this is generally true. Men lack a language for emotion altogether: 'Since we don't have a language in which to identify our emotional and sexual needs and since the very recognition of needs compromises our masculine control, we seek to satisfy our different needs without really being able to identify them' (Metcalf and Humphries 1985: 161). Is this because emotion is necessarily unsayable or do some modern men find themselves sole survivors of the lost planet of pre-masculine emotional relations, the only speakers of a lost language?

In David Leavitt's novel *The Lost Language of Cranes* (1987), from which I took the idea for the title of this chapter, one of the characters reads the case history of a baby boy who was left isolated for long periods in his cot by his single-parent mother. Outside the window he could see large cranes moving rhythmically on a construction site. When the boy's plight was discovered and he was taken into care, he could only communicate by moving his limbs in crane movements. He never learned to speak. His language of cranes was too private to become a language, and the lack of human interaction had left him without ordinary language. He tried to teach people his language, but it looked to them like meaningless, robotic gestures. Boys' comics showed us a milder fantasy version of this dilemma. In the remainder of this chapter I shall show how we might reconstruct the significance of these fantasies of loss by showing first that the inwardness of emotion is not simply a non-rational authenticity as is commonly assumed, and then considering emotion as a social structure that shapes many gender divisions in social life.

THE AUTHENTICITY OF FEELING

Modern common sense tells us that emotion is valuable when it is inward and authentic, manifesting the deepest inclinations of an individual. A journalist, Celia Dodd, researching a book on the relations between mothers and daughters says: 'the basic idea was to prompt so-called ordinary people to talk directly about their emotions' (*Observer*, 18 February 1990, p. 30). Their emotions would be the truest, most individual expression of their lives. TV interviewers ask the disaster victim: 'What do you feel?' The most authentically individual response is an emotion the victim is asked to name and, if possible, display for the audience. Emotion is the guarantee of their discourse's integrity. The key element in many contemporary therapies that aim to heal the psyche is the acknowledgement and full cathartic expression of inner emotion. A cathartic discharge of emotion can supposedly create a true inner self in harmony with itself. Such sentimental commonplaces have frequently provoked scorn from men intellectuals. The possible emptiness of such confidence in emotion was recognized by Adorno and Horkheimer in a particularly astringent comment on modern life in *Dialectic of Enlightenment*:

> The way in which a girl accepts and keeps the obligatory date, the inflection on the telephone or in the most intimate situation, the choice of words in conversation, and the whole inner life as classified by the now somewhat devalued depth psychology, bear witness to man's attempt to make himself a proficient apparatus, similar (even in emotions) to the model served up by the culture industry. The most intimate reactions of human beings have been so thoroughly reified that the idea of anything specific to themselves now persists only as an utterly abstract notion: personality scarcely signifies anything more than shining white teeth and freedom from body odor and emotions.
>
> (Adorno and Horkheimer 1979: 167)

Even these two critics of the enlightenment seem to have a nostalgia for some intimate authenticity, and their choice of example, the girl on a date, also suggests that they retain the traditional assumption that emotion is feminine. Their suspicion that the emotions might form part of the proficient apparatus of an ideologically manipulated robotic individual was taken up by Michel Foucault in volume one of *The History of Sexuality* where he proposes that theories of sexuality are an extension of society's control over the individual (Foucault 1981: I, 10–11). Widespread popular faith in the integrity of emotion as a measure of a person's individuality tends to produce theoretical aversion to all claims for the validity of feeling.

Behind the commonsense idea that emotion expresses an inner essence is the Romantic paradigm of the expressive self. Charles Taylor locates its emergence in Germany in the 'Sturm und Drang' period and describes it like this:

> To talk about the realization of a self here is to say that the adequate human life would not just be a fulfilment of an idea or a plan which is fixed independently of the subject who realizes it, as is the Aristotelian form of a man. Rather this life must have the added dimension that the subject can recognize it as his own, as having unfolded from within him . . . man as a conscious being achieves his highest point when he recognizes his own life as adequate, a true expression of what he potentially is.
>
> (Taylor 1975: 15,17)

The problem with the expressive paradigm is not only that it presupposes a self-transparent archetypal subject, and obscures the importance of language, but that it has a metaphoric substrate drawn from analogies with childbirth, and is similar to other masculine appropriations of femininity for aesthetic theory like the idea of genius (Battersby 1989). This ghostly maternal fantasy lurking in the paradigm should make us wary of modern philosophical and literary theories which exalt emotion. They may involve denials of the material conditions of men's lives, especially of dependency and relationship.

Such denial is evident in the use of emotion as a bedrock of inner authenticity by the theory of ethical 'emotivism'. According to some modern philosophers the modernist morality which MacIntyre believes to be incoherent is fine. Morality could not be anything other than 'emotivist'. According to a recent defence by Stephen Satris, emotivist ethics unites art and science because it relies not only on 'one's logical capabilities and one's cognitive abilities with respect to natural facts, but also on resources that science must refrain from calling into play, such as one's ordinary social (non-scientific) understanding of people and one's emotional sensibilities' (Satris 1987: 121). The major exponent of the theory was the American philosopher Charles L. Stevenson.

> In Hume's terms, Stevenson could agree that reason (cognition) *per se* is inert, while passion (conation-affection) provides motives to the will. Consequently, since morality (or rather, what one recognizes as moral) must determine or influence the will, this must of itself be passion-determining, or as Stevenson would say, moral judgements must have emotive meaning.
>
> (Satris 1987: 122)

In a critical account of emotivism in *After Virtue*, Alasdair MacIntyre argues that emotivism assumes that moral statements are simply 'expressions of attitude or feeling' (MacIntyre 1985: 12). A debate about morality finally comes down to what different people feel. There can be no general principles on which rational argument can base a judgement. What people feel is final and irreducible. If this were true, political differences could never be referred to general rational principles (like equality or freedom) which could be defended by rational argument, but only to emotional commitments to one belief or another (this is surely one reason why the idea of 'commitment' has been so important to radical social movements). The resulting individualism would make libertarian political appeal to principles impossible to sustain. MacIntyre still assumes that emotion is a form of inner expression, however, and in doing so actually goes further than Stevenson who speaks of 'attitude' rather than emotion, and emphasizes that

> although the controversial aspects of ethics spring from disagreement in attitude – a factor which, having been too little heeded in traditional theory, will here require constant attention – they rarely if ever spring from this kind of disagreement alone. Beliefs are the guide to attitudes.
>
> (ibid.: 18)

Since these are beliefs about facts, truths, scientific knowledge and so forth, Stevenson is closer to believing that emotion is moral (and rational) than that morality is emotional. Nevertheless Stevenson thinks that emotion is individualistic authenticity, and so MacIntyre is right to characterize emotivism as incoherent individualism. But if emotion were recognized to be socially structured his criticisms would be much less effective.

The literary equivalent of emotivism dominated literary studies during the heyday of Leavisite and New Critical humanist criticism. At its worst humanist criticism overstressed the importance of affect at the expense of textual logics and intertexuality. Critics sometimes held literary emotions upto the critical gaze in wonder as if the emotions themselves were of inestimable value. The difference between New Criticism and recent literary theory could be represented not so much in terms of their different understanding of the relation of the subject to language, but their different understanding of the role of emotion in language and texts. (I will not discuss the complex case of recent reader-response criticism because I believe it is either wholly psychoanalytic, or maintains the best of the earlier New Critical concern with emotion in a more psychoanalytically informed framework, without examining the theoretical issues surrounding its interest in emotion. A more extended account of masculinity, emotion and literary theory would certainly need to give extended attention to this often subtle and somewhat unfashionable form of criticism.)

New Criticism can appear to be anti-emotivist because of its emphasis on reason and intelligence, but on closer examination its emotivism is evident.

The best-known critique of affective criticism, W.K. Wimsatt and Monroe Beardsley's essay 'The Affective Fallacy' (1967) is not opposed to the idea that literature is patterned emotion, but to the extreme kind of criticism that celebrates visceral emotional effects (like A.E. Housman's facial bristles standing on end for shaving, when he thinks of a good poem) and allows the critic to talk like a revivalist preacher. Wimsatt and Beardsley believe that good criticism discusses 'shades of distinction and relation between objects of emotion' (1967: 34) (David Hume defined an object of emotion as the mental image to which an emotion is directed). Indeed they define poetry quite explicitly as a 'discourse about both emotion and objects, or about the emotive quality of objects', and therefore describe poets as scientists of emotion: 'leading expositors of the laws of feeling' (38–9). Taking law in a broader sense, these critics are like the psychoanalyst, mediators between the laws of feeling and the client. Perhaps because of this Wimsatt and Beardsley claim New Criticism is a cognitive method because it analyses paradox, irony and symbol. They use Cleanth Brooks's discussion of Tennyson to demonstrate that Brooks has to refer to symbols and other textual details to reveal 'the reasons for the emotion' he analyses (in this case sadness). For Wimsatt and Beardsley, critical analysis of the textual logics provides a diagram of the poem's emotional circuitry, showing where and how it produces emotions in the reader. Emotion is the field of study for their critical method despite its emphasis on reason and formal structures.

A similar strategy is evident in some of F.R. Leavis's literary criticism. He praises Keats's 'Ode to Autumn' for its intelligence rather than its emotional power: 'The strength appears here as critical intelligence, something intimately related to the sureness of touch and grasp', and 'more serious than mere aestheticism' (Leavis 1936: 262). The text is not discussed in relation to autumn (or metaphorical analogues), or as a biographical moment. Instead it is used to represent an ideal condition of life, one in which mind (intelligence) and body (touch and grasp) are 'intimately related'. His valorizing terms become more and more intimate: 'sensuous richness', 'concrete vigour', 'sensuous firmness', 'warm richness' (ibid.: 262–4). The significance of these is summed up by a curious negation – Keats's art is 'unvoluptuous' (ibid.: 264). Such critical terms are usually read against the terms of praise used by predecessors like the Keats critic John Middleton Murry. Another possibility is evident in the context of our discussion of masculinities. Voluptuousness is an almost exclusively female category. To be unvoluptuous may not automatically be masculine but it signals an escape from overt feminine sexuality. Leavis's word-pairs offer a masculine trait – richness, vigour, firmness – humanized by a feminine trait, just as traditional sexual politics said that women could humanize men. The word-pairs are familiar to us from decades of practical criticism spent discussing literature's virtues, its use of concrete imagery and its sensuous detail, its vitality. Yet in this passage we can read another more somatic text, an erotic body wary of voluptuous eroticism. Its eroticism is a male eroticism, a more phallic firmness and maturity than most poets are capable of. We can now see why Leavis insists on the critical intelligence (the very quality of the critical reading also) even though all the examples he chooses to analyse from Keats's poem are chosen for their non-intellectual qualities. Like the 'reasons' in Brooks's example, the intelligence is necessary to make the textual pleasure legitimately masculine. For Leavis, Keats's poetry reveals an emotional pattern of carefully controlled male eroticism. Emotion is made respectable by the intelligence which releases it, and made masculine by the treatment of the text as an erotic male body.

For a literary theorist like Terry Eagleton, emotion's expressivist individualism is a sign of inauthenticity: 'Like aesthetic judgements for Kant, ideological utterances conceal an essentially emotive content within a referential form, characterizing the lived relation of a speaker to the world in the act of appearing to characterize the world' (Eagleton 1990: 94). Bourgeois art and morality are limited by an emotivism largely abandoned by recent literary and cultural theory. Eagleton assumes that emotion is a source of epistemological distortion, and speaks for a common contemporary theoretical position in doing so. The earlier humanist critics, however, often did recognize the social structures of emotion but lacked a social or political discourse, and so they frequently collapsed the social dimension back into the individualist and expressivist paradigm. Influential New Critical works like Wayne Booth's *The Rhetoric of Fiction* (1961) emphasize emotion as a means for discussing both reader response and social relations. The central demonstration of authorial rhetoric in *The Rhetoric of Fiction* is entitled 'Distance in *Emma*', and glosses 'distance' as 'emotional distance' and effectively treats it as a discursive space (compare Paul de Man who treats rhetoric as if it were primarily ratiocinative):

> While only immature readers ever really identify with any character, losing all sense of distance and hence all chance of an artistic experience, our emotional reaction to every event concerning Emma tends to become like her own. When she feels anxiety or shame, we feel analogous emotions. Our modern awareness that such 'feelings' are not identical with those we feel in our own lives in similar circumstances has tended to blind us to the fact that aesthetic form can be built out of patterned emotions as well as out of other materials. It is absurd to pretend that because our emotions and desires in responding to fiction are in a very real sense disinterested, they do not or should not exist.
>
> (Booth 1961: 248)

Emotion becomes a term for various forms of social relation, most obviously that between reader and text. Wayne Booth is quite clearly talking of morality and moral norms at times, but cannot conceptualize them in anything but emotivist terms. This becomes the justification for claims whose masculine bias is sometimes painfully obvious: 'marriage to an intelligent, amiable, good, and attractive man is the best thing that can happen to this heroine' (ibid.: 260). Such solecisms are a reminder that the demise of humanist criticism also coincided with the emergence of feminist literary theory. Feminist theory made the humanist literary claims for emotion seem not only ridiculous but worse, a veneer for male fantasies. Much of the discussion focuses on the reader's irritations with Emma Woodhouse's imperfections. *Emma* is made to provide a space for the man reader to enjoy playacting emotions that are safer than the real ones which might blind him with mad passion. Literary emotions are more like the passions aroused by games: exciting simulacra but having no lasting consequences in the real world. Literary emotion becomes a game first because its sociopolitical dimension is overlooked and then because the rationality and significance of these relations is unrecognized. If aesthetic form is built of patterned emotions, the man reader's exasperation with Emma (sexist feelings that every woman needs a man) can be justified by arguing that the text needs the man reader's emotions in order to be read properly.

Rhetoric is emotion for the humanist Wayne Booth, but it is a form of rationality for the next generation of critics, like the poststructuralist Paul de Man, albeit a negativity that deconstructs the metaphysics based on the logical certainties of grammatical order. The first essay in de Man's *Allegories of Reading* (1979) explores the conflict between rhetoric and grammar through a series of examples drawn from high and low culture, and turns rhetoric into a vertiginous emotional disturbance of intellectual certainty, without ever quite naming this disturbance as anything other than language.

Paul de Man's first example is drawn from American television. The sitcom male chauvinist, Archie Bunker, is irritated with his wife for understanding his dismissive remark, 'What's the difference?' literally, when she asks him how he likes his shoes laced. De Man teasingly assumes a metalinguistic perspective to explain an anger already present in the initial rhetorical question, 'What's the difference?' an anger Bunker directs at his wife's unwanted solicitude: 'The very anger he displays is indicative of more than impatience; it reveals his despair when confronted with structures of linguistic meaning that he cannot control' (de Man 1979: 10). Archie Bunker's anger refuses his wife access to his inward life (where his wishes concerning shoe lacing are, she presumes, to be found). A little further on de Man concludes: 'Rhetoric radically suspends logic and opens up vertiginous possibilities of referential aberration. And although it would perhaps be somewhat more remote from common usage, I would not hesitate to equate the rhetorical, figural potentiality of language with literature itself' (ibid.: 10).

The 'rhetorical, figural potentiality of language' is equivalent to literature, and rhetoric 'suspends logic'. The echo of Coleridge's formula – the suspension of disbelief – creates parallels between logic and disbelief, and between rhetoric and belief. Rhetoric is so disorienting it leads to 'vertiginous possibilities of referential aberration'.

Like the sublime, vertigo has a long history of being used as a liminal physiological condition to represent psychic disorientation, moments when the mind falls, perhaps into error, perhaps into unconsciousness. The anthropologist Michael Taussig gives a fine example of its history in his account of the demonization of indigenous peoples by the colonizers, when he cites a historian of Cuba, Fernando Ortiz (1906):

> Despite the 'advanced psychology' of the whites in Cuba, writes Ortiz, 'the superstitions of the blacks attract them, producing a type of vertigo so that they fall into those beliefs from the height of their civilization; as if the superior planes of their psyches first drown and then become detached, returning to primitiveness, to the nakedness of their souls'.

(Taussig 1987: 217)

The mind falls when it is drawn from its safe heights by a strong attraction, and it ends up naked, primitive, uncivilized. The mind is returned to the body. We can trace this constellation further in the story of a man whose vertigo is narrativized as a fear of women. As Teresa de Lauretis has observed (1987: 110), it is hard not to think of Hitchcock when reading this passage from Paul de Man. One of the greatest studies of 'vertiginous possibilities', Hitchcock's *Vertigo* (1958), is the story of a man whose attacks of vertigo begin when he nearly falls from a roof during a chase. Scottie, a detective played by James Stewart, is hauled to safety by his partner, but at the same time accidentally pulls the other man off the roof to his death. Stewart is then drawn into a complex plot in which his vertigo (conveyed by using rapidly telescoping vertical shots) becomes a significant contributory factor to a murder. Hitchcock ordinarily uses vertical shots to present people as objects for scrutiny. The moment in *Rear Window* when James Stewart is shown from above instead of eye level is the moment when his appraisal of events can no longer be trusted. Stewart is finally to be gazed at, not the means of our gaze. Vertical shots are commonly used to show death (as at the end of *Dangerous Liaisons*). In filmic logic, vertigo is the inability to control the gaze that would make the other person an object of analysis. Instead, the object under analysis threatens to overwhelm the subject's ability to construct objects. Stewart's vertigo began when he killed his male partner. Men kill one another all the time (the accidental death occurs during a chase in which both detectives and criminal are using guns to try and kill each other), but this time the dead man was a *partner*, someone for whom Stewart felt strong affection (Mulvey (1985: 814) points out that he has 'freely chosen' to be a policeman having previously been a lawyer, a choice that is only the first in a number of similar complicities with a violent, dominant and voyeuristic masculinity). The accidental killing of a man he cared for results in the loss of control of the objectifying gaze. During the murderous chase of a male enemy the murderousness gets out of control, and Stewart begins to suffer referential aberration. He cannot tell which woman he is following or, later, is in love with. His dilemma is only resolved when he is able to convict another man of pushing his wife to her death off a high tower, thus convicting that part of himself which murdered the man closest to him. Throughout the film, Stewart is portrayed as a man afraid of women and any emotional commitment to them. He is afraid of feeling, and the death of his partner instigated feelings that threaten to overwhelm him altogether. *Vertigo* suggests that referential aberration results from the inability to face the murderous intent men feel towards other men, and more generally from the loss of the ability to make others into objects under the stress of overwhelming emotion. Such emotion destroys the hegemonic ability to treat subject–subject relations as subject–object relations. The failure of the male gaze induces vertigo in its would-be possessor.

What is the object the critic's gaze cannot objectify and what masculine violence might have caused it? Consider the hostile incompatibility Paul de Man attributes to grammar and rhetoric in his second example, the ambiguous final line of Yeats's poem 'Among School Children': 'The two readings have to engage each other in direct confrontation, for the one reading is precisely the error denounced by the other and has to be undone by it' (de Man 1979: 12). De Man assumes that because grammar and rhetoric are not identical it is possible to produce grammatical and rhetorical readings which behave like battling independent readers. Empirically it is certainly possible to read less than what is available in the text and to envisage a circumstance when two empirical readers manage to exclude exactly that element of the text the other emphasizes. But this is empirical. De Man is claiming something much stronger: the text will necessarily be read this way. The opposition of rhetoric and grammar is a sort of transcendent structure imposed on any empirical reading. I am not claiming, as David Lehman (1991: 131) does in his polemical book on deconstruction, that Yeats is an 'unwitting mouthpiece' for Paul de Man. The confrontation is real enough, but not quite so transcendental. There is a gut feeling to its gendered hostility. But what makes the readings confrontational? In the final two stanzas of Yeats's poem several metaphoric strands are woven together by the words 'labour' and 'worship'. Mothers give birth to babies in labour and then worship what their bodies have created, just as nuns worship at shrines decorated with sacred images. Women's worship is an act of passion that becomes knowledge. But where are the men? They break into a passionate apostrophe in the final section and address, not the women, but their creations, these babies/ sacred images, and by doing so place themselves in the position of mothers/ nuns. These men tell the 'presences', as the babies/sacred images are now called, that 'labour is blossoming or dancing' when the body is not sacrificed to an ideal, or 'beauty born out of its own despair'. Labour (understood as both parturition and creativity) is metaphorically equated with dance if certain conditions are met. One of these is that despair is not the mother of beauty; despair does not give birth. Another condition is that 'body is not bruised to pleasure soul', a bruising all too common in actual childbirth, although whether it is done to pleasure the soul is questionable. The masculine voice whips the recalcitrant babies/images into line. The women doted on them too much and were therefore ruled by them. Further apostrophes follow, to the chestnut tree and 'the body swayed to music', and effectively parallel tree and body with the presences addressed earlier. De Man claims the final line fissions into two opposed statements. On the one hand, form and experience are one, and on the other we desperately need to distinguish signs and what they refer to, and need to know how to do it. Therefore, if, as I suggest, this is a masculine voice responding to maternal passion and its conventional sublimations, the passion generated between the two readings has a prior cause, just as Archie Bunker's anger arose from his wife's mild insubordination in daring to gaze into his masculine certainties. If separating the dancer and the dance is what the masculine voice wishes to do, he assumes from the start that only passion (the word 'know' has already been valorized as the act of passion) can do it, because he assumes the dancer produces dance as labour produces a baby or a mother worships the image which is her baby. If, on the other hand, the masculine voice is saying that we cannot separate dancer and dance, then passion fails. The masculine voice can never know what the relation between woman and offspring is like. That produces its own despair. De Man's hostility between the readings is a prior hostility to the women who command the only real creativity: maternity. The possibility of two readings is a counsel of despair for the masculine voice that can never be sure of his own capacity for self-birth or self-creation.

In the Archie Bunker example the man's anger at his wife makes the confrontation possible. The elaborate abstract theorization of the critic's analysis moves us away from this everyday exercise of male power. What is the significance of this emotion generated by the relation between grammar and rhetoric, and what is its relation to the vertiginousness of language? James Stewart killed his partner accidentally and then suffered vertigo. Could it be that logic has killed rhetoric and now suffers referential aberration? The killing of Stewart's partner was precipitated by an atmosphere of male violence. In de Man's rhetoric the two readings behave like the opponents of and collaborators with an oppressive, violent regime, each ready to denounce the other, because of the general state of hostilities. Deconstruction is initiated by mutual fear and anger, whose sources are never addressed.

Paul de Man argues that this emotion is a form of the sublime. It is not language, but a sudden awareness of our incapacity for knowing what the infinite immensity of language is doing, that produces these emotions:

> Any question about the rhetorical mode of a literary text is always a rhetorical question which does not even know whether it is really questioning. The resulting pathos is an anxiety (or bliss, depending on one's momentary mood or individual temperament) of ignorance, not an anxiety of reference – as becomes thematically clear in Proust's novel when reading is dramatized, in the relationships between Marcel and Albertine, not as an emotive reaction to what language does, but as an emotive reaction to the impossibility of knowing what it might be up to.
>
> (de Man 1979: 19)

The demand for understanding in the face of the rhetorical functioning of a literary text will (just like the mind faced with the sublime according to Kant) meet a momentary check and be forced backwards by the unrepresentability of what it experiences. The result is emotion, not as a direct result of what the text says (the traditional affective model), but as a result of what cannot be understood. The cause is rhetoric. De Man's conclusion introduces a further element, the element of self-transformation: 'Literature as well as criticism . . . is condemned (or privileged) to be forever the most rigorous and, consequently, the most unreliable language in terms of which man names and transforms himself' (ibid.). Rhetoric is a name for human transformation – or perhaps self-transformation – hence the surprising conclusion implicit in his reasoning: deconstruction occurs when emotion overwhelms reason.

Rhetoric was once, as de Man notes, a major part of a good education, not because literary ornament was prized, but because the arts of verbal persuasion, in largely oral cultures, were essential in the public sphere. Rhetoric was the art of affecting listeners, and that meant skills in both logical argument and emotional relations. The difference between rhetoric and grammar is the difference between an account of language as a relation between speakers and hearers, and an account of language as an abstract knowable system. Grammar is by definition knowable. It is the structure of the system constructed in order to study and guide language use. Rhetoric is the use of language in terms of its modes of address. Rhetoric is the means by which the emotional relations of the intersubjectivity on which our reading and writing depend are negotiated. The effects of the sublime would then translate as moments when intersubjectivity becomes so vast and incomprehensible as to seem overwhelming, an intersubjectivity which begins to look remarkably like the discarded emotional relations of earlier criticism.

MAD PASSIONS

Common sense may value emotion as a sign of authenticity but strong feelings are not always assumed to be automatic connections to the deepest sources of life. Popularly, emotion is often reckoned to be a disturbance of the rational order of being, flooding away reason with tears or blinding it with rage. From the exhortation, 'Big boys don't cry', to government fears of the mob emotions of large demonstrations, there is a recognition that mature reason may not mix easily with emotion. Gender also plays a strong part in the commonsense pictures of emotion. Emotion has commonly been identified with femininity, and masculinity then defined negatively as a repudiation of it. Not surprisingly, modern men philosophers have often left emotion out of their accounts of logic and reason altogether: 'The ingredients of an emotion are only sensations and images and bodily movements succeeding each other according to a certain pattern. With this conclusion we may leave the emotions and pass to the consideration of the will' (Russell 1921: 284).

With this characteristically robust judgement in *The Analysis of Mind*, Bertrand Russell relegates the emotions to that mere vehicle of mind, the body, and passes on to higher and more significant issues. His dismissal is only a blunter version of the philosophical assumption which finds its most authoritative statement at the opening of Kant's *Critique of Pure Reason*. Transcendental philosophy is 'a philosophy of pure and merely speculative reason. All that is practical, so far as it contains motives, relates to feelings, and these belong to the empirical sources of knowledge' (Kant 1933: 161).

Kant was actually very interested in emotion, as the *Critique of Judgement* and the lecture notes *Anthropology from a Pragmatic Point of View* demonstrate, but he kept it clear of the basic arguments about mind and the *a priori* conditions of experience. For Kant and Russell the problem is emotion's connection with the body, and what is at best the body's irrelevance to the structures of reason and at worst its power to incapacitate the mind emotionally.

Contemporary literary and cultural theory is also sceptical about the theoretical significance of emotion. Once prominently and proudly displayed as part of a discourse of sensibility and later of sexual liberation, emotion is now rarely mentioned. Emotions belong to the body, and the body is widely believed to be an apparatus whose self-awarenesss is constructed by external discourses. Desire is assumed to be a more precise, more theoretically defined term for the phenomenon. How could something as primitive as a discussion of feelings in literature and criticism any longer be a serious subject? When the Italian critic Franco Moretti discusses what he calls 'moving literature' in *Signs Taken for Wonders*, he admits that his own feelings were the basis of his choice of texts, as if he were another humanist critic. Early in the chapter he winningly says: 'But why precisely this group

179

of texts and not others? Because – let theory addicts try to stay calm at this point – only these texts have made me cry' (Moretti 1983: 158). But crying is soon revealed as a subterfuge: 'Crying enables us *not to see*. It is a way of distracting us from the sight of what has upset us, or rather of making it disappear' (ibid.: 179). The rest of the essay is satisfyingly theoretical and concludes that the tears these novels induce are a false resolution of real contradictions. Moretti is not after all holding up his feelings to our admiring gaze. The strong emotion of grief, promoted by these novels as a value in itself, induces a condition of politically disabling self-obliviousness. The question the chapter does not ask is whether other more fruitful responses than emotionally induced blindness might be possible. Perhaps such blindness is not an inevitable consequence of emotion, but a result of certain kinds of inability to articulate emotion, inabilities particularly common to modern masculinities. Emotions are assumed by Moretti and most recent theorists to be personal, intimate, humanist, sentimental and old-fashioned. Feeling therefore lies outside postmodern theories of the subject in language, because they are predicated on a structure of logic and desire. Desire is the only legitimate term for a universal motivational force in human interaction; desire is a 'fundamental pattern of being that discards any possibility of satisfaction' (de Man 1983: 17).

Moretti is probably remembering Sartre's theory of emotions when he finds such emotional literature to be deceptive. One obvious step for men philosophers to take as an alternative to the humanist inflation of the value of individual emotion and the emotivist destruction of any basis for moral argument was to deny the significance of emotion altogether. Jean-Paul Sartre argued in *Sketch for a Theory of the Emotions* that emotion plunges consciousness into a magical retreat from the real world of politics: 'All ways are barred and nevertheless we must act. So then we try to change the world; that is, to live it as though the relations between things and their potentialites were not governed by determinate processes but by magic' (Sartre 1963: 63). In one example he describes how a patient of the psychiatrist Pierre Janet sobbed rather than confess her problems to the doctor: 'In this case, then, the emotion of sadness is a magical play-acting of impotence' (ibid.: 70). But doesn't Sartre's interpretation ignore the power relations and gender differences between doctor and patient? Surely her impotence is real enough and it is the doctor, not the patient, who is failing to comprehend her social and emotional position? Sartre's attempt to rescue political debate from the extremes of humanist individualism, by feminizing emotion and denying any reliable axiological or epistemological capacity to it, is itself open to the charge that he is rationalizing what some feminists have identified as a marked tendency amongst modern men either to ignore the emotional life around them or to treat it as women's magic:

But . . . 'it' is not just there by nature or magic. It is there because our

society raises girls to provide it. . . . Boys come to experience emotional nurturing as part of the fabric of life. It is one of those invisible 'laws'
of patriarchal culture. Boys' and men's emotional dependency needs
are less exposed and more continually met. . . . Boys are not raised to
develop the emotional antennae which girls acquire.

(Eichenbaum and Orbach 1984: 75)

Jessica Benjamin describes the dynamic this gives rise to in many relationships: 'The ideal mother-wife protects the autonomous individual from
having to admit his needs by meeting them in advance; she protects him
from the shame of exposure, allowing him to appear independent and in
control' (Benjamin 1990: 205).

While cultural theory has become suspicious of emotion because it produces political self-deception, and because the language of feeling seems to
belong to a discredited humanism, alternative psychotherapies based on the
expressivist model of the self have gone to the other extreme, but for very
similar reasons. They focus on emotion because it both manifests the
authentic inner person and, when out of control, can mislead, even overwhelm reason. The key therapeutic tool they use for making it visible to the
inward gaze of reason, and for dispelling the aporias it produces in the
effective functioning of consciousness, is catharsis. Many psychotherapies
go in for heavy doses of it. They assume that emotional energies can
accumulate to dangerous levels and therefore need bodily release in the form
of crying, angry physical activity, trembling, laughter or even yawning, to
free up the mind's reasoning processes. These therapies recognize that the
bodily affect associated with some emotions is not just a signal of the
presence of that emotion, but a form of discharge, the means by which the
emotion's power to disturb intellectual functions is reduced, a distinction
many philosophical theories of emotion (and some psychological ones also)
have found difficult to make. Too often an emotion like sadness has been
treated as if its somatic registration, tears, were only a communicative
gesture.

As far as I can abstract an account of what is still largely an oral tradition
of psychotherapy, the current theory of catharsis goes something like this.
Someone who suffers a serious trauma experiences a range of emotions
necessary to come to terms with the shock (emotion is protective of the
integrity of the person, not necessarily a weakness), but these emotions
temporarily overwhelm consciousness and the power of reasoning. Part of
the mind locks solid. Only some of this emotion may find a way to discharge
at first. Safety, some sense of inner strength, of self-love and self-respect are
needed before the mind has the strength to become fully aware of the
dangerously overwhelming emotions. A listening witness is almost essential
to provide a counterbalance to the pain, and to sustain articulation.
Psychotherapeutic catharsis starts as the mind slowly acknowledges the

hitherto unbearable stored-up responses, and the body acts as a kind of earth or lightning conductor for the emotions as they discharge. Catharsis may proceed through several phases of different kinds of bodily discharge, not necessarily all at once or in order of intensity. It may take hours, days or years. The understanding is more and more able to assess the traumatic event now that emotions are down to negotiable levels. Gradually the memories can be articulated. If the catharsis had not been allowed to occur, as for example might be the case in combat, some area of memory and the mental functioning associated with it would be locked solid, effectively dead until catharsis were possible. Whatever the situation of the person inhibited from discharge, the cathartic process would be clamouring for an opportunity to be carried out, even over long periods, drawing awareness back to itself to clear up the emotional mess. Thoughts and actions would constantly recur to the general site of the trauma, caught in a repetition compulsion whose sign would be some bearable association to the trauma. The suppression of catharsis maintains a condition of localized mental blindspots and may result in unconscious attempts to set up a situation in which emotional discharge can occur. A person with an angry grievance may instigate physical violence as a release for the anger. If you prevent people from articulating their feelings, and sometimes even from displaying them at all, you effectively ban most kinds of emotional discharge, and therefore can powerfully mould a person for the future. If you 'make education an aggressive game of simu-lated warfare', as Suzette Henke (1990: 56) describes Stephen Dedalus's school, and the young man learns to suppress emotional discharge, then you can powerfully shape him to the needs of a repressive social system (unless he rebels and becomes the artist observing it from exile).

There are problems with the catharsis model once we consider everyday life and history. Most emotional disturbances don't arise from one-off shocks. They accumulate through years of deprivation, barely noticed cruel-ties, small disorienting lies. There are no specific traumas to decathect. Because catharsis works in some cases doesn't mean that emotion is only an inner charge of energy needing release. Emotion is much more complex than that. The quantitative energetics of the expressive model of psychic experi-ence assumes that emotion already exists in some stored form, rather than as a potential within relational structures. But emotion is not only discharge and it is not all reawakened childhood patterns of response or old traumas. Some of what is termed discharge is probably better understood as a present-moment display of emotions precipitated out of the social structure in which a person is situated. As many critics of the cathartic model of psychotherapy have noted, there is rarely some clear inner feeling waiting for release. The process of healing is a long unravelling of memories, thoughts and feelings in which catharsis plays a role, which is partly why psychoanalysis acknowl-edges catharsis only as an incidental feature of the working through of cathexes in the transference. Catharsis theories ignore the potential that the emotions have for rationality, communication and sociality. Nevertheless these catharsis theories draw attention to a significant area of emotional function neglected by much mainstream theorizing.

Sartre's dismissal of the woman patient's tears is therefore also an inadvertent ban on catharsis. We can find similar male restrictions given philosophical authority by other modern philosophers, notably Ludwig Wittgenstein in *Philosophical Investigations*. In the course of his argument about the impossibility of a private language and the difficulties raised by the language for inner mental events, he makes a passing reference to cathartic grief:

> 244. How do words *refer* to sensations? – There doesn't seem to be any problem here; don't we talk about sensations every day, and give them names? But how is the connexion between the name and the thing set up? This question is the same as: how does a human being learn the meaning of the names of sensations? – of the word 'pain' for example. Here is one possibility: words are connected with the primitive, the natural, expressions of the sensation and used in their place. A child has hurt himself and he cries; and then adults talk to him and teach him exclamations and, later, sentences. They teach the child new pain-behaviour.
>
> 'So you are saying that the word "pain" really means crying' – On the contrary: the verbal expression of pain replaces crying and does not describe it.

(Wittgenstein 1976: 89)

Wittgenstein begins with a dualist Cartesian model of the relation between mind and body. For Descartes an emotion had two parts, the bodily event in which some physiological change occurred (like a trembling in the limbs), and a mental event, the registration of what was going on down below. Instead of challenging the dualist model of mind on psychological grounds Wittgenstein translates its claims into linguistic terms. Words actually refer to inner bodily sensations and feelings. To show that the referential model of language is misleading he then retranslates this argument into a question about learning (a manoeuvre similar to that in psychoanalysis: to understand the present psychic structure we examine its development). The example carries other implications as well. Wittgenstein assumes that language is an adequate replacement for the emotional discharge which crying facilitates. The description becomes powerfully prescriptive by using the oppositions between primitive and civilized, emotion and reason. Language is made a superior substitute for emotion. The problem is that emotion won't go away. Emotion haunts language still and it seems to haunt Wittgenstein's arguments.

In section one of book two of *Philosophical Investigations* Wittgenstein argues that emotions are not simply the mental acknowledgement of bodily affects, and uses the cathartic processes as his key examples of such affects.

He claims that the shivering sensations of fear are quite distinct from the verbal expression 'I am frightened', for example. Although it makes sense to say, 'For a second he felt violent pain', it does not make sense to say, 'For a second he felt deep grief', because the word 'felt' is used in quite different senses: ' "Grief" describes a pattern which recurs, with different variations, in the weave of our life' (Wittgenstein 1976: 174). By making language a replacement for emotion, the text makes emotion *other* to language, mysterious, silent, private and therefore the cause of seemingly unaddressable disturbances. The text produces the very phenomena it has tried to repress, in the form of these examples which refer to emotion, examples inside protective quotation marks that make them simulacra of affectively charged dialogic utterances. They might be playacting emotion.

If emotion is irrational and disturbs reason, this need not mean that it is not intelligible when considered from outside, by a rationality in full possession of itself. Historically, some thinkers analysed emotion as a rationally comprehensible system outside reason and consciousness altogether, a physics of the mind's sustaining body. Spinoza's theory exemplifies this approach, and has had a considerable influence on modern theories of the unconscious as a result. His materialist theory of emotion can also help us understand why contemporary theories of emotion insist on the rationality of emotion (to use Ronald de Sousa's (1987) phrase). For Spinoza, emotions are passive, they are caused by external objects: 'We are driven about by external causes in many manners, and . . . like waves driven about by contrary winds, waver and are unconscious of the issue and of our fate' (Spinoza 1986: 127). Treating the self as a material body, Spinoza imagines emotion to be a form of energy that enables the self to persist in a particular condition, in the same way that momentum enables the state of a material body to persist. A contradiction then develops in Spinoza's theory between the autonomy of purposiveness that characterizes desire, and the reactivity of emotion, a contradiction like that in the catharsis theory of emotion. A similar lacuna exists in Freud's work, because it is unable to account for the autonomy and reliability of reason in the face of desire and the unconscious. Freud's work easily leads to an extreme Nietzschean position on the illusory nature of truth and reason, and therefore has difficulties locating its own psychoanalytic rationality. Spinoza's theory treats emotion as a rationally comprehensible system of purposiveness which leaves the rationality or logic of consciousness unaltered, however much emotion might occlude it.

REASONABLE FEELINGS

Luce Irigaray has written: 'the bodily in man is what metaphysics has never touched' (Jardine 1985: 61). One reason for this hands-off policy should be obvious. Those hands risk becoming contaminated with the madness of emotion if they come too close to the body. Irigaray's claim is a little too sweeping, but there have been few counter-examples (William Blake perhaps, or the theory of the sublime?) until recently. Contemporary philosophers (not that they would call themselves metaphysicians) have at last set about showing that emotion is not to be so readily dismissed as both metaphysicians and behaviourists have imagined. The implied dualism of body and mind will not stand close scrutiny. Philosophers, psychologists and sociologists have done extensive work on emotion in the past thirty years, but much of it remains resolutely confined to its specific discipline, and much remains unresolved. Emotion, like mind in general, is so complex a phenomenon, and so resistant to existing forms of scientific investigation, that, as Thomas Nagel puts it, 'with respect to mental phenomena our objective understanding is undeveloped, and it may never develop very far' (1986: 19). I feel the same sense of inadequacy as many other investigators have, both in the face of the complexity of the phenomenon itself, and the complexity of the existing heterogeneous theory. In what follows I shall make certain simplifications in order to keep the discussion manageable. I shall take a psychologist, Nico Fridja, and two philosophers, William Lyons and Ronald de Sousa, to represent existing theories (their heterogeneity is brought out by the fact that the psychologist's extensive bibliography doesn't list William Lyons whose book was published several years earlier by the same university press; and neither gives much space to the extensive psychoanalytic and phenomenological literature on emotion). I shall also use the terms affect, emotion, feeling and passion interchangeably. They have been used with different meanings at different periods by different thinkers, but not consistently. I have tried to recognize and maintain specific contexts for these terms, but I also want to emphasize continuities and similarities.

Despite the defence of boundaries between disciplines, and the sometimes incompatible theoretical paradigms, contemporary theorists do agree on a number of points. William Lyons, in his summary of what he calls a 'full-blooded' theory of emotion (1980: 207), argues that emotion is fundamentally evaluative: 'the central evaluative aspect gives rise to emotional behaviour via a rational, and causal, link with desires' (ibid.: 53). Nico Fridja defines emotion as:

> awareness of some mode of action readiness of a passive and action-control-demanding nature, involving readiness to change or maintain relationships with the environment (or intentional objects generally); which action readiness is experienced as motivated or caused by situations appraised as relevant, urgent, and meaningful with respect to ways of dealing with it; which situations are felt to affect the subject, and affect him bodily.
>
> (1986: 257)

For both philosopher and psychologist, emotion is capable of awareness. It makes judgements of all kinds, especially evaluative responses to the environment. Emotions are active and make things happen. Emotion doesn't simply play over a person who remains passive, like a breeze over a wind chime; it can be self-generated (although it is not clear from these definitions how that can happen). It is an occurrent (or ongoing) experience rather than a character trait. Although neither definition has much to say about the social and linguistic character of emotion, they avoid treating it as a purely objective material phenomenon.

By showing that rationality is not so neatly exempt from emotional influence as earlier theories would have it, contemporary theorists of emotion have given renewed prominence to the work of the philosopher David Hume (whose direct influence Lyons acknowledges). Hume's double-edged recognition of the directive role of emotion in the operations of reason remains one of the most important theories of emotion because it faces up to the far-reaching consequences of this recognition. The result is not only a decentred subjectivity but also a scepticism about the foundations of knowledge that still remains challenging, however much specific argumentative strategies have been queried. Hume's *Treatise* is not just an argument in favour of scepticism, but a different theory of the ground of human society from those which found it on some kind of rationality. His scepticism is aimed at the seeming truths and certainties on which the masculine worlds of law, science, politics and religion are based, showing that they depend on beliefs (in cause and effect for example), which in turn depend on what he calls the passions. He concludes that there are no general truths because he cannot shake off the idea that emotion is individual and arbitrary. He relies on the eighteenth-century cult of sensibility for a confidence in the potential value of emotion, but that is not why he places them centrally. Hume, whose own father died when he was 2 years old, grew up in a world dominated by his mother, who ran the small family estate herself. According to E.C. Mossner's biography, little is known of this period in his life, so we can only conjecture about the contrast between this world and the men's world he entered at the age of 11 when he went with his brother to university in Edinburgh, and was directed to take up the law and follow in his father's footsteps, at the age of about 14. At the age of 18 he suffered a nervous breakdown (he wrote in a letter in his twenties that his experiences must have echoed those of certain French mystics, because 'this kind of Devotion depends entirely on the Force of Passion, & consequently of the Animal Spirits' (Mossner 1980: 70)), and only recovered by living outside his own world (in France) and writing a long account of human nature and society in order to explain what must have seemed to him impossible conflicts. Raymond Williams describes this as 'an attempt to restore the identity of social and personal virtues' (Williams 1988: 141). Hume's philosophy, says Williams, depends upon 'the shared conventions of humane feeling; the certainty that these are embodied in the common language of approval and disapproval; the conviction that moral activity is the use of this language, and that reasoning is necessary mainly to confirm this use and to expose the inadequacy of other definitions of morals' (ibid.: 134). Williams believes that Hume tried to reconcile 'reasoning and experience' (the latter a term Williams considered using instead of 'structure of feeling' in his own theoretical schema) within his philosophical writing, and used emotive language not to affirm his own personal beliefs or to browbeat the reader, but to signal an already shared common ground. I speculate that this can also be understood in terms of Hume's changing situation in relation to dominant genders. As a boy he lived first in a locally matriarchal world for a long while relative to most boys' development, and then was switched abruptly to a patriarchal one, while remaining on very close terms with the world of his mother (he lived at times at the family house with her, and later with his sister and brother). The *Treatise* is the closest thing to a reconciliation of masculine and feminine versions of the self to appear in English until this century. Hume's scepticism is not so much epistemological as the result of learning two incompatible ways of recognizing social structures, and finding the claims of the man's world of the law schools unsupportable in the face of his inside knowledge of the alternative.

Hume's dictum – 'Reason is, and ought only to be the slave of the passions' (Hume 1969: 462) – arises from the consideration that it must be the passions which initiate the actions of reason. For Hume, emotions provide motives. Reason can't because it has no connection with desire or 'volition' (as Hume calls it). Pain and pleasure are the initial causes of action, and reason's role is to advise on the best ways to achieve the possibilities to which the consequent emotions draw attention. An original pain or pleasure stimulated by an object attracts or repels us in relation to it and we are then impelled by the emotion to find other objects 'connected with its original one by the relation of cause and effect' (ibid.: 461). Reason is able to work out what these relations might be, so that the emotions can 'extend themselves to the causes and effects of that object, as they are pointed out to us by reason and experience' (ibid.: 462). Without the emotional involvement we would not bother to work out the relations. He concludes that 'as reason is nothing but the discovery of this connexion, it cannot be by its means that the objects are able to affect us' (ibid.: 462). Reason needs some motive for its attentions to specific concerns because otherwise all concerns would be equally important and equally indifferent to it.

Every emotion has both an object and a cause. A man becomes angry with the government (the object of the emotion) for cutting educational spending, but his anger is caused by a sleepless night. Like Saussure's theory of the sign, Hume's theory is actually an account of a relationship between two mental events because both the cause and the object of an emotion are ideas. Since ideas correspond to objects, emotion makes clear to reason the importance of the relation between objects which can then be intepreted by the mind. Despite the importance of emotion for reason the two processes are quite distinct. A 'passion is an original existence, or, if you will, modification of existence, and contains not any representative quality, which renders it a copy of any other existence or modification' (ibid.: 462). Emotion therefore has no relation to truth understood as a correspondence between idea and object. Its incapacity for representation means that an emotion has no reference to any other object: 'When I am angry, I am actually possesst with the passion, and in that emotion have no more a reference to any other object, than when I am thirsty, or sick, or more than five foot high' (ibid.: 462–3). Emotion may be accompanied by representations but has no truth content in itself, and is what he calls 'an original existence'. This places passion or emotion in a curious position of authority because ideas, as representations, are by definition secondary and determinate, whilst emotion is not dependent on anything else for its being. Two different forms of determination produce what appears to be a paradox. Emotion has a cause but is not a sign of something else. Emotion is so completely true to the world that it cannot provide true knowledge of it. Here a note of uncertainty enters. Reason should 'serve and obey' its sovereign, the passions. 'Should' because Hume himself is unsure of this point: 'Reason is, and *ought only to be* the slave of the passions' (my emphasis). If reason is the slave of the passions as his argument proposes, it is because reason has no volition. There is no possibility of a rebellion that needs to be held back by the moral restraint of an 'ought'. The superfluous insistence on its appropriateness betrays the persistent uncertainty about the relation between emotion and idea that runs through Hume's account. If reason is even remotely capable of some Spartacist revolt then it must have other motivating powers than emotion. He doesn't put emotion on the throne to denigrate reason. He admires reason. It is reason's claims to self-sufficiency or self-grounding certainty that he cannot believe in. Something else sustains it.

Many of Hume's ideas about the emotions are still current in some form. His distinction between the object and the cause of an emotion is widely endorsed. Other distinctions exist in forms which seem to have lost sight of Hume's care for the interrelations between society, reason and emotion. The strong claim about the dominance of the passions finds an altered but recognizable formulation in the psychoanalytic claim that reason is the slave of childhood passions. His claim that emotion is not a form of representation because emotions lack the ability to represent truth, even though they are mental events, is echoed in Kant and in poststructuralism, and probably underlies the widespread idea that (in Novalis's words), 'feeling cannot feel itself' (Bowie 1990: 182). If it could feel itself then it would be able to represent itself. If, however, as contemporary philosophers propose, emotion is rational, then the picture alters. Representation may not exhaust the possibilities of self-consciousness. The rationality of emotion may not take the form of self-reflexive consciousness.

Nico Fridja points out that 'emotional experience, in its more direct manifestations, is not conscious of itself' (1986: 188). Awareness itself is a complex phenomenon. Fridja describes emotions as forms of awareness (ibid.: 256), but this awareness requires education. If emotions are intentional in structure, a failure to recognize the scope of the intentions at work in an emotional event would result in the appearance of a split between behaviour and consciousness. A person who had reached maturity without much emotional development would be vulnerable to social control of his or her emotions, and to being co-opted into organizations whose purposes run counter to his or her own well-being. Fridja also emphasizes that not all consciousness need be self-consciousness. Irreflexive experience need not be unconscious either: 'A subject is usually part of his own awareness; however, he then plays the part more as condition of experience and subject of action than as subject of experience' (ibid.: 189). If emotional experience is usually not directly self-conscious this does not mean it is therefore unconscious, although it can be.

If emotion is partly rational then it may also be educable. Tom Brangwen's educated feelings may be an instance of a general possibility. Several recent philosophers have explored this aspect of emotion. Ronald de Sousa, in his wide-ranging synoptic account of emotion, *The Rationality of Emotion*, offers a new version of the educability thesis in his discussion of the rationality specific to emotion. He argues that emotions 'act like models': 'Whatever their own susceptibility to rational criticism, they themselves give us frameworks in terms of which we perceive, desire, act, and explain. Their reputation for irrationality is partly due to their power to reinterpret the world' (de Sousa 1987: 24). He names this modelling process a 'paradigm scenario' because he believes that we learn from earliest childhood to recognize situations to which certain emotions are appropriate. We learn to think about emotions in terms of the dramas they arise from: 'We acquire the capacity to talk about emotions in terms of the stories that give rise to them' (ibid.: 183). Emotion has an axiological dimension (as opposed to deontological, thus making it a similar claim to MacIntyre's) different from cognition or instrumental reason. The world projected by the emotions is complementary to, but different from, that of rational knowledge or strategic manipulation. De Sousa's description of emotion goes about as far as the subject-based approach to emotion can go in recognizing the social dimensions of emotion. Instead of the emotional object being a discrete material object like a dangerous dog that evokes fear (which is roughly what Hume's cognitive theory of emotion proposed), the notion of object has been expanded to name a whole set of relationships with others in time and space. Nevertheless, it only pictures this process from the one point, the zero point subject of the emotion, and for that reason will need to be supplemented by other more socially structured phenomenologies to represent the consequences of masculine emotional pathologies.

If emotion is educable it can also suffer arrested development, or even a manipulated underdevelopment. As I said earlier, some feminists have argued that women learn very early on, as girls, to sustain the emotional relationships around them while boys and men simply expect this sustaining and, because they don't learn it, treat it as magic, or don't see it at all (Chodorow 1978; Eichenbaum and Orbach 1984; Dinnerstein 1987; Segal 1987). Such men notice its absence but not its presence. According to this theory, men live in a world whose emotional structure is largely maintained by women. As one man puts it in the essay by Wendy Hollway (1984: 252) (she herself is not an explicit advocate of this theory), 'My relationship with Jeanette, who I lived with for many years, developed in such a way that she was responsible for doing the feelings'.

In *Men*, a book written for the general reader, Mary Ingham says: 'Women are beginning, however, to resent their continuing support of men. Without perhaps fully appreciating male lack of skill, both verbally and empathetically, women are expecting men to give the same emotional input into relationships that they do' (1985: 223). Men are allegedly lacking in both empathy and its language, as if they, not women, were closely ident-ified with the pre-linguistic. Relationships need emotional labour, yet men have apparently been trained not to express emotion. Men are largely absent from the lives of young children, who therefore grow up emotionally supported by women. Because boys learn to separate from their mothers without finding a father ready to pass on emotional skills, unlike their sisters, they are not given much opportunity to learn them. Men's absence, and inexperience, perpetuate the situation, so that boys grow up unable to provide intramasculine emotional support (except perhaps in sport and war, which therefore become particularly attractive).

The potential for conflict is obvious. As a woman friend of mine likes to put it, men have a lot of emotional housekeeping to do (Agnes Heller (1979: 199) also uses the phrase in her book on the emotions). Emotional support is not the whole story. As we shall see, some men (soldiers and killers for example) positively embrace emotional obliviousness. Their power, as Hollway (1984) says, derives partly from this cultivated occlusion of self-reflection. Theirs is only an extreme form of something widespread, a refusal to allow that emotion is actually and permissibly sayable for men. Emotion is not simply an inner event. Whole areas of our lives are constituted out of emotional relations: politics, economics and culture, to begin with. A lack of emotional development might result in complex social structures whose forms were a kind of social pathology. The issue is not whether people actually have emotions, but whether they are aware of them, and to what degree. Educating the emotions means at least two quite different things: learning that certain objects, situations and people are part of specific networks of emotion, and learning what they entail in consequent words and actions. Strictly speaking, emotional silences and states of oblivion are not conditions of absent emotion; they are conditions of absent awareness.

Contemporary philosophers and psychologists show us that emotion is rational, aware, educable and capable of interrupting and even suspending some cognitive processes if its demands become too great as a result of trauma and mistreatment. What might the consequences be for modern men? Some postmodernist theories can be interpreted as an attempt to answer this question without naming it as men's problem. The theories of the sublime (including versions of it like Julia Kristeva's theory of the 'chora', the pre-linguistic maternal space out of which signification arises) are, albeit in their different ways, investigations of the role of emotion in the linguistification of thought. Yet all these theories still treat emotion as a phenomenon belonging to the singular subject. Emotion, however, is not so simply private. The switching off and frozenness of men's feelings may be a constitutive element of social formations as well as individual male psyches. The male violence that forms a horizon for the psychoanalytic encounter between male analyst and male analysand is a disturbance of men's relations with one another. If those relations are partly figured as structures of feeling, then we should look for ways in which relations between men are inscribed within theories of the grounds of self-consciousness, language and representation. But first we need to look in more detail at the way men have represented emotional dysfunction within literary and theoretical representations of subjectivity.

MEN SWITCH OFF

The young man interviewed by Tim Beneke (1989) who could just turn off his emotions when he didn't want to acknowledge an unpleasant feeling of unimportance in the eyes of a beautiful woman seemed to be capable of a deliberate self-forgetting. The young man thinks of emotion as an internal machine that can be switched off. Is that the case or are emotions still there unacknowledged and possibly out of his control altogether? Whatever the mechanism, the result is stark. He can contemplate rape as a painless experience for a woman. What does it mean to switch off one's emotions? How is it represented to consciousness and what sort of consciousness does it produce? Is this what the men's movement mean when they say modern men are out of touch with their feelings? Dorothy Richardson wrote: 'a lifetime might well be spent in annotating the male novelists, filling out the vast oblivious in them' (1979: IV, 240). Could obliviousness be a key element in certain masculine pathologies? Such an idea has widespread currency amongst feminists and feminist men. A cartoon sold as a postcard in London a few years ago, titled 'Dealing with the Male Ego', shows a clean-cut young man saying to an equally smartly dressed young woman, 'I just want to shut out the world and lose myself in you, babe'. The woman is saying, 'That's very sweet of you', while thinking, 'Not another emotionally dependent bloke looking for a mother figure!' The man wants to forget himself, become oblivious to self-consciousness, and switch off the inward gaze. Only a female lover can help. She is aware that he can only do it if she takes over the responsibility for emotional awareness, and becomes mother. It is misleading to say as Sartre does, that 'a consciousness becoming emotional is rather like a consciousness dropping asleep' (1963: 78). Only if it turns off its awareness is that true, and unlike a sleep walker, it is even then still capable of much of what passes for conscious, intentional action.

Men's writing offers innumerable instances where this state of self-forgetfulness is actively courted through the experience of a strong emotion which overwhelms consciousness. The male lover on the postcard hopes sexual intimacy with a woman will wipe out his self-consciousness. In the following scenes from an American private-eye novel, *An Infinite Number of Monkeys*, a novel which is a little more self-conscious than most but typical enough, and satisfactory enough, to win the prize for the best first private-eye novel in 1986, sex with a woman helps a man switch off his feelings and embrace obliviousness. Passionate sex with a woman is an anaesthetic, not a stimulant. These passages might have come from a hundred contemporary novels written by men for popular consumption, novels with no pretensions to art, but plenty of pretensions to masculine authenticity. The man (or private eye – the associations with gazes and private languages will be obvious) meets the woman and describes her:

> She wasn't tall, perhaps five foot four, but she moved with the grace of a much taller long-legged woman. Her eyes were an impossible, unbelievable green with an iridescent blue undercast to them, and were set wide apart beneath her broad forehead. Her cheekbones were classically sculptured, worthy of either of the Hepburn ladies, and her mouth was full and almost pouty and begged to be kissed and nibbled and caressed, and her blond hair had a just-tossed look that made me want to put my face in it and leave it there for a long time. Yet there was a sadness about her, a sort of bruised and aching look that for me added up to the overwhelming sensuality of one of the most striking women I'd ever seen in my life. Her look was not inviting; just the opposite, it said she'd been hurt a lot and please keep your distance.
>
> (Roberts 1989: 8–9)

Less crude than many such literary descriptions of beautiful women, which often only gaze at the obvious erogenous zones, it still manages to represent her face as an erotic map of her body. The judgements are the explicitly subjective responses of the male narrator to the woman, responses that are not as simply a desire for sexual intercourse as the narrative would have them appear. The eyes for example are 'impossible, unbelievable'. Belief is an important component of this masculine sexuality and her eyes are exciting

192

because they are a challenge to his belief that they can be possible, that he can believe in them, and also an extreme threat that cannot be acknowledged to exist. Eyes are overdetermined as sexually open legs, windows of the soul, and the power of the gaze. Her gaze is ultimately unbearable because its sexual invitation not only beckons inward to her soul, it also gazes inward at his naked self. The fear of her gaze adds to his wish for something much more desirable than sexual intercourse. He wants to lose himself in her, to immerse his face in her hair, and efface his own awareness of body and consciousness by cancelling out his own face and eyes. He needs 'stratagems to thwart the gaze's bedazzlement' (Kristeva 1987: 360), and so looks to her hair to calm him, like a canary who falls asleeps when a cloth is thrown over its cage. How unerotic this trance in which erotic stimulation is suspended seems (very like Stephen Dedalus's aesthetic stasis in *A Portrait of the Artist as a Young Man*), when we look closely at his wishes. Her overwhelming beauty, from which he longs to hide his eyes, produces such strong feeling he wants to switch it off.

These motifs are developed in the later obligatory bedroom scene. Usually such scenes entirely ignore the man's own self-consciousness of his reactions and feelings, while stressing the appearance and behaviour of the woman partner at length. This scene opens with the lovemaking finished and the reflective voice of the narrator commenting on the 'little affectionate kisses' the woman is giving his chest and neck. Unusually, we are offered a little reflexive comment on the male narrator's self-consciousness, comment that reveals a fear of feeling too much:

> there was no come-on in the kisses, just the affection, and it felt monstrous pleasant, as if a persistent and chronic itch had finally been scratched; it felt even better than the sex had (if such a thing were possible, because sex always feels good and sex with someone who obsesses you feels better than that).
>
> (Roberts 1989: 69)

This affectionate touching feels better than the sex, but the parenthesis indicates an unease about admitting such a heretical possibility, as does the revealing use of 'monstrous' to describe the affectionate contact. This affectionate, nurturing care feels better than sexual intercourse, yet also threatening. Consciousness of the woman's non-sexual affection is what he really wanted, but the wanting is ironized as an itch, as a mere bodily reflex satisfied, warding off any suggestion that this is a mutual encounter of conscious subjects. The treatment of the sexual act which follows this moment of affection is similarly narrated as a matter of the physical movement of bodies, mostly the woman's:

> and when I finally penetrated the warm wetness of her she arched her body against me as though a duality was at work, as though she wanted

193

to resist me almost as much as she wanted all of me she could get inside her, and though we strained and moved against each other for a long while, she didn't climax until I eased myself off her and out of her . . . she climbed astride me and with her hands put me inside her again and this time there was no hesitation, this time there were no qualms, just a hunger that was equally sharp in both of us . . . and within moments I reached my own apex, so good that it seemed as though I'd never done it before, so good that it made me wish it was my first time.

(ibid.: 70)

There is considerable speculation about what the woman feels (resistance, desire, qualms), yet little about what the narrator might know with at least some certainty, his own feelings. Why doesn't the male narrator say more about his feelings or fantasies during intercourse than simply the general and evasive comment that it was 'so good that it seemed as though I'd never done it before'? Maybe he has no language for them and isn't able to know what they are? Sex scenes are aimed at a voyeuristic male reader, so the narrator needs to remain a fairly empty vessel into which the reader can project himself, but it would be a mistake to consider it only in that way. The narrator doesn't talk much about his feelings for the same reason that he has never done 'it' before. This feels like the first time because it is the first time he is conscious of certain feelings of dependence and need (the monstrous itch that he is only just able to acknowledge). Even now he is only tentatively able to become self-conscious of the feelings he has for his lover. This male lover's body is usually an instrument, not the place where emotion, language and sexuality emerge. This private-eye novel records a moment when oblivion is tentatively set aside and is therefore unusual. More often the record of sensations and pleasures in the woman's imagined feelings are the sum total of this heterosexual erotic masculinity.

Emotional oblivion can be a prelude to violence as Tim Beneke's (1989) young man showed us. Numbness or indifference to the pain of others is a useful prerequisite for male violence. A clear example of the dangers of such self-embraced emotional oblivion is presented by Klaus Theweleit in his study of men and militarism, *Male Fantasies*, where he examines the writings of men who were experienced killers in the German Freikorps, the freelance military clubs he claims (it is a much contended claim) formed the basis of the Nazi SS. Discussing a passage from a Freikorps novel, Theweleit concludes:

The soldier male murders differently [to the Communist enemy]. He's not altogether present. One might say that he is *intensely absent*. He doesn't really murder. . . . Yes, the men pulled the triggers, but not as an act of will; they were *somewhere else entirely* in their minds . . . but where? [ellipses in original]

(Theweleit 1987: 203)

194

Theweleit's murderous modern soldiers suffer a kind of emotional overload which leads to obliviousness and even total self-forgetfulness. The overload of emotion trips the fuses and no emotion can get through. Intense emotion can result in its opposite: emotional numbness.

The serial killer Dennis Nilsen describes a very similar experience to Theweleit's soldiers: 'I seem not to have participated [in the killings], merely stood by and watched them happen – enacted by two other players – like a central camera' he wrote in response to the repeated requests to go over the details with the authorities (Masters 1986: 144). Nilsen's necrophilia gave him the greatest pleasure: 'I thought only of the sublime pleasure these feelings gave me. . . . The pure primitive man of the dream world killed these men' (ibid.: 260). And he insists: 'There was no sadistic pleasure in killing. I killed them as I would like to be killed myself. . . . If I did it to others I could experience the death act over and over again' (ibid.: 277). Cameron and Frazer (1987) draw attention to Nilsen's use of Romantic categories of subjectivity, especially the gaze, to represent his own murderousness. His pleasures are sublime and he achieves them mainly by gazing on the corpse, whose objectivity in death doubly confirms his own subjectivity. I shall suggest that the sublime is a term for the self-awareness of extreme emotional states, but first we need to consider more generally the terms modern men artists have used for the self-awareness of strong passions and their absences.

Modern literature and philosophy both manifest similar fascinations with emotional obliviousness, but, unlike the popular fiction, are much more concerned to question it. T.S. Eliot, creator of many of the paradigms of mid-century literary studies, frequently returned to this very issue. Indeed he almost makes this a mark of the modernist (and perhaps his traditional predecessors also) in his essay 'Hamlet' (first published in 1919): 'The intense feeling, ecstatic or terrible, without an object or exceeding an object, is something which every person of sensibility has known; it is doubtless a subject of study for pathologists' (Eliot 1975: 49). The pathologists were not to be allowed exclusive rights on this experience of being overwhelmed by excessive emotion. Eliot developed a poetic technology for the careful handling of emotion – impersonality. The artist could treat his own emotions the way a scientist treats the chemical agents in laboratory experiments where the chemical reaction depends on an inert catalytic substance. The mind can act as a catalyst, 'the shred of platinum' (ibid.: 41), during poetic experiments: 'The elements which enter the presence of the transforming catalyst, are of two kinds: emotions and feelings' (ibid.: 41). Emotion is dangerous stuff, explosive like the gases in the experiments Eliot was remembering from his schooldays. The poet handles them with great care, careful not to be contaminated: 'the more perfect the artist, the more completely separate in him will be the man who suffers and the mind which creates' (ibid.: 41). Despite the danger they pose, emotions are vital to the poet because they are the very foundation of the poet's activity, the material from which the poem is constructed. Somehow they must be converted by the artist into what his collaborator on *The Waste Land*, Ezra Pound, called 'equations for the human emotions' (Pound 1952: 14). In the *The Waste Land* one of the voices describes an experience very like that of the private eye. Coming back from a hyacinth garden with a girl, the speaker was overwhelmed with feeling and could neither speak nor see, felt neither dead nor alive, and forgot everything he knew. The poem never specifies the gender of the speaker, and treats the moment as an exemplary modern experience of sterility. It fits very well alongside the masculine experiences of emotional oblivion as a consummation devoutly to be wished.

Jim, Wendy Hollway's (1984) interviewee who had trouble with the frozenness of feelings, suffered from emotions he couldn't switch on, rather than feelings which switched off his consciousness. Many modernist and postmodernist men writers also describe a struggle to switch emotions on, and put man and mind back in touch. Art is a means of bringing emotions into the light of reason and language, a way of 'doing them', to echo Sam, another of Hollway's informants. The poet Robert Creeley said in an interview what many modernist poets have believed to be true of poetry: 'It's all an attempt to articulate some complex of feelings that are gained through the writing, that are otherwise not to be gained' (Creeley 1973: 102). Without poetry the complex of feelings will not be 'gained'. Robert Creeley's language of gain is significant. Emotional articulation needs to be struggled for, and once achieved becomes a valuable possession. Amerigo, the Italian prince in *The Golden Bowl* is contemptuous of 'the doing by the woman of the thing that gave her away' (James 1966: 61) because unguarded emotional expression is a gift of one's self in a capitalist society where all human relations are based on gain and possession: 'It was her nature, it was her life, and the man could always expect it without lifting a finger. This was *his*, the man's, any man's, position and strength' (ibid.: 61). A man would invest his emotions wisely, not give them away. If poetry is the articulation and maintenance of feeling, then it can be a means of avoiding the contempt of men like the prince, by making emotional revelation a valuable commodity whose aesthetic value can be claimed to transcend mere financial worth. Without poetry, or some other art, emotion remains invisible or inaccessible. W.B. Yeats put it firmly in his essay 'The Symbolism of Poetry':

> An emotion does not exist, or does not become perceptible and active among us, till it has found its expression, in colour or in sound or in form, or in all of these, and because no two modulations or arrangements of these evoke the same emotion, poets and painters and musicians and in a less degree because their effects are momentary, day and night and cloud and shadow, are continually making and unmaking mankind.
>
> (Yeats 1980: 46–7)

In the second 'Duino Elegy', Rainer Maria Rilke presents the loss of feeling as a specifically modern failing compared to what was possible in the classical world, and to what the angelic figures of possibility can still manage:

> But we, when moved by deep feeling, evaporate; we
> breathe ourselves out and away; from moment to moment
> our emotion grows fainter, like a perfume.
>
> (Rilke 1987: 156–7)

> (Denn wir, wo wir fühlen, verflüchtigen; ach wir
> atmen uns aus und dahin; von Holzglut zu Holzglut
> geben wir schwächern.)

No object can sustain the emotion he wants to feel. Yet Rilke obviously considers poetry a useful temporary expedient for the maintenance of emotion. The goal would be, as the critic Carl Rapp claims was the goal of the later William Carlos Williams, to find: 'a form that would permit feeling to be and at the same time represent the complete triumph of subjectivity over its own manifestation' (Rapp 1984: 111).

The Romantic theory of the sublime can be interpreted as a representation for consciousness of the moment when strong feelings induce oblivion and produce a consequent desire to shut out the emotion-provoking external stimulus. For Kant (1952: 91) the sublime is 'a momentary check to the vital forces . . . an emotion that seems to be no sport, but dead earnest in the affairs of the imagination'. It emerges when discrete representation fails:

> The beautiful in nature is a question of the form of the object, and this consists in limitation, whereas the sublime is to be found in an object even devoid of form, so far as it immediately involves, or else by its presence provokes, a representation of *limitlessness*, yet with a super-added thought of its totality.
>
> (ibid.: 90)

The sublime makes the mind feel inadequate because these infinities cannot be adequately presented in perceptual terms. The result is a kind of mental vertigo. A note of qualification is needed here in the midst of all this talk of minds, ideas and reason. Kant insists that 'we say of a man who remains unaffected in the presence of what we consider sublime, that he has no *feeling* [*Gefühl*]' (ibid.: 116). The recent revival of interest in the sublime has been due to a postmodern fascination with Kant's admission of the failure of representation marked by the sublime.

Kant's description of the sublime experience makes it a moment of alternating consciousness and unconsciousness. The mind encounters something beyond its powers of comprehension, something which signifies the limitations of its conceptual understanding. The mind reels and then recovers itself by turning inward because it 'has been incited to abandon sensibility'. Then the mind triumphs over its setback by reassuring itself that the problem is not the overwhelming, external experience but the limitations of external experience itself (the 'intuitions' or sensory information that are all the mind can know); its failure to provide representations for the mind's infinite capacity for understanding. What we learn from the sublime is that 'sublimity, therefore, does not reside in any of the things of nature, but only in our own mind' (ibid.: 114). For example, the absence of evidence of the full pattern of nature's laws becomes paradoxical proof of them. Kant has taken an experience like that of the private eye, or the murderous 'I', overwhelmed by feeling, and analysed it as a mini-version of the intellectual crisis brought on by the new post-theological age of scientific enquiry, whose laws of space and time reach far beyond the limits of the human ability to verify their embodiment in the material world. The sublime becomes a name for the self-awareness peculiar to states of emotional overload.

Postmodernist aesthetics returns to the sublime, ostensibly to open out the metaphysics of representation, but with a renewed preoccupation with states of liminal subjectivity. A disturbance of traditional certainties is attributed to the necessary condition of subjectivity, rather than the lessening authority of white male intellectuals, by reconfiguring emotional pathology as linguistic indeterminacy. In the best-known account of postmodernism, *The Postmodern Condition*, Jean-François Lyotard identifies the sublime with postmodernity and describes it as a form of masochism. His description interweaves many of the themes we have traced in the formation of masculine subjectivities, although his text remains unconscious of the degree to which his metaphoric structures are gendered:

> The sublime sentiment [*le sentiment sublime*], which is also the senti-
> ment of the sublime, is, according to Kant, a strong and equivocal
> emotion: it carries with it both pleasure and pain. Better still, in it
> pleasure derives from pain. Within the tradition of the subject, which
> comes from Augustine and Descartes and which Kant does not radi-
> cally challenge, this contradiction, which some would call neurosis or
> masochism, develops as a conflict between the faculties of a subject, the
> faculty to conceive of something and the faculty to 'present' some-
> thing. Knowledge exists if, first, the statement [*l'énoncé*] is intelligible,
> and second, if 'cases' can be derived from the experience which 'corre-
> sponds' to it.
>
> (Lyotard 1984: 77)

This interpretation of Kant's *Critique of Judgement* makes the sublime a neurotic pathology resulting from the failure to produce a sign for an inner conception. Such a conception is therefore wholly inarticulate, a form of subjectivity inaccessible to language. Lyotard's sublime could be a private language of emotion. The emotion of the sublime arises when the intellect is trapped inside itself without any expressive outlet, because 'the imagination fails to present an object which might, if only in principle, come to match a concept'. According to Lyotard, the World, infinity or a state of pure simplicity would all be such concepts. Each one is also an example of an extreme of subjectivity's ambition to dominate everything, whether by inclusion (knowledge of the infinite) or exclusion (knowing what all possible contaminants of a pure simplicity are). The sublime is a feeling of failed relationship, an inarticulacy hiding a megalomaniacal intellectual project of complete understanding, and therefore complete elimination of whatever is other to the subject. The sublime is the natural condition of all those would-be rulers of the universe like Mongul in the *Superman* comic story I discussed earlier (see p. 37), would-be rulers whom our comic-book super-men have to defeat. Lyotard's discourse echoes the traditional appropriation of maternal metaphors to describe men's creative labour. The sublime is a conception which cannot be born (the pun insists upon itself). For moder-nists, says Lyotard:

> The emphasis can be placed . . . on the power of the faculty to conceive, on its 'inhumanity' so to speak (it was the quality Apollinaire demanded of modern artists), since it is not the business of our understanding whether or not human sensibility or imagination can match what it conceives. The emphasis can also be placed on the increase of being and the jubilation which result from the invention of new rules of the game, be it pictorial, artistic, or any other.
>
> (Lyotard 1984: 80)

If conception is inhuman it is so only for men. The increase of being is a reminder of the human process of childbirth from which men are for ever excluded, and for which they repeatedly claim creative substitutes. Lyotard's insistence on spelling out the genitive equivalent of the phrase, 'sublime sentiment', underscores the extent to which the sublime is a form of pre-linguistic emotion. The sublime appears when emotional understanding is not matched by the intellect. Postmodernism is in part a reactive shadow of feminism constructed by highly self-conscious men, aware of the disturb-ances of rationality within their discourses.

EMOTIONAL POLITICS

Thomas Mann's artist hero, Tonio Kroger, utters a typically modern double-edged sentiment when he says: 'Spring is a bad time for work; and why? Because we are feeling too much. Nobody but a beginner imagines that he who creates must feel' (Mann 1955: 152). Tonio Kroger is an artist whose art results in his exclusion from the healthy emotional lives of the bourgeois world around him. The passage that I've quoted is part of a very long speech delivered to another artist, a woman, who finally replies in exasperation: 'You are a bourgeois on the wrong path, a bourgeois manqué' (ibid.: 161). The male artist who dismisses emotion is shown by a woman that he secretly longs to feel it. But is his woman friend right? Is emotion bourgeois?

The widespread use of discourses of emotion in political life might suggest that emotion is bourgeois in the broadest sense, a central feature of the politics of modernity. Benedict Anderson explains modern nationalism as the emergence of 'imagined communities' that 'command such profound emotional legitimacy' (1983: 13–14) they can provide motives for war and self-sacrifice on behalf of the nation. 'Amor patriae' is similar to 'the other affections, in which there is always an element of fond imagining' (ibid.: 140). When news of the end of the Communist Party's monopoly of power in Czechoslovakia was announced, a BBC radio journalist asked one of the celebrating crowd in Wenceslas Square a question which was broadcast as part of that day's news report. 'What are you feeling?' she said. 'We have freedom. It is wonderful,' replied the anonymous man. This display of emotion was major political news. For much of Prime Minister Margaret Thatcher's time in office, newspapers reported her supposed emotional reactions to events as if the emotion itself was a major political occurrence. A typical headline would read: MAGGIE FURY AT LONRHO AFFAIR (*Daily Mail*, 3 April 1989). Why is her anger news? Why do emotional responses matter in politics? Are we meant to fear her wrath as we might fear that of an absolutist monarch? Emotional expressions permeate the ordinary discourse of politics as it is presented in accessible form to the public. George Bush was asked about his emotions after an important summit meeting with Mikhail Gorbachev in Malta, and replied: 'It's hard for me to find words for my feelings about it. I'm not an articulate emotionalist' (BBC Radio). To be in politics you clearly don't have to be an 'articulate emotionalist' (Stephen Dedalus's clumsy friend Temple is a self-confessed 'emotionalist' (Joyce 1988: 205) – not much of a recommendation as far as the novel sees it), but a discourse of emotion is apparently expected of the news media and will be supplied by the commentators if the politicians are tongue-tied. These emotions people in the news are asked to express seem to provide some guarantee of the significance of political actions.

The playwright Edward Bond, who criticized the actors working on his play *The Woman* for 'hugging feelings to themselves' and 'gazing at themselves', is alert to the risk of calling all emotion bourgeois, as Tonio Kroger's friend did. Bond tries to describe the social character of emotion as a possibility to be chosen:

At the first run-through of *The Woman* at the NT I was astonished at the way the acting forced the play into the ground, buried it in irrelevant subjectivity. Much of the acting still belonged to the nineteenth century. The company were acting emotions, hugging feelings to themselves, gazing at themselves, speaking to themselves, even when they shouted. . . . A concept, an interpretation (of the situation, not the character) must be applied to an emotion, and it is this concept or interpretation or idea that is acted. This relates the character to the social event so that he becomes its story teller. When this is done emotions are transferred to the surface. Instead of being hidden in the heart or the gut (or other corners of the bourgeois soul) they go to the hands, feet, face, head, and become living, creative energy.

(Bond 1978: 8–9)

This can be compared with the Jungian analyst James Hillman's reference to his first book, a scholarly review of modern theories of emotion:

In my book *Emotion* (1961) emotion and affect are differentiated. I conceived emotion as a total event of the personality, activating all levels and therefore a symbolic kind of transformed consciousness with 'body' in it . . . emotion raises, transforms and symbolizes. Emotion is essentially a purposive creative state which has affect in it.

(Hillman 1970: 130–1)

Hillman's account comes close to identifying emotion too much with the self, because his welcome emphasis on the body and teleological subjectivity seems to preclude emotional interaction. He tries to overcome this by arguing that because the unconscious is 'collective', 'then the unconscious could no longer be conceptually confined within the individual and emotions would belong to the unconscious aspect of our entire situation rather than only to the individual's subjectivity' (Hillman 1968: 93). This attractive attempt to describe the social structures of emotion and their complex relation to reflective awareness too readily abandons consciousness, and makes it hard to imagine emotion playing an intelligent part in social and political life. Bond's description is valuable because he is not working within the usual frameworks of psychology, philosophy or literary theory. Emotion can be turned inward or outward, and so depends on interpretation as well as the body. Only if both are in play is an actor's portrayal of an emotion going to be a social emotion and therefore work theatrically. Brecht, who is usually remembered for his suspicion of theatrical exploitation of the infectiousness of emotion, actually believed something closer to Bond: 'the epic theatre is not against the emotions, it tries to examine them, and is not satisfied just to stimulate them. It is the orthodox theatre which sins by dividing reason and emotion' (Brecht 1974: 162).

Yvonne Rainer, the former dancer, and maker of postmodern films, offers further elucidation of these points from the standpoint of a performer who has had to formulate a working hypothesis about the social character of emotion. As a choreographer she is best known for *Trio A*, a dance with a series of transitions lacking the standard 'accents' of classical ballet, occurring too fast for the eye to assimilate all at once and compelling the viewer to respond in non-visual as well as visual terms. Her working principle as a choreographer, the 'mind is a muscle', was a dancer's version of the mind as a system of libido, a system with no place for emotion. Reflecting on the reasons for her transition into film making in a letter written after the completion of her first full-length movie, she makes clear how far she had moved from the muscular mind:

> As a dancer the unique nature of my body and movement makes a personal statement, but . . . dancing could no longer encompass or 'express' the new content in my work, i.e., the emotions . . . dance was not as specific – meaning-wise – as language. . . . Dance is *ipso facto* about *me* (the so-called kinesthetic response of the spectator notwithstanding, it only rarely transcends that narcissistic-voyeuristic duality of doer and looker); whereas the area of the emotions must necessarily directly concern both of us. This is what allowed me permission to start manipulating what at first seemed like blatantly personal and private material. But the more I get into it the more I see how such things as rage, terror, desire, conflict, et al., are not unique to my experience the way my body and its functioning are. I now – as a consequence – feel much more connected to my audience.
>
> (Rainer 1974: 238)

Like Bond, Rainer discusses emotion in terms rarely used by the professional theorists. Her sense that emotions are a language, a space for interaction, and yet still bodily and personal, is a good clue to the way to think of the social character of emotion.

Rainer associates language and emotion. Rom Harré and a number of collaborators have recently argued for a social constructionist theory of emotion which sounds like the answer to what we are looking for. Harré argues that emotions depend on the context in which they appear, the local language and moral order. He then proposes a method derived from ordinary language philosophy: examining how words and phrases for emotions are actually used in different contexts. Emotion is not interestingly bodily at all:

> Emotion concepts . . . are not purely psychological: they presuppose concepts of social relationships and institutions, and concepts belonging to systems of judgement, moral, aesthetic and legal. In using emotion words we are able, therefore, to relate behaviour to the complex background in which it is enacted, and so to make human actions intelligible.
>
> (Harré 1986: 30)

This approach is fine, but limited, as the observations on emotion by the non-professionals (the artists) suggest. Harré's description of the social

202

system imagines it all at one level, the intellectual assessment of situations. A more rounded account of the social character of emotion will need to describe how emotions link people together in other ways also.

One celebrated description of postmodernism describes its condition as a 'waning of affect' (Jameson 1984: 61). Fredric Jameson's formula assumes that the emotions produced in otherwise similar situations can alter over time, something Rom Harré also implies when he insists that most emotions are not universal but local to a culture and a history. For my purposes a comparison of modern ideas of emotion with those of classical Greece would be especially interesting because it was a culture where the importance of social bonds, of citizenship and the polis, were well understood, and because it is a culture very far distant from our own, yet extremely well documented. Harré's claim that emotions are culturally specific is a warning that the problems of translation are likely to be severe, given the great distance between our culture and theirs, despite the wealth of scholarship. For the non-specialist there are almost insuperable difficulties in drawing conclusions from Greek sources. Relying on secondary accounts and translations I shall simply draw attention to the thoroughness with which Greek philosophers understand emotion as a social phenomenon.

A.W. Price in *Love and Friendship in Plato and Aristotle* shows that for Aristotle even *eudaimonia* (well-being), the aim of one's life, was an irreducibly social concept. It is 'not success in pursuing one's own projects whatever they may be' (Price 1989: 127) but is to be found in social relations like loving friendships, in which one is able to identify with the friend 'by making his acts also one's own as realizations of choices that one shares with him' (ibid.: 130): 'His activity displays the character we share, and the fact that we share it' (ibid.: 124). This emphasis can be found in most of Aristotle's discussions of emotion. Like Plato, Aristotle thinks of the passions as educable and, as a corollary, that it is possible to remain in an emotionally undeveloped condition. Some emotions are only fitting for youth. According to the *Nicomachean Ethics*, shame is appropriate only to the young because 'they live by passion and therefore commit many errors, but are restrained by shame' (Aristotle 1980: 105). One passion can restrain others. It is possible to live according to the passions, but this does not mean that one is living according to an involuntary nature. Aristotle is at pains to stress that the passions are voluntary. We choose to perform the acts that arise from anger, for example. A passion is not a wholly determining cause of one's actions. Aristotle clearly recognizes the cognitive element of emotion. Rage, for example, is usually the result of 'apparent injustice', a socially interpreted event. His account of pride in the *Nicomachean Ethics* is not an account of an abstracted mental or physical function, but of the proud man: 'It makes no difference whether we consider the state of character [dispositions] or the man characterized by it'. Pride can only be fully understood in terms of its social action. This favourable account of pride is presented from society's standpoint, not as a judgement on the behaviour of the man who feels it. His pride is society's pride in him. The negative accounts of pride in post-Renaissance philosophical discussions of emotion are a mark of the shift from social to individual theories of emotion in modern times. Aristotle views it as a valuable passion because of its role in leadership. Modern philosophers condemn it because they no longer recognize the importance of its social role, and indeed often fail to recognize the relevance of such considerations when constructing models of the self. For the Greeks, emotion was relational. For the moderns it is what hinders relation, and is intensely and divisively personal. By contrast, emotion often appears central to Aristotle's conception of social life, as in this summary of moral virtue:

> For instance, both fear and confidence and appetite and anger and pity and in general pleasure and pain may be felt both too much and too little, and in both cases not well; but to feel them at the right times, with reference to the right objects, towards the right people, with the right motive, and in the right way, is what is both intermediate and best, and this is characteristic of virtue.

(ibid.: 38)

Virtue is a form of social feeling.

In *The Republic* Plato describes a tripartite soul, in terms of three classes of society. Reason corresponds to the ruler, appetite to the merchants, and a middle term, *thumos* or spirit, is 'reason's natural auxiliary'. *Thumos* is in modern terms emotion. The auxiliaries, a restraining force somewhat like a modern bureaucracy, carry out the decisions of the ruler and police them. As psychology it was questioned both by Aristotle and even, in a sense, by Plato himself in other dialogues. Its interest for us lies in its emphasis on the importance of a process rather like emotion understood in social terms. Emotion, understood in social terms, becomes the active agent of intelligence. This enables Paul Ricoeur to recycle the concept of *thumos* as a name for the otherwise hard-to-describe workings of certain social structures of feeling.

Greek psychological and social thought is too enmeshed in hermeneutical problems to make a direct contribution to a theory of emotion. We need to turn to contemporary societies and political events like that which prompted the ecstatic demonstrator in Wenceslas Square to tell the interviewer, 'We have freedom – it is wonderful.' In doing so he answered a question about feelings with a political observation about the collective condition of the crowd and the country. Emotion was evident in the tone of his voice, but his answer only partially conformed to the interviewer's framework of expectations ('wonderful' but also 'freedom'). The demonstrator's wonder was not just a cue for the audience's shared identification with otherwise hard-to-comprehend events, but part of what Raymond Williams called a 'structure of feeling'.

What does Williams mean by a structure of 'feeling'? Although he used the term constantly throughout his career he seems to have given little thought to ontological or epistemological questions about emotion, relying instead on the commonplace assumption that emotion lies beyond the borders of reason. The originality of the concept of the structure of feeling lies not so much in his valorization of feeling (common enough in the literary milieu in which he trained) but in his association of this value with social structure and social change. A recent article by Miranda Fricker defends the emphasis on the importance of feelings in the women's movement in similar terms. Anger for example is a highly political emotion. In his lecture notes, *Anthropology from a Pragmatic Point of View*, Kant says that at least one form of anger, the 'desire for vengeance' is a straightforward analogue of 'appetite for justice [*Recht*]' (Kant 1974: 137). In her study of Kant, Susan Meld Shell (1980: 122) points out that Kant believes anger 'underlies morality. By universalizing anger, right [justice] transforms a physically destructive self-forgetting into a morally constructive one'. A recent critique of expressivism in contemporary psychotherapy, Carol Tavris's *Anger: The Misunderstood Emotion*, argues that rage is essential to launch new political movements. Anger is needed because 'in the beginning, there is no word: there is only private, unarticulated experience' (Tavris 1982: 248). Only anger can urge people forward to unite and begin to understand how change might be possible. A 'group becomes defined by its anger' (ibid.: 248). She emphasizes the political importance of anger because she fears that in a culture where therapy replaces politics, anger may become an end in itself, given the commonplace therapeutic belief that inner feelings are one's authentic inner being and need full expression, whatever the social relations in which one is placed. Like Tavris, Fricker is also careful not to celebrate some idealized pure feeling. She sees the need to avoid stigmatizing emotions as mere resultants of external conditions like language and social structure (as Adorno and Horkheimer (1979) do in their reference to the 'proficient apparatus' of the moderns whose emotions are all pre-scripted), or by an unconscious structured in early childhood and working according to fixed laws. Fricker says:

> Emotions and their interpretations certainly are conditioned to some extent, but they are not wholly *determined* as long as we do not fail to listen to each other's stories and question the suitability of the publicly available modes of interpretation. Only then may emotion become a political force for changing how we interpret the world. If we achieve this, then we can assert that our emotions – if we listen to them – are not only an expression of the world, but also active participants in how the world is shaped.
>
> (1991: 18)

Fricker's difficulty in making this case is that she can only assert, and not explain, what she claims is the manifest ability of emotion to resist dominant ideology better than reason. She says: 'to refute this would be to fly in the face of evidence, since CR [consciousness-raising] groups and other ways of listening to personal stories have brought about many changes of consciousness' (ibid.: 18). This still doesn't explain why emotion, and not reasoning, should be credited with the major role. Tavris, aware of the same difficulty, repeatedly emphasizes in a Humean fashion the need for reason to complement anger, to point out possibilities, choices, causes and above all strategies. Both writers effectively argue for the recognition and fostering of a reciprocal relation between emotion and reason.

Raymond Williams (1979: 157) uses the term 'structure of feeling' to describe what happens when a new cultural grouping emerges to challenge the existing social order. The group is linked by a common preoccupation with both forms of cultural expression and 'the deep community that makes communication possible', and its structure of feeling is formed by that deep community, whether or not it is aware of itself, because it 'is what is actually being lived, and not only what it is thought is being lived'. The structure of feeling is a state of unfinished social relations not yet capable of reflexive self-comprehension. It is 'a structural formation at the very edge of semantic availability' (Williams 1977: 134), because of its strong distinction from the 'official or received thought of a time'. So the structure of feeling becomes the zone of incomplete articulation, and a form of mediation between experience and language: 'The peculiar location of a structure of feeling is the endless comparison that must occur in the process of consciousness between the articulated and the lived' (ibid.: 167). The zone is comprised of 'what is not fully articulated, all that comes through as disturbance, tension, blockage, emotional trouble' (Williams 1979: 168).

Emotion need not be unsayable, unrepresentable and private – it can slowly emerge from the 'zone of incomplete articulation' through the construction of new social movements and their initial phases of self-comprehension in new art movements. It can be social without simply being a structure of manipulation as Adorno and Horkheimer assumed. Little has been said about the significance of the emotional dimension of the structure of feeling by contemporary theorists but the term itself now enjoys wide currency because it answers to an unfilled need for a theory of emotion in contemporary literary and cultural studies. Rachel Blau DuPlessis argues that: 'Female aesthetics begins when women take, investigate, the structures of feeling that are ours. And trying to take them, find also the conflict between these often inchoate feelings (coded as resistances . . .) and patriarchal structures of feeling' (1985: 267). Structures of feeling are the disputed territory of art, and they can be patriarchal structures.

Williams uses the term 'structure' to signify that this is an intersubjective (and in literature, intertextual) feeling that transcends individuals. A refusal to specify this structure in any more detail for the general case (Williams has plenty to say about specific instances) leaves a deliberate ambiguity in the term, an ambiguity exploited in its widespread current usage to mean anything social that is not specifically recognizable as a social structure, like a company or a political party. It implies both an aggregative structure resulting from the multiple contributions of many individual feelings and, more significantly, the organization by this general structure of certain relevant feelings experienced by individuals into socially active processes. One process is bottom up, the other top down, so they seem mutually exclusive, but it is likely that both poles of this opposition were meant to be included in Williams's concept.

Williams's theory of the importance of emotion for social change leaves much about emotion itself unclear. Is it simply pre-reflective consciousness or is it some kind of intersubjective bond, and if it is, how does it work? A possible answer to these questions can be found in Paul Ricoeur's little-known discussion of emotion in *Fallible Man* (1960) (it is not listed in the bibliographies of Lyons (1980), de Sousa (1987), Amelie Rorty (1980) or Fridja (1986), although de Sousa does list his book on Freud). Many of the features of emotion only recently established in the philosophical literature (that emotion has an intentional structure, can be rational, is educable, and can be a valuable form of relation to others) are anticipated by Ricoeur. He proposes the hypothesis that society is partially constituted by affective relations which are made tangible as the spheres of economics, politics and culture, because many of the emotions are essentially 'interhuman, social and cultural' (Ricoeur 1986: 111). He constructs his theory out of seemingly traditional elements: Plato's concept of *thumos* (usually translated as 'spirit' or 'feeling'), Kant's genealogy of passions in the *Anthropology*, and Hegel's history of *Geist* ('spirit') in *Phenomenology of Spirit*. The result is far from traditional. He demonstrates that some emotions are an integral part of all forms of social structure. He calls these emotions the passions to distinguish them from emotion proper, which belongs to the body. The passions are devoted to the will. Ricoeur doesn't maintain this distinction between the terms strictly, and I want to argue, like Robert Solomon, that the distinction is neither necessary nor sustainable, so I shall refer to the passions as emotions in what follows, in order to underline the possibility of using his ideas aspart of an account of masculine structures of feeling.

Ricoeur's argument begins with the claim that emotion and reason are reciprocal. He bases this on an observation, possibly derived from Hume, that:

> the power of knowing, by hierarchizing itself, truly engenders the *degrees* of feeling and pulls it out of its essential confusion. On the other hand, feeling indeed generates the *intention* of knowing on all its levels. The unity of sentir, of Fühlen, of feeling, is constituted in this mutual genesis.
>
> (Ricoeur 1986: 83)

Reason is able to clarify emotion, and emotion provides the drive behind reason. Emotion immerses us in the world, while reason separates us by objectifying the world, making distinct the divide between subject and object, knower and known. Since 'representation is not all that a *thing* is capable of' (ibid.: 112), emotion also has an important part to play in our relations with things. This is Ricoeur's way round Hume's consequent relegation of emotion from the intellectual plane because it is non-representational, and the subsequent relegation in Hegelian, and post-structuralist theory (which cannot imagine knowledge without representation).

In the *Anthropology* Kant distinguishes two sorts of passion, those of natural (innate) inclination, and those inclinations derived from human culture. By passion Kant means an emotion directed at others. There are three of these, passions for possessions, power and honour, in order of their sophistication. Kant actually calls them manias (*Sucht*) because, as Ricoeur puts it, Kant is interested in their fallen and therefore visible condition. Kant's relatively pedestrian exposition has not had a great influence on the philosophical tradition. Ricoeur perceptively seizes on the idea of cultural passions in order to make a fundamental point about emotion. Using Plato's idea that *thumos* mediates between reason and desire, he suggests that these passions are emotions in the role of *thumos*, and then concludes that these passions are 'a class of feelings that cannot be accounted for by a simple derivation from the vital feelings' or libido (it was this claim that led Ricoeur to write a hermeneutic study of Freud). These passions are not sublimations of instinct. For Freud, as one analyst describes it, 'instincts *represent* organismic stimuli; they are not these stimuli themselves. Ideation and affect *represent* instincts, and neither of the former should be confused with the latter' (Green 1983: 179). Ricoeur believes that not all affects represent instincts. The love of money may be partly anal fixation, but the equation of money and faeces does not exhaust the affective relations centring on money. Even Freud speaks of 'transformations of instinct'. At the end of *Freud and Philosophy*, where Ricoeur summarizes his ideas on the cultural passions, he interprets Freud's notion of transformation as a tacit acknowledgement that 'the regressive instinct of our desires does not replace a progressive genesis concerned with meanings, values, symbols' (Ricoeur 1970: 512).

Ricoeur then adds the third element of his argument, the Hegelian model of social development. Ricoeur proposes that each of these three passions constitutes a sphere of intentional objects of emotion (using another term from Hume), only one of which is actually a sphere of material things. His explanation of how this constitution takes place is strictly Hegelian, although he does not share Hegel's conviction that:

it is quite inadmissible for anyone to appeal simply to his feelings. He who does so withdraws from the sphere, common to all, of reasoned argument, of thought, of the matter in hand, into his particular subjectivity which, since it is essentially passive, is just as receptive of the worst and most irrational as it is of the reasonable and the good.

(Hegel 1971: 75)

The assumption that the emotions are passive, irrational and essentially individual sets Hegel apart from contemporary philosophers like William Lyons and Ronald de Sousa. Ricoeur is less opposed to this view but as far as the rationality of the passions is concerned, he thinks quite differently from Hegel. Take the case of the passions of 'having' which help form the sphere of economics:

We may say, then, that man becomes self-consciousness insofar as he experiences this economic objectivity as a new modality of his subjectivity and thus attains specifically human 'feelings' relative to the availability of things as things that have been worked upon and appropriated.

(Ricoeur 1970: 508)

Neither this sphere, nor those of power and culture, are constituted by libidinal cathexis (ibid.: 507). Passion is double-structured, both externally as an intention, and internally as an affect. Therefore passion does not work directly off perception as some theories of emotion seem to suppose. Instead its medium is the internalization of 'object-relations that pertain . . . to an economics, a politics, a theory of culture' (ibid.: 508). Agnes Heller describes something similar in *A Theory of Feelings* (1979) when she explains what she means by 'emotional housekeeping':

the feeling objectivations of every society, the tasks to be solved by the individual belonging to a given class or state and the dominating feelings developing along with these objectivations determine the 'frame', or rather area of movement, within which the individual may keep in order his 'emotional household'.

(Heller 1979: 199)

Her account's dependence on Hegelian Marxist terminology makes it hard to extend out of its specific context, and yet it does offer a useful gloss on Ricoeur's Hegelian account of feeling, giving his abstractions a little more tangibility.

Economics, politics and culture are in part constituted by passions, emotions capable of great range and complexity. For my purposes Ricoeur's description of power is especially relevant:

The objectification of man's power over man in an institution is the new *'object'* that can serve us as a guide in an immense world of feelings that manifest affectively the diverse modalities of human power according to which it is exercised, opposed, courted or under-gone. All the social roles that man may exercise initiate situations that political institutions consolidate into an object. Affectivity interiorises these situations as intersubjective feelings that modulate indefinitely on the theme of commanding-obeying. . . . There is no end to construct-ing and ordering the varieties of feelings that revolve around the exercise of power, through all the modalities of influence, control, direction, organization and compulsion. Psychological segmentation is endless; the ordering principle can come only from the 'object', which here is nothing other than the form in which the interhuman relation of power is realized.

(Ricoeur 1970: 119)

Our place in a political system is also a place in a network of feelings engaging with, and indeed helping form, that system. This sphere of power is not *necessarily* oppressive, even if its usual manifestations are Kant's manias: 'I can conceive of an authority which would propose to educate the individual to freedom, which would be a power without violence' (Ricoeur 1970: 120). Ricoeur assumes that violence occurs within the affective re-lations of power. Understanding male violence would require an under-standing of these emotional relations.

Ricoeur's theory is irreducibly speculative because of its dependence on Hegelian dialectic and the somewhat arbitrary tripartite division of the passions borrowed from Kant (presumably partly to lend authority to such daring proposals), but the basic analysis doesn't depend on this invocation of philosophical authorities. There could be more or less than three passions as long as they were relatively autonomous and yet built into a hierarchy. A looser, less dialectical model of human interaction emerging out of affective as well as rational relations would suffice. Ricoeur repeatedly stresses the significance of social interaction and the impossibility of thinking of it as simply based on visual recognition and its epistemological pretensions: 'A reflection that would end the intersubjective constitution of the thing at the level of the mutuality of seeing would remain abstract. We must add the economic, political and cultural dimension to objectivity' (Ricoeur 1970: 112). The desiring gaze, as libido-motivated power, is not sufficient to account for social structures.

Although Ricoeur's theory of affective social structures makes plain the limitations of explaining all emotional relations as regressive desire, and shows how social structures could be formed out of emotional relations as well as needs and ideology, it is by no means wholly convincing. Commentators have pointed out that Ricoeur also offers a limited descrip-tion of emotion – he prefers to consider emotion involuntary although, according to Robert Solomon, his own analysis often assumes that it is voluntary. Ricoeur participates in what Paul Connerton calls in another context the 'etherealization of the body' (Connerton 1988: 205) in modern social theory and, like Sartre, regards emotion as 'bad imagination' (Solomon 1979: 15). The fundamental difficulty is Ricoeur's wish to distinguish three forms of affect – emotion belonging to the body, the passions to the will, and feelings to imagination (by feelings Ricoeur means roughly the capacity to intuit complex images). This tripartite division threatens to reinstate an unnecessary dualism of mind and body, and obscure the achievement of his analysis. As Solomon notes, Ricoeur is drawn back repeatedly to consider emotion, but seems to do so reluctantly. In that way he shares a problematic with many modern philosophers for whom modernity is unthinkable without uneasy appeals to shared emotions. For Heidegger: 'Dasein as Being-in-the-World is "fearful". This fearfulness is not to be understood in an ontical [*ontisch*] sense as some factical [*factisch*] "individualized" disposition, but as an existential possibility of the essential state-of-mind of Dasein in general' (Heidegger 1962: 182). Michael Murray glosses such difficult passages as meaning that the experience of Being 'is precipitated by special moods like dread, radical boredom, or joy' (Murray 1978: 83). Adorno and Horkheimer (1979: 16) talk of the general modern fear of 'outsideness' as a defining characteristic of post-Enlightenment societies. For Bataille and Derrida (Derrida 1978: 256) the emotions of laughter can challenge dialectics. And for Fredric Jameson (1984: 61) postmodernism is a 'waning of affect'. Emotion is a means of describing fundamental existential orientations of a collective subject that cannot be easily attributed to any linguistically derived subjectivity.

We live within structures of emotion. Emotion is far more than sensibility, sensitivity or the behavioural display of bodily affect. Tears and rage are the exception. These networks of emotion are mostly below the level of self-conscious reflection, but we nevertheless learn them, embed our purposes in them, and treat them as substantive elements of our lives. The moment-by-moment consequences of interdependence are registered by emotion. We negotiate them through the reflexive activities of language in many ways. When we discuss feelings we are refining, adjusting and establishing the situation of our emotions. Our language and behaviour are permeated with emotion signs which we learn to interpret at both self-conscious and unself-aware levels. All speech has an emotional inflexion, however attenuated. Oliver Sacks recounts that he watched a group of aphasic patients, who were unable to understand words at all, laughing at President Reagan on television because they could still register the falsity of tone and feeling in his speech. Ordinary speech, he says, is 'embedded in an expressiveness which transcends the verbal' (Sacks 1986: 77), and much of this expressiveness is what we mean by emotion. In addition, much ordinary conversation is likely to be a showing and discussing of emotions to establish a significance rarely fully disclosed at once. The process is inherently one of exchange and dialogue, inherently intersubjective. Emotion does not depend for its existence on self-awareness but its power over us, the possibility that mania will replace passion, is much more likely if we are oblivious to the forces which surround us. Disturbances of emotion like those affecting men will have far-reaching social and political consequences.

MASCULINE STRUCTURES OF FEELING

A cross-cultural study of emotion in different European and Israeli societies showed that the differences between men and women were much greater than the cultural differences: 'we were surprised to see how similar both the antecedents and the responses for the various emotions were across all the cultures' (Scherer *et al.* 1986: 188). Men in most Western cultures are not supposed to show any emotion in public other than anger, except in certain ritually defined circumstances, because anger is masculine power at its most impressive. Otherwise men should control themselves, and maintain a firm jaw in the face of trouble. Women commonly can show any emotion except anger. From early childhood boys and girls learn these restrictions. Marianne Grubracker's diary of her daughter's growing up in Munich and Berlin, records many such moments. Here is one:

> St Nicholas Day is upon us again and four children are waiting. All of them, two girls and two boys, are a little timid. Then Thomy, the eldest, is persuaded to come forward with the comment, 'Come on, a boy can't be scared of St Nicholas.'
>
> (Grubracker 1988: 76)

Boys must not show fear. On the other hand boys are tacitly encouraged to express anger and its aggressions. A little boy, Schorschi, has been grabbing toys violently from her daughter Anneli. Grubracker observes:

> Shoving and taking other children's toys away from them seems to play a special part in the social life of small male children. The fact that Anneli does not hit him back surprises me at first, until I leaf through my diary and see how often I have told her not to.
>
> (ibid.: 40)

Girls may be just as angry as boys but they are constrained from showing it in public. The creation of women's and men's structures of feeling starts early. In this final section I shall discuss some well-known theoretical paradigms for self-consciousness, language and deconstruction, and suggest that they are also phenomenologies of the disturbances to the social structures of feeling caused by male violence, and the methods used to restore the resulting broken continuities.

What happens to the structures of emotion when two or more men are gathered together? One frequent result is the mock abuse described ironically by a popular novelist, Barbara Michaels, in her novel *Search the*

Shadows: 'The affection between them was plain to see, but how odd men were, expressing friendship with insults and blows' (Michaels 1987).

A more sophisticated version of this is to be found in the work of the grandfather of postmodernizing theory, Hegel, whose Master/Slave dialectic reads like the archetypal encounter of two male egos stripped for action as each prepares to force the other to acknowledge his dominance. The near-obsessive preoccupation with this one passage, in modern European, especially French, thought, is usually attributed to its paradigmatic summary of class, sadism and the intersubjectivity of self-consciousness. Its charisma is also due to its display of masculine prowess in a wrestling match like those which boys love, where masters like Hulk Hogan merge real fighting and playacted melodrama (the playacting makes it all the more convincing). The Master/Slave passage of the *Phenomenology of Spirit* grounds the emergence of self-consciousness in a metaphoric battle to the death between two male figures, who can only contemplate a relation of mastery and oppression between themselves. Self-consciousness is represented as the result of men fearing one another. Indeed fear is the key to the whole process, the unexplained motive force that drives the whole process of the emergence of self-consciousness. The Master/Slave dialectic is of course an allegory. Hegel is not using it literally, and therefore, like all allegories, an excess of dissimilar material is built into the narrative which provides the exemplary comparison. The masculinity of the struggle is not intended to be paralleled with the emergence of self-consciousness, and could therefore be dismissed as inevitable given the historical circumstances (men held public roles), and it could be claimed that since the model applies to both sexes, a different, androgynous example could have been chosen. This possibility is undercut by another feature of the Master/Slave dialectic. The master narrator Hegel's relation to the inarticulate figures, who are emerging as self-conscious subjects in historical time, initiates the struggle between men. The masculinity of the model is not incidental.

The *Phenomenology of Spirit* shows successive stages whereby spirit realizes itself. The early stages are difficult to represent because they possess no self-consciousness, and therefore cannot represent themselves. The philosopher narrator of the dialectic of spirit has to speak for them. His method requires that the narrative show how on their own terms these stages are contradictory, and contain the drive towards a more complete form of self-understanding. Speaking for the pre-linguistic consciousness becomes a problem in the Master/Slave passage because there finally a bedrock for articulacy can begin to form itself. To represent this crux Hegel has to bring together three different standpoints, and in doing so encourages the interpretative ambitions which have so dominated subsequent thought, especially Lacanian versions of literary and cultural theory. The first mode is the master narrator's (or philosopher's) ostensive gesture at the material. Having told us that the Lord 'takes to himself only the dependent aspect of the thing and has the pure enjoyment of it', and therefore the 'other consciousness' (the bondsman) is 'expressly something unessential', he then is able to say: 'Here, therefore, is present this moment of recognition, viz that the other consciousness sets aside its own "being-for-itself", and in so doing itself does what the first does to it' (Hegel 1977: 116). The philosophical guide is able to stop the action and analyse it. By this gesture the reader is drawn into a textual moment other than the moment of the gesture. As with a stage direction, we are made as readers to share a privileged separation and a separate time from the time of the bondsman and lord.

The second mode is the narrative enacted by these two figures. Things have happened to them. Most notably the bondsman has experienced some-thing for which there has been no precedent in the *Phenomenology* so far, fear:

> For this consciousness has been fearful, not of this or that particular thing or just at odd moments but its whole being has been seized with dread; for it has experienced the fear of death, the absolute Lord. In that experience it has been quite unmanned, has trembled in every fibre of its being, and everything solid and stable has been shaken to its foundations.
>
> (ibid.: 117)

Such suffering is the most authentic representation of self-awareness that Hegel can give within the constraints of his exposition. Emotion allows history to begin and it starts off with a loss of manhood made evident by the unmanly show of fear and the resultant deathly humiliation. It is the show of fear that is significant. President Saddam Hussein of Iraq acknowledged the force of this masculine double-bind when he said before the Gulf War: 'We would rather die than be humiliated.' For Hegel, therefore, the emergence of self-consciousness depends on the loss of male inexpressiveness. So we're then told, in the analytic mode of timeless expository argument, that this melting away is intrinsic to the beginning of self-consciousness: 'But this pure universal movement, the absolute melting-away of everything stable, is the simple, essential nature of self-consciousness, absolute negativity, pure *being-for-self*, which consequently is *implicit* in this consciousness' (Hegel 1977: 117). The context of this third mode doesn't allow its claim to absolute independence to go unchallenged. Without undergoing such an experience as the bondsman's, the general statement wouldn't be possible. The bonds-man's shaking is not an example of a specific instance of this general observation. Hegel, unusually, is quite emphatic about this, saying that for the bondsman the moment of 'pure being-for-self' is 'explicit' and that this is not a dissolution in principle, but 'in his demise he *actually* brings this about' (ibid.: 117). What would in other contexts (Kant's *Critique of Pure Reason*, for example) be read as a timeless, non-narrativized statement within an argument is here altered by its relationship to the primitive form of narrative into a statement of the conditions at a momentary stage in the transformation related by the narrative. The statement is no longer timelessly true. Hegel's language makes this even more evident when he uses verbs of transformation in his description of the bondsman: 'Through work, however, the bondsman *becomes* conscious of what he truly is' (Hegel 1977: 118; my emphasis). The bondsman is appropriating the argument because he is 'becoming conscious of what he truly is': 'It is in this way, therefore, that consciousness *qua* worker, comes to see in the independent being [of the object] its *own* independence' (ibid.: 118). The phrase 'comes to see' stitches together at that point the bondsman, the reader, the philosophic narrator and the exposition, so that in the next paragraph when we are told: 'Now, however, he destroys this alien negative moment' (ibid.: 118), the emphatic word 'now' leaps out at us. Description, narrative and argument coalesce and the narrative takes over. Hegel's language remains master only on the surface but is challenged subversively from within. The philosophic master narrator does the bidding of the former slaves to his design. Now reason is the slave and the passions are the master, as Hume demanded. The unsayable, emotion, resists mastery and begins a conflict between masculine figures. In the *Phenomenology* Hegel accepts the banishment of emotion from the realm of metaphysics begun by Hume and completed by Kant, and makes up for its suppression by naming self-consciousness 'desire'. The close embrace between self-consciousness and desire banishes the third member of the triangle, emotion, which then haunts the relationship like a discarded lover. In the Master/Slave dialectic the emergence of consciousness coincides with the fear of annihilation by other men. To know yourself as a man is to know that other men may enslave and destroy you. Masculinity does need to deny emotion. Otherwise it would have to confront the fear it wants to forget. The connection between self-consciousness and the social structures in which male violence disrupts the structures of feeling is made especially evident, and is surely one reason for the continuing fascination with Hegel's philosophical allegory.

Henry James described the relation of author to text in terms similar to these in the preface to *The Golden Bowl*, in the often quoted passage about the godlike role of author.

> It's not that the muffled majesty of authorship doesn't here *ostensibly* reign; but I catch myself again shaking it off and disavowing the pretence of it while I get down into the arena and do my best to live and breathe and rub shoulders and converse with the persons engaged in the struggle that provides for the others in the circling tiers the entertainment of the great game.
>
> (James 1966: 8)

The distant echo of images of gladiatorial combat (from sources like Swinburne's 'Faustine' perhaps) disturbs the sense of order which the reference to muffled majesty evokes. What then is this author doing down in the arena: interviewing the combatants for the pleasure of others, or worse, taking part and joining the deadly games? This image of the novel as a game in which the contestants may die, a deadly game for the pleasure of others, should give us pause before consigning impersonality to a category of benign outmoded poetics. Henry James shows that this art is a game, but the kind of game in which the combatants may suffer and die, and a game in which both reader and author participate. The author is both the sovereign who has ordered the games and a participant. When the male sovereign subject leaves his throne and goes into the arena he becomes the object of his own gaze and its delight in violence. The image of this process is one of murderous male conflict, yet for most readers of a novel so lacking in incident and devoid of what we ordinarily understand by physical conflict, this must seem hyperbole. That of course is the point. Contact with others in the emotional arena is experienced as potentially deadly by many men, for whom James speaks in the preface. *The Golden Bowl*, James's last completed novel, could be described as the most extreme form of the fiction of such Hegelian relations between private selves in a public medium, in which the attempt to know what others are thinking and feeling leads to an intense, overwhelming self-deception. Maggie Verver invents the speeches, the reactions and the emotional crises of those closest to her, in her efforts to know what apparently cannot be known, the true state of another inner self whose emotions can only be known when expressed, and when expressed, are always subject to that self's absolute controlling censorship. James has to use a woman as the proponent of this investigation to maintain a plausible plot. No man could plausibly be expected to undertake such careful researches in empathy within the limitations on publicly acceptable masculinities.

Postmodernist theorists and writers return again and again to the basic structure on which the Master/Slave dialectic was constructed, the conflictual emotional relations between men (often male violence), out of which the very possibility of self-consciousness and representation arises. Commonly this manifests itself as a reworking of the Hegelian narrator's mastery into various forms of utopian bond between men, figured by implicit relations such as that of reader and text, and as a growing recognition of the disturbance of discursive certainty produced by the unacknowledged diremptions of men's structures of feeling caused by the threat of male violence. Such recognition is rarely discursively explicit. Even men writers with a clear commitment to a radical sexual politics rarely talk openly about the relations between their experiments in discursivity and their sexual politics. One exception is the 'language poet', Charles Bernstein (it was a language poet, Bob Perelman, whom Fredric Jameson chose as a representative postmodernist writer in his *New Left Review* essay on 'Postmodernism, or the Cultural Logic of Late Capitalism'). For Bernstein, the disrupted linguistic surface of language poetry, 'where grammar can be reforged', has a sexual politics:

the project of much current poetry that attempts to rupture conventional grammatical and narrative patterns can be understood in terms
of just such a sexual politic [sic]. At the same time, *as a man*, I have
been concerned with resisting any establishment of new and positive
identity formations through such writing practices.

(Bernstein 1989: 191–2)

Bernstein's explanation of the linguistic strategies of language poetry is
persuasive but far from the only one offered by language poets, even
Bernstein himself. The most familiar explanation is that the sign has become
as reified as a commodity in contemporary America, and that only a poetry
which denies itself the use of the reality effect of ordinary referentiality (now
heavily ideological) can be considered politically radical. So what Bernstein
is doing in effect is to co-opt an existing radical practice and propose it as a
radical male feminist writing. He argues this by claiming that men need to
promote a negativity of maleness:

The 'imaginal' values of maleness have not been suppressed/
discredited/denied but rather vaunted: the struggle for men is to
unlearn masculinity, without substituting any positive value to this
gender differential since positive values for maleness (as distinct from
'humanness') remain suspect, at least for the present, as socially adapt-
ive strategies to maintain control and power.

(Bernstein 1989: 192)

How does he go about this postmodernist practice of unlearning masculinity? To begin with, he is cautious about the status of his own poetic
claims. He might well be responding to a critique of expressivist theories of
emotion when he says: 'I have tried, in my work, to understand who and
what I am without assuming the authenticity of my feelings or sexuality.
This has afforded me an unlimited amount of pleasure in writing' (ibid.:
192). He has repeatedly insisted, in his discursive essays and in interviews,
that his poetry makes the reader an active partner in the formation of
meaning and its subjectivities. The poetry's disrupted surfaces are an invitation to participative interpretation that also constructs a relation between
male author and readers. A male reader who would try to speak like the
Hegelian narrator for the emergent subjectivities is made to enter this zone
of incomplete articulation in the process of unlearning his masculinity, but it
all depends on the assumption that there is a prior relation between male
reader and male-authored text. The parallel between the reality effect and
masculinity that Bernstein creates by his appropriation of the earlier radical
programme for sexual politics means that masculinity is equated with reality
effect. Bernstein mostly uses forms of socially recognized discourse,
arranged in ways that refuse any statement from him. For example his poem
'The Klupzy Girl' is assertive at all points – it begins with the powerful

217

reflexive claim that 'poetry is like a swoon, with this difference:/ it brings you to your senses' (Bernstein 1986: 285). These assertions are not guaranteed by any framing voice. The sentences – 'Yet his/ parables are not singular. The smoke from/ the boat causes the men to joke. Not/ gymnastic: pyrotechnic' (ibid.: 285) – refuse to integrate into a coherent assertion. Assertion is the material the poem works with, both assertions of fact and assertions of self, but the poem is not simply pure disruption, or pure unlearning, any more than it is a set of pure assertions. When the poem says, 'It has more to me than please to note acquits/ defiant spawn' (ibid.: 287), the previous quotation (from an irritable memo about unrecorded telephone use in an unnamed organization) provides a ghostly context, but the sentence's badness disrupts its grip on clear assertion. The semantic murk seems to come from the 'I', as if the self were speaking too animatedly, or emotionally, to articulate clearly. Bernstein's language poems can be read as representations of the actual failure of masculine structures of feeling to be coherent. The apparent reality of these structures, like those of society as a whole, is a smooth meaningful surface (real, referential) only within the dominant ideologies. Once challenged, the continuities made possible by ideologies of masculinity disappear leaving fractured structures of feeling. A new relation between men is needed, and it begins with confusion and a will to make sense, and a recognition that more is needed than the narrative mastery of a Hegelian dialectic.

My last postmodernist is the philosopher Jacques Derrida. Like Bernstein's poems his texts not only anticipate reading strategies, they choreograph them, keeping the reader moving quickly through a complex series of reflexive addresses to the conditions of the making of the dance of subjectivity. Yet feminist critics have suggested that his work has not reflected upon all the conditions of its making, and that an anxiety of male authorship can be discerned in many of the texts. Postmodernist masculinities can be found doing their own 'Danse Russes' if we look (see p. 47 for my discussion of William Carlos Williams's poem 'Danse Russe'). Alice Jardine (1985: 191, 199) argues that Derrida associates femininity and undecidability: 'wherever the metaphysical writer's text oscillates is where the "essential virility" of metaphysical discourse is shaken'. She suggests that when Derrida analyses Mallarmé's *Mimique* in 'The Double Session' (1981) he invites strong feminist reactions. He writes about a man who murders his wife, he ignores the homosexuality in the text, he ignores the stereotyping on which his own textual play depends, and he misses the opportunity to implicate any part of the male body. Jardine concludes that Derrida has taken Lacan's 'feminine jouissance' and replaced it in a new hysterical body, 'the text as écriture' (Jardine 1985: 192). I will show that Derrida's text also plays with masculinities.

Feminine textuality is synonymous with what Derrida calls 'undecidability', but what is undecidability, and why is it associated with gender at all, especially femininity? Is this simply a new version of woman as mystery? In all his discussions of gender, whether in Mallarmé, Nietzsche or Heidegger, Derrida does not introduce the sexual terms himself. They are not designations applied from without. It's the attribution of a reflexive philosophical claim to these terms that is an act of external imposition. Mallarmé clearly emphasizes the importance of the 'hymen' in his own text, and associates it with mime, mimesis, and writing itself. Derrida says that the undecidability of the hymen is not due to its semantics but the 'formal or syntactic *praxis* that composes and decomposes it' (Derrida 1981: 220). Only in Mallarmé's text is Derrida's mastery of the word undecidable. Words which function like 'hymen' (Derrida instances others – *pharmakon, supplément, différance*) 'mark the spots of what can never be mediated, mastered, sublated or dialecticized through any *Erinnerung* or *Aufhebung*' (ibid.: 221). Derrida adds that:

> these play effects, these words that escape philosophical mastery . . . have, in widely differing historical contexts, a very singular relation to writing. These 'words' admit into their games both contradiction and noncontradiction (and the contradiction and noncontradiction between contradiction and noncontradiction).Without any dialectical *Aufhebung*, without any time off, they belong in a sense to both consciousness and to the unconscious, which Freud tells us can tolerate or remain insensitive to contradiction.
>
> (ibid.: 221)

Undecidability, of which the hymen (sign of a relation to men and masculinity) is an instance, is not simply present in the word as a sedimentation of etymology, but results from its use, whether in a text or, more generally, in the symbolic code. It results moreover from the attempt to master, or decide, meaning, from the attempt at domination by rationality. Rationality belongs to consciousness and the unidimensionality of its truths. A 'play effect', like Mallarmé's use of the word 'hymen', is a language-game where the philosophical player cannot win, because the rules (roles) make play to win impossible. This kind of play, or mimesis, is associated with a part of the female body, not by Mallarmé, but by Derrida himself, for it is his text which universalizes a general 'serial law' as he calls it, from these textual usages. The metalinguistic absolutism of 'what can never be mastered' is Derrida's. The anxiety is that of contemporary masculine philosophy. It is the man philosopher who wants to decide and cannot, whose anxiety is prompted by an effect which appears to be both conscious and unconscious.

The feminizing of this process which escapes reason is less evident in 'The Double Session' than in *Spurs*, as Jardine and others have noted. Derrida (1979: 51) takes up Nietzsche's claim that 'truth is like a woman' and elaborates on the version of truth which this implies. It is hard to separate Derrida and Nietzsche in this essay, because the French philosopher at once

219

speaks through the voice of the German philosopher, and to him, and in opposition to him. As so often in his work, Derrida seems to be speaking in his own voice (while denying that there is such 'voice'), making asseverations which carry his authority as warrant, only to suddenly reveal that he has just stepped out from behind reported speech (or writing) as the philosophical interviewer relaying his interviewee's thoughts to the reader. When Derrida says: 'indeed, if woman *is* truth, *she* at least knows that there is no truth . . . and she is woman precisely because she herself does not believe in truth itself, because she does not believe in what she is, in what she is believed to be, in what she then is not' (1979: 53), we do not know who is saying this, Jacques Derrida or Friedrich Nietzsche, Jacques Nietzsche or Friedrich Derrida.

The textual commentary enacts a relation between men which in Derrida's master narrative becomes the hymeneal mark of undecidability. This mark could also be paradigmatic of the attempt to overcome the divisions in the social fabric caused by male violence. Derrida suggests that Heidegger misses the function of sexual terms in Nietzsche (in a more recent essay Derrida argues that Heidegger missed the significance of the desexualization of being in *Being and Time* (Derrida 1991: *passim*)). Like Amerigo, the prince in *The Golden Bowl*, Derrida thinks that women can be understood in relation to what they give away. Or is it Nietzsche who does? His sexual lexicon 'might be called a process of *propriation* (appropriation, expropriation, taking, taking possession, gift and barter, mastery, servitude, etc.)' (ibid.: 109):

> not only is propriation a sexual operation, but *before* it there was no sexuality. And because it is finally undecidable, propriation is more powerful than the question ti esti, than the veil of truth or the meaning of being . . . propriation is all the more powerful since it is its process that organised both the totality of language's process and symbolic exchange in general.
>
> (ibid.: 111)

Any return to a 'pre-critical relation to the signified' (ibid.: 112) would fail to grasp this process. The 'pre-critical' is linguistic, but thinks it is not, and in this delusion of 'natural language' believes it can return to a state anterior to language, some unsayable 'chora' of emotion. This philosopher has to warn those who are attracted to such a course that it is only illusion. He insists from his position of mastery that there is nothing logically prior to the critical phase.

Propriation is that process which the comic-book heroes know so well, the mark of a point where conscious and unconscious meet in an embrace which is also masculinity's inability to recognize itself with love and not a blow. The undecidable hymen or propriation is the discovery of something that cannot be spoken for, cannot be performed by propriating Nietzsche. It is the attempt to speak with Nietzsche's voice, and give his words enough intelligibility and credence to be effective, that makes the feminine other to Derrida's argument also. A relation to Nietzsche dresses up as a relation to an excluded category of being, woman. That other category then emerges as the disembodied spirit of his own argument. Derrida uses feminine meta-phors to negotiate the difficult relation with another man thinker who has already taken the step of writing woman as other. The recuperation of this already existing sexism is not able to take the form of a recognition of the relation between two men, once a sexual discourse for relations to the other (referents, truth, laughter) has been initiated by the other man's writing. Undecidability of the bond between the men is not considered as a possible cause of difficulty, and so the tensions of this relation become exemplary of men's relations between one another because exemplarity is already encoded into the argument. Undecidability is projected onto the traditional face of femininity, even though it arises out of the attempt to find a textual figure for the relation of one man with another. Undecidability is a moment which contemporary philosophers like Derrida recognize as the unwanted residue of previously confident imperial systems of logic and reason, and then assimilate to the long tradition of categorizing such necessary foundations of inspiration and irrationality as feminine, in the hope of overthrowing the imperial power. In doing so they put a name to loss: undecidability. The lost language of certainty, the pre-critical language and mastery are actually unattainable. Their postmodernist answer is to insist that something called simply language, which has lost its loss (its historicity, emotion and mascu-linity) is master over the postmodernist, the modernist and temporalization itself, mismirroring all.

But male postmodernists are wary men. They know they may be held accountable for their gender, and so tend to keep out of the fray, with the result that they explore dilemmas of modern masculinities with an analytical rigour not matched by boldness in identifying them as men's problems. Some of the most rigorous phenomenologies of modern masculinities can be found in the work of thinkers less agonized about the politics of gender, but no less scrupulous about language, representation and the unsayable. In *Philosophical Investigations* for example, Wittgenstein creates a thorough demonstration of the overlays of morality, emotion, reason in modern masculinity, because its discussion of the self centres on the presentation of emotion. The *Philosophical Investigations* makes evident that many modern masculinities can understand their own bewitchments only as a disturbance in the logic of their own reasoning, and otherwise remain unable to articulate these disturbances. But of course as I say this I know that for most readers it does none of these things. For most readers this is to misread a philosophical work which scrupulously avoids just such claims. I am sympathetic to that desire to keep men thinkers like Wittgenstein away from readings like this one, but I think it should be resisted. By limiting the universality of such arguments as Wittgenstein's to his specific circumstance as a man philosopher, it becomes possible to see the scope of his thinking as a triumph over limits. Masculinity need not be simply unalterable fate. I believe that *Philosophical Investigations*, and indeed much else in Wittgenstein's corpus, shows a remarkable fidelity to men's issues. I also want to encourage others to address such questions about men's self-reflections, to men thinkers like Wittgenstein. Such a procedure could even be said to fall within Wittgenstein's legitimate concerns if, as G.P. Baker and P.M.S. Hacker say, 'men in different epochs, different cultures, have different forms of life' (1983: 243). His own philosophy must also be open to a reading from within a different form of life which then questions the 'distinctive forms and norms of representation' evident in his investigations. We now live in a somewhat different form of life to that in which he wrote, one shaped by feminism.

Throughout the *Philosophical Investigations* language is said to mislead us. Philosophers who use words like 'being' have to be checked. Philosophy should be a 'battle against the bewitchment of our intelligence by means of language' (Wittgenstein 1976: 109/47; the first number refers to the section and the second to the page). Wittgenstein variously locates the problem of bewitchment in grammar (an idea which echoes Nietzsche), and in the inaccurate images with which language pictures its own activities. There is another way of interpreting this metaphor of bewitchment. Witches are usually feminine; men do battle. Philosophy could then appear as the masculine struggle against the bewitchments of feminine language. But how could language do this, and why should it be feminine? Shortly after his remark about bewitchment, Wittgenstein qualifies his remark about the role of philosophy by saying: 'There is not *a* philosophical method, though there are indeed methods, like different therapies' (ibid.: 133/51). Philosophy is therapy, but for what neurosis? Wittgenstein says that language can bewitch us, and yet also assumes that language is the place where we transact our social relations. The two propositions seem to be in conflict. If human beings made language, why and how could we deceive ourselves? Wittgenstein doesn't think of this as a question in need of an answer because he is directing his attention at men philosophers who have illegitimately extended the meanings of ordinary words into philosophical discourses and produced monsters. It is, however, a question that can be asked, because Wittgenstein insistently addresses the reader as part of a collective prone to these mistakes. Our rationality needs philosophical therapy. Looking at the way this therapy works will tells us more about the alleged causes of bewitchment. Section IX of the second part of the book, for example, begins: 'If you observe your own grief, which senses do you use to observe it?'

The *Philosophical Investigations* is marked by an interrogative intensity whose source is hard to locate. Although such questions as this are not intended to have any personal element, the interrogative depends upon the possibility, the plausibility, of such an emotional investment. Both grief, and the need to 'know how to know it' (Hollway 1984: 249), are assumed to be addressable realities. What is it then that gives rise to these questions? The proper answer would be philosophy or, more specifically, the mistaken reasoning of earlier empiricist philosophers. The insistent use of emotion as the locus of argument suggests another way of investigating this investigation (Wittgenstein was a devoted reader of *Detective Story Magazine* (Monk 1990: 422), where the stories emphasized the convergence of action and thought in criminal investigations. Like boys' comics, these stories justify masculinity's character, especially its violence, in the name of the law that makes investigation meaningful). The interrogative intensity could be said to arise from a passionate engagement with the beliefs and contradictions of modern masculinity as it renegotiates the relations between reason and emotion.

The question and answer dialogue of rational enquiry becomes the ideal model of human interaction because it provides believable occasions for philosophical statements to be made. The argument is insistently dialogic, taking place within the relationship of a speaker and respondent, sometimes using the reader as one party to this dialogue, and sometimes controlling both sides of this dialogue in the text. As we saw earlier, for Wittgenstein language replaced emotional catharsis; words replaced crying. Feelings lose their communicative component of non-verbal expression, and therefore disappear off the verbal map altogether, only to reappear as the sites under discussion. They are reified as mere exempla of linguistic use. The result of tacitly identifying language with what is opposed to emotion is that the text everywhere produces the very phenomena it has tried to repress. Examples that refer to emotion proliferate. Doubts about human relationships proliferate with them. 'I tell someone I am in pain. His attitude to me will then be that of belief; disbelief; suspicion; and so on' (Wittgenstein 1976: 310/ 103).

Disbelief and suspicion soon overwhelm belief. To assume that all we can do is believe that someone has a particular feeling is itself a measure of alienation. It discounts the possibility of empathy, and leaves us only with uncertainty. Characteristically we are told: 'So much, however, is true: we can often predict a man's actions from his expression of a decision. An important language-game' (ibid.: 632/163). How else could we do it? This doubt, and the distancing provided by the second sentence, are linked with the difficulties created by emotions. The uncertainty arises from the inability to find a way of representing emotion within this linguistic mapping of social relations.

These features are even more evident in the passage cited earlier in my discussion of catharsis (p. 183), about the problem of instantaneous feeling:

'For a second he felt violent pain.' – Why does it sound queer to say: 'For a second he felt deep grief'? Only because it so seldom happens? But don't you feel grief *now*? ('But aren't you playing chess *now*?') The answer may be affirmative, but that does not make the concept of grief any more like the concept of a sensation. – The question was really, of course, a temporal and personal one, not the logical question which we wanted to raise.

(Wittgenstein 1976: 174)

The parenthetic example is intended to illustrate the acceptable use of the word 'now', but it also has the side-effect of associating grief with chess. Linguistic and philosophical objection to the statement 'for a second he felt deep grief' also suggests some objection to the idea that he felt grief at all. There is a definite hierarchy at work. At the top are logical questions, and beneath are the merely temporal and personal. Why does it sound queer to utter this sentence? Wittgenstein's implied answer is that it violates the language-game rules for the use of 'now', but another answer would be that men are not allowed this language-game. The question asked of the person who felt grief is not to be a personal (emotional) one, but a logical (rational) one. This whole passage is concerned with the correct, rational way that powerful emotion should be discussed, but its structure is one of avoidance.

If these examples are put alongside the material I cited earlier from the men's movement, their preoccupations can look remarkably similar. Remember Victor Seidler's claim on behalf of men that: 'Since we don't have a language in which to identify our emotional and sexual needs and since the very recognition of needs compromises our masculine control, we seek to satisfy our different needs without really being able to identify them' (1989: 161). This describes well the subjective experience of feeling thwarted by language from saying what you feel, but it is not a lack of language that's the problem. As the Wittgenstein passages show, there is plenty of language but it sounds queer. (I will have to comment on that pun. The offending sentence sounds like a homosexual way of talking because gay men *have* developed subtle languages for expressing emotion.) The self is unable to locate its relation to expressions of feeling, so they remain alien objects of investigation, rather than means of interaction. Seidler recalls that he learnt to conceal his fear as a child, confirming Grubracker's observation of the little boy, Thomy, I mentioned earlier: 'I learnt not to show my fear to others as I learnt to hide it from myself' (1988: 150).

Wittgenstein also considers the concealment of fear when he discusses the fallacy of thinking that fear is something inwardly tangible noticed by a mind (in the way, for example, a person notices a road sign). One can conceal fear behind a masking smile:

'I must tell you I am frightened.'
'I must tell you: it makes me shiver.' –

And one can say this in a *smiling* tone of voice too.

And do you mean to tell me he doesn't feel it? How else does he *know* it? – But even when he says it as a piece of information he does not learn it from his sensations.

(Wittgenstein 1976: 174)

The effect of hiding fear from oneself and others could be the loss of the power to recognize the signals of one's own fear. This is the very issue Wittgenstein is concerned with. How does this man know he is afraid? Wittgenstein's answer is to separate out sensations of shivering, the emotion of fear, and the verbal expression of fear, treating each as a discrete phenomenon. As a result, shivering loses its voice, feeling loses its voice, and the voice itself has to learn from elsewhere what it feels. The passage tries to assert that the man is certain of what he knows, yet manages to leave an aura of doubt. How can he know that he is afraid? The text tries to seal off these questions from such existential politics, and place them as merely rational enquiries of logical significance only. We can see from the context provided by Seidler's recollections, that these questions can be understood as part of the crisis of a masculinity whose model of reason excludes affect from its communications. Its silence becomes only the more eloquent, resounding between the inverted commas of a suppression that highlights its predicament. In the following example the interlocutor's voice takes on a note of near hysteria at the direction of the philosopher's arguments, as if misunderstanding them to have a personal significance directed at the interlocutor:

583. 'But you talk as if I weren't really expecting, hoping, *now* – as I thought I was. As if what were happening *now* had no deep significance'. – What does it mean to say 'What is happening now has significance' or 'has deep significance'? What is a *deep* feeling? Could someone have a feeling of ardent love or hope for the space of one second – *no matter what* preceded or followed this second? – What is happening now has significance – in these surroundings. The surroundings give it its importance. And the word 'hope' refers to a phenomenon of human life. (A smiling mouth *smiles* only in a human face.)

(Wittgenstein 1976: 153)

The multiplying questions presuppose a lack of rapport, of a kind that emotional isolation would produce. The only answer is the provision of context ('surroundings').

One of the main difficulties presented by Wittgenstein's philosophy has been deciding what the contexts of his arguments should be, so much so that a common exegetical strategy is to provide a specific context as the opening move in an interpretation. Yet the writing doesn't have the air of disembodiment one might expect. It so insistently takes the form of negotiation, of dialogue and verbal conflict, that it always seems on the verge of breaking into a personal or historical context for its arguments. The writing is almost as dependent on relationships between its anonymous speakers as Plato's philosophy is on his very much named citizens. The *Philosophical Investigations* demonstrates that the 'inner life' and its representations can only be understood in the social terms of language. It demonstrates this by examining in detail the implications of particular non-specialized linguistic usages, without explicit recourse to a systematic theoretical framework. At certain points it proves necessary to offer some more general explanatory metaphors for the operations of language, because Wittgenstein wants to make clear that this is a general principle. Language can only be properly understood within actual ordinary situations. In order to describe these transindividual, but not universal, contexts, he coins the apparently non-metaphysical, and certainly non-specialized term, *Sprachspiel*, or 'language-game' as it has become known in English. It is the only term whose recurrence in the *Philosophical Investigations* has anything approaching the status of a key heuristic concept. Wittgenstein emphasizes that the term's value lies in its open-ended descriptiveness of transactions that do not necessarily share any specific defining characteristic.

When the going gets tough the tough get going, is the saying. When the philosophical going gets tough the tough (masculine) philosopher goes gaming. When Hume finds himself 'ready to reject all belief and reasoning, and can look upon no opinion even as more probable or likely than another', and finds himself asking 'Where am I, or what?' he abandons the isolation of sceptical philosophy to play backgammon with friends (Hume 1969: 316). Undecidability cuts him off from the playfulness of men. Ludic man has been a favourite of modern philosophers, especially in aesthetics, because, from Schiller to Derrida, and from Freud to Lacan, play is equated with freedom and comradeship. Play is opposed to the goal-oriented work of care-burdened adulthood. It carries a special charge for men, because for most men play is their only access to childhood, since they don't have extended time with children in which to re-enter (and possibly renegotiate) those early foundations of their psychic life. Could it be that these men enjoy the pleasures of boyish games so much that they are ambivalent about submitting them to analytic scrutiny; making games and play central to their work but not looking too closely at the pleasures of play? Are they a little bit like Charles Darke, the politician in Ian McEwan's recent novel *The Child in Time* (1988), who mysteriously reverts to boyhood, and retires to the country? He plays in a tree house while his wife keeps his behaviour secret from the world. Stephen, the protagonist of the novel, is never quite sure what has happened to his friend. Is he mad or is he playacting? Charles Darke's behaviour has an odd air of research about it, as if he had 'combed libraries, diligently consulted the appropriate authorities to discover just what it was a certain kind of boy was likely to have in his pockets' (ibid.:

113). The nostalgia implicit in philosophical theorizing that depends on playing games needs to be countered by the recognition that many children's games are 'aggressive games of simulated warfare' (Henke 1990: 56), rather than celebrations of innocence and freedom. There is a reminder of this in the *Philosophical Investigations*. In the following example of a language-game of emotions, a hypothetical questioner replies to Wittgenstein's suggestion that the questioner's words do not refer to feelings: '582. If someone whispers "It'll go off now", instead of saying "I expect the explosion any moment", still his words do not describe a feeling: although they and their tone may be a manifestation of feeling' (Wittgenstein 1976: 582/153).

The half-glimpsed setting of this observation is a battle, a scene of the kind Wittgenstein must have witnessed on the Russian front (the front he was lucky to survive, given the fate of so many men like the Rat Man). Wittgenstein's example assumes that this setting is nothing extraordinary. This is the kind of thing his readers will know. But the setting is special in one sense; it is a moment when men are both close to one another (they whisper comradely warnings) and killing one another (with explosions). Games create similar but non-destructive opportunities for closeness and aggressive competition. This is probably why men thinkers don't think too hard about the games they use for their rhetorical purposes. The masculine issues are too loaded.

Hans-Georg Gadamer, for example, takes aesthetic philosophy in the same direction as Wittgenstein, by narrowing play to game-playing. The subjective experience of playing games is, he claims, parallel to the experience of art. Like art, a game imposes a flexible, changing normative structure on the players: 'the game tends to master the players' (Gadamer 1979: 95). This mastery attributed to the game is similar to the mastery of the Hegelian narrator, and to the uncomfortable mastery of the philosophical post-modernist, a mastery which hides a fatalistic submission to unexamined dominant masculinities. Gadamer's theory of art depends as much as Wittgenstein's theory of language on the assumption that games are a universal mode of human activity. But are they? Aren't games specific to certain areas of human life? When games are extrapolated as analogies for all forms of life, unconscious masculine preoccupations are inscribed within the analysis.

Games are a means of representing other social activities without their usual consequences, and so provide a rehearsal for other more lasting social interactions. After a football game the players go home. After a battle the political map is usually redrawn, and some combatants may never go home. Competition, simulation and rule observance are all common (but not necessary) components of games. The game model of language is meant to stress heterogeneity, the absence of universal paradigms, and the limited, temporary nature of the governing rules which require consent for play to be possible. Other unnoticed restrictions are also present. Modern masculinities impose limits on the social interpretation of language through the 'language-game' model. They become limitations because Wittgenstein wants to establish the bonds between language and social relations very firmly: 'The common behaviour of mankind is the system of reference by means of which we interpret an unknown language' (Wittgenstein 1976: 206/82).

Wittgenstein's starting point is the social space of human activity. Any restricted representation of that space will have consequences for the discussions of language and rationality. If language is like a game, then it is not the primary space where social transactions occur; it is the space where they are rehearsed. They are removed from the ordinary fray of actual consequences in everyday life. Ordinary language would then be lacking in the dense relationships of human life, especially affective embodiment in the history of relationships with others. This language-game behaviour might be very emotional, but it would remain pretence in the way games are pretences. There would be no serious relational consequences to follow. These implicit assumptions arise from the semantic domain of the term 'game', but they also reproduce very accurately the two features of ordinary modern masculinity evident in Wittgenstein's reference to war. Masculinity, as we have seen, maintains much of its power by affective anaesthesia. It often produces combat instead of affection. In modern capitalist societies the insecurities of manhood have been exploited to stimulate competition between men in the marketplace of the economy. The most visible everyday social form of masculinity is competition, and its accompanying dialectic of submission and dominance.

It is important to acknowledge that ordinary speech, irrespective of the gender of the speaker, is likely to be as competitive as the social life of the society where it occurs. One influential theorist of drama, Keith Johnstone (1981), has suggested that the basic element of all theatre depends on the competitive conflict of speakers, in what he calls a 'status game'. Without compelling status games, a theatrical performance seems bland and unconvincing to a modern audience. With them, even a script lacking in plot and range can grip an audience. According to Johnstone, even in ordinary conversation what is said is much less important than the degree to which it makes the speaker more or less important than his or her addressee. The idea that ordinary language use is a game reproduces this version of human conversation. The game model both acknowledges this feature of ordinary utterances and redirects it in a masculine direction.

In his resolute refusal of systematization and philosophical misappropriation of ordinary language, Wittgenstein uses other models of language which qualify the term 'language-game'. Explaining the use of terminology in aesthetics and ethics, and the difficulty their indeterminacy faces us with, he says:

In such a difficulty always ask yourself: How did we *learn* the meaning of this word ('good' for instance)? From what sort of examples? in what language-games? Then it will be easier for you to see that the word must have a family of meanings.

(Wittgenstein 1976: 77)

This passage presents a constellation which is characteristic of the *Philosophical Investigations*: difficulty, learning, self-questioning, word and family. The term 'family' itself is not used much, but its association with intimate, personal life is typical of a network of other terms. Explicitly the text is saying that knowing how families work we will have an idea of how meanings are connected. Implicitly this extends the space of social relations represented by language-games. 'Family' is also used in the course of his exposition of the interconnected heterogeneity of language-games:

I can think of no better expression to characterize these similarities than 'family resemblances'; for the various resemblances between members of a family: build, features, colour of eyes, gait, temperament, etc. etc. overlap and criss-cross in the same way. – And I shall say: 'games' form a family.

(ibid.: 67/32)

'Game' is used more literally than the concept of family. Here language-games are only considered to be analogous to people in a family. Language actually functions as a game, according to the other metaphor. Language-games: 'are *related* to one another in many different ways. And it is because of this relationship, or these relationships, that we call them all "language" ' (ibid.: 65/31). The language-games only form language because of their relationships, just as individuals only form a society because of *their* relationships. The initial emphasis on competition and the distantiated rehearsal of relationships is qualified by this other emphasis on the intimate, personal character of language use:

When philosophers use a word – 'knowledge', 'being', 'object', 'I', 'proposition', 'name' – and try to grasp the *essence* of the thing, one must always ask oneself: is the word ever actually used in this way in the language-game which is its original home –
What *we* do is to bring words back from their metaphysical to their everyday use.

(ibid.: 116/48)

'One must *always* ask oneself': this is a powerful obligation to take words back to their original home. How does language come to be separate from us, leaving home to confuse and resist us? Could it be that this language really is man-made in the more limited sense of that term, and that it

229

commonly lacks the feminine understanding of emotion which the maternal home can provide?

Wittgenstein's conception of language is partially articulated in terms of games. The masculine preoccupation with games so evident in modern thought colludes with this rhetoric to present ordinary utterances as both competitive and make-believe. Since language-games sustain forms of life, those too are presented in terms of a masculine gaming. These language-games are like the homes of words; patterns of language use form into families. Misuse and confusion result when words leave home and play in places other than their proper ones. Away from the mothers who could mediate their emotional lives for them, they become confused. The language-game model represents all linguistic social relations in terms of competition and the rehearsal of actual relationships in a pretend form. Several forms of linguistic exchange become hard to represent this way. Non-competitive forms of affection go missing. So does the sense that language use can be a place where relationships actually occur. Wittgenstein's model curiously reproduces the secondariness which afflicted the mimetic theory of language, and against which his philosophy is directed. It is not that words are signs of real other things, but that using language is like playacting some drama which has existence elsewhere. Wittgenstein's theory of language does not, despite its aims, represent the totality of social life, because it only thinks of this life in terms of competition and play. This, however, becomes its great strength as an account of masculine forms of modern rationality. As a descriptive phenomenology of modern masculinity in language there is little to compare with it. One of the forms of life it traces with such acumen is a modern masculinity.

CONCLUSIONS

Recent theories of subjectivity are also struggles with dominant conceptions of masculinity. The fantasy of centred, full subjectivity, so widely and confidently deconstructed by recent literary and cultural theory, is also a masculine fantasy of inwardness. But deconstruction may not be enough to expose its masculine bias. Masculinity has a vested interest in blocking unheroic, masculine self-analysis. Poststructuralism may sometimes boost the power of masculine subjectivity by discrediting all attempts at self-reflexion. As masculinity is more and more widely investigated there are signs that poststructuralism is no longer so confident that it has the one true theory of subjectivity. Men are beginning to gaze at their subjectivity and power in a spirit of self-critical examination, using less masterful, more tentative and heterogeneous theoretical concepts. Much of this new self-consciousness of gender is not immediately recognizable as a discourse on masculinity. There are few names for the effects on men's subjectivity of the vertiginous male gaze. The men's movement has identified it as emotion, a useful name for individually based therapy, but one that doesn't break free of the image of the self-sufficient individual enough to represent social life and political urgencies, or adequately recognize the rationality of emotion. Postmodernism itself is partly driven by this need to understand a baffling division in subjectivity that arises from within as well as without. Just as hitherto marginalized groups challenge the white male subject's sovereignty, so does the act of gazing inward at masculinity in order to unlearn its ideologies and acknowledge its possibilities. The result need not be stasis. Here and there the makings of a discourse are visible. A new politics of masculinity is possible if the dilemmas of masculine self-reflection are confronted critically and empathically. Then much-needed alliances between heterosexual men and gay men, between men and feminists, and First World men and the oppressed peoples of the colonialist legacy can be constructed with more confidence. Men could make more thoroughgoing contributions to the long overdue transformation of the conflicts between public and private space. Men could take more responsibilities for the care of children, a task we men so widely avoid. Denying the masculinity in the mirror won't help. It won't go away. And theory can help as long as it doesn't become a new position of mastery for those whose positions of sovereignty have been so thoroughly challenged.

But I cannot keep up a polemical tone for long without becoming all too aware that mine is a voice in a debate. It is for discussion between all of us, not for individuals, to decide future action. Instead I want to end with a reflection on the making of this book. I thought at first of ending by telling you how and why I wrote it, especially about the need to understand the awful self-destructiveness haunting the lives of men friends, and more generally the inescapable fact that it has consistently been men who kill. But I find I cannot speak of such things here. It is all either too personal or too familiar. It needs a novel or large-scale empirical research. The short story I began with hinted at the possibilities. It implied that boys learn to be men by representing themselves as the subjects of violently competitive masculinity, and thereby prevent analysis from addressing the process of self-representation because it begins up in the air of men in battle with one another. Instead of offering such reflections I shall tell you about my maternal grandfather.

He served as a private in the Balkans and Palestine for several years during what one of his medals called the 'great war for civilization'. He was a telegraphist, and he seems to have spent most of his time waiting in makeshift shelters to send and receive messages. When I was a child he told me the exciting story of how one night he was keeping watch when an enemy soldier silently materialized in the wireless tent and threatened to kill him. My grandfather explained to me that the other man didn't really want to kill him because that would rouse the camp. He simply wanted to cut off their communications. So my grandfather kept quiet and watched the intruder destroy the equipment and then steal away as silently as he came. I don't know what happened then. Later in the war my grandfather was in a party of men stranded without food. They found a railway wagon full of condensed milk and lived on it for two weeks before they were rescued. As a child I thought this must have been wonderful and was intrigued by his refusal to eat this wonderful food (does condensed milk symbolize concentrated nurture?) when we had it for Sunday lunch. War had given him the chance to eat it to such satiety that he never needed it again. I imagined that war had satisfied a powerful desire so completely that it disappeared. When I was grown up I learned from my mother that his return from the war had been very difficult because he came back to watch the wife he had married shortly before his departure die very soon of tuberculosis. These are common tales in every family: men struggling to maintain communication and threatening one another with death; the loss of relations with women and children; and the boys themselves finding men's battles seductively appealing. This has been the reality of modern men's lives – struggles to articulate themselves and love others in ways that often seem to negate those intentions. I have tried to trace those struggles in this book.

BIBLIOGRAPHY

2000AD (1986) *2000AD Monthly* 5, February.
—— (1987) *2000 AD*, 17 January.
Abbott, Franklin (1990) *Men and Intimacy: Personal Accounts Exploring the Dilemmas of Modern Male Sexuality*, Freedom, Calif.: The Crossing Press.
Abbott, Laurence L. (1986) 'Comic Art: Characteristics and Potentialities of a Narrative Medium', *Journal of Popular Culture* 19/4.
Adams, Parveen (1979) 'A Note on Sexual Divison and Sexual Differences', *m/f* 3.
—— (1983) ' "Mothering" ', *m/f* 8, 41–52.
Adler, Alfred (1929) *The Practice and Theory of Individual Psychology*, London: Routledge & Kegan Paul.
Adorno, Theodor W. and Horkheimer, Max (1979) *Dialectic of Enlightenment*, trans. John Cumming, London: Verso.
Anderson, Benedict (1983) *Imagined Communities: Reflections on the Origin and Spread of Nationalism*, London: Verso.
Aristotle (1948) *The Politics of Aristotle*, trans. Ernest Barker, Oxford: Clarendon Press.
—— (1980) *The Nicomachean Ethics*, trans. David Ross, J.R. Ackrill and J.O. Urmson, Oxford.
Astrachan, Anthony (1986) *How Men Feel: Their Response to Women's Demands for Equality and Power*, Anchor City, NJ: Doubleday.
Auden, W.H. (1966) *Collected Shorter Poems 1927–1957*, London: Faber.
Baker, G.P. and Hacker, P.M.S. (1983) *An Annotated Commentary on Wittgenstein's Philosophical Investigations*, Oxford: Blackwell.
Barker, Martin (1989) *Comics: Ideology, Power and the Critics*, Manchester: Manchester University Press.
Barrett, Michele (1980) *Women's Oppression Today: Problems in Marxist Feminist Analysis*, London: Verso.
Barthes, Roland (1977) 'The Death of the Author', in Stephen Heath (ed.) *Image-Music-Text*, London: Fontana.
Batman (1990) *Batman v. the Joker: The Greatest Joker Stories Ever Told*, London: Hamlyn.
Battersby, Christine (1989) *Gender and Genius: Towards a Feminist Aesthetics*, London: Women's Press.
Baumli, Francis (1985) *Men Freeing Men: Exploding the Myth of the Traditional Male*, Jersey City: New Atlantis.
Bellah, Robert, Madsen, Richard, Sullivan, William M., Swidler, Ann and Tipton, Steven M. (1988) *Habits of the Heart: Middle America Observed*, London: Hutchinson.

233

Beneke, Tim (1989) 'Men on Rape', in Michael S. Kimmel and Michael A. Messner (eds) *Men's Lives*, New York: Macmillan.

Benhabib, Seyla (1986) *Critique, Norm and Utopia: A Study of the Foundations of Critical Theory*, New York: Columbia University Press.

Benjamin, Jessica (1990) *The Bonds of Love: Psychoanalysis, Feminism, and the Problem of Domination*, London: Virago.

Bernstein, Charles (1986) 'The Klupzy Girl', in Ron Silliman (ed.) *In the American Tree*, Orono, Me: National Poetry Foundation.

—— (1989) 'Poetry and (Male) Sex', *Sulfur* 24.

Bloom, Harold (1976) *Poetry and Repression: Revisionism from Blake to Stevens*, New Haven, Conn.: Yale University Press.

Bly, Robert (1990) *Iron John: A Book about Men*, New York: Addison-Wesley.

Bond, Edward (1978) 'Us, Our Drama and the National Theatre', *Plays and Players*, October.

Boone, Joseph (1989) 'Of Men and Feminism: Whose is the Sex that Writes?', in Linda Kauffman (ed.) *Gender and Theory*, Oxford: Blackwell.

Boone, Joseph A. and Cadden, Michael (1990) *Engendering Men: The Question of Male Feminist Criticism*, London: Routledge.

Booth, Wayne (1961) *The Rhetoric of Fiction*, Chicago: Chicago University Press.

Bowie, Andrew (1990) *Aesthetics and Subjectivity: From Kant to Nietzsche*, Manchester: Manchester University Press.

Bradbury, Malcolm and McFarlane, James (1976) *Modernism: 1890–1930*, Harmondsworth: Penguin.

Brecht, Bertolt (1974) *Brecht on Theatre*, ed. John Willett, London: Methuen.

Brittan, Arthur (1989) *Masculinity and Power*, Oxford: Blackwell.

Brittan, Arthur and Maynard, Mary (1985) *Sexism, Racism and Oppression*, Oxford: Blackwell.

Brown, Carolyn, Cullis, Ann and Mumford, John (1985) *Laws of Gender. Concerning Some Problems Encountered in Studying Representations of Masculinity*, Birmingham: Centre for Contemporary Cultural Studies, Birmingham University.

Browning, Robert (1981) *The Poems: Vol. 1*, ed. John Pettigrew, New Haven, Conn.: Yale University Press.

Bush, Ronald (1976) *The Genesis of Ezra Pound's Cantos*, Princeton, NJ: Princeton University Press.

Butler, Judith (1990) *Gender Trouble: Feminism and the Subversion of Identity*, London: Routledge.

Cameron, Deborah and Frazer, Elizabeth (1987) *The Lust to Kill: A Feminist Investigation of Sexual Murder*, Oxford: Polity.

Carruth, Hayden (1970) *The Voice that is Great Within Us: American Poetry of the Twentieth Century*, New York: Bantam.

Chapman, Rowena and Rutherford, Jonathan (1988) *Male Order: Unwrapping Masculinity*, London: Lawrence & Wishart.

Chodorow, Nancy (1978) *The Reproduction of Mothering: Psychoanalysis and the Sociology of Gender*, Berkeley: University of California Press.

Christensen, Jerome (1987) *Practicing Enlightenment: Hume and the Formation of a Literary Career*, Madison and London: University of Wisconsin Press.

Cohen, David (1990) *Being a Man*, London: Routledge.

Collins, Jerre, Green, J. Ray, Lydon, Mary, Sachner, Mark and Skoller, Eleanor Honig (1985) 'Questioning the Unconscious: The Dora Archive', in Charles Bernheimer and Claire Kahane (eds) *In Dora's Case*, London: Virago.

Connell, R.W. (1987) *Gender and Power: Society, the Person and Sexual Politics*,

Oxford: Polity Press.

Connell, R.W. (1989) 'Masculinity, Violence and War', in Michael S. Kimmel and Michael A. Messner (eds) *Men's Lives*, New York: Macmillan.

Connerton, Paul (1988) 'Freud and the Crowd', in Edward Timms and Peter Collier (eds) *Visions and Blueprints: Avant-garde Culture and Radical Politics in Early Twentieth Century Europe*, Manchester: Manchester University Press.

Cousins, Mark (1978) 'Material Arguments and Feminism', *m/f* 2.

Creeley, Robert (1973) 'A Colloquy with Robert Creeley', interview by Linda W. Wagner (1963–1965), in Donald Allen (ed.) *Robert Creeley: Contexts of Poetry: Interviews 1961–1971*, Bolinas: Four Seasons Foundation.

Cullingford, Elizabeth Butler (1990) 'Thinking of Her . . . as . . . Ireland: Yeats, Pearse and Heaney', *Textual Practice* 4/1: 1–21.

de Beauvoir, Simone (1983) *The Second Sex*, trans. H.M. Parshley, Harmondsworth: Penguin.

de Bolla, Peter (1989) *The Discourse of the Sublime*, Oxford: Blackwell.

de Lauretis, Teresa (1987) *Technologies of Gender*, London: Macmillan.

de Man, Paul (1979) *Allegories of Reading: Figural Language in Rousseau, Nietzsche, Rilke and Proust*, New Haven, Conn.: Yale University Press.

—— (1983) 'Literary History and Literary Modernity', in *Blindness and Insight: Essays in the Rhetoric of Contemporary Criticism*, London: Methuen.

—— (1987) 'Hegel on the Sublime', in Mark Krupnick (ed.) *Displacement: Derrida and After*, Bloomington: Indiana University Press.

de Sousa, Ronald (1987) *The Rationality of Emotion*, Cambridge, Mass.: MIT Press.

Derrida, Jacques (1978) *Writing and Difference*, trans. Alan Bass, London: Routledge & Kegan Paul.

—— (1979) *Spurs: Nietzsche's Styles/ Eperons: Les Styles de Nietzsche*, Chicago: Chicago University Press.

—— (1981) 'The Double Session', in *Dissemination*, trans. Barbara Johnson, Chicago: University of Chicago Press.

—— (1991) '*Geschlecht*: Sexual Difference, Ontological Difference', in Peggy Kamuf (ed.) *A Derrida Reader*, Hemel Hempstead: Harvester Wheatsheaf.

Descartes, René (1931) 'The Passions of the Soul', in *The Philosophical Works of Descartes Vol. I* trans. Elizabeth S. Haldane and G.R.T. Ross, Cambridge: Cambridge University Press.

Dinnerstein, Dorothy (1987) *The Rocking of the Cradle and the Ruling of the World (The Mermaid and the Minotaur)*, London: Women's Press.

Dollimore, Jonathan (1991) *Sexual Dissidence: Augustine to Wilde, Freud to Foucault*, Oxford: Oxford University Press.

Dunlop, Francis (1984) *The Education of Feeling and Emotion*, London: George Allen & Unwin.

DuPlessis, Rachel Blau (1985) *Writing Beyond the Ending: Narrative Strategies of Twentieth-Century Women's Writers*, Bloomington: Indiana University Press.

Eagle (1987) 'Dan Dare', 26 September.

Eagleton, Terry (1990) *The Ideology of the Aesthetic*, Oxford: Blackwell.

Easthope, Antony (1986) *What a Man's Gotta Do: The Masculine Myth in Popular Culture*, London: Grafton Books.

Eichenbaum, Luise and Orbach, Susie (1984) *What Do Women Want?*, London: Fontana.

Eliot, T.S. (1963) *Collected Poems 1909–1962*, London: Faber.

—— (1975) *Selected Prose of T.S. Eliot*, ed. Frank Kermode, London: Faber.

Ellmann, Maud (1987) *The Poetics of Impersonality*, Brighton: Harvester.

Ellmann, Richard (1949) *Yeats: The Man and the Masks*, London: Faber.

Fairbairn, W.R.D. (1952) 'The Repression and the Return of Bad Objects (with Special Reference to the "War Neuroses")', in *Pyschoanalytic Studies of the Personality*, London: Tavistock.

Felski, Rita (1989) *Beyond Feminist Aesthetics*, London: Hutchinson.

Fernihough, Anne (1990) 'The Tyranny of the Text: Lawrence, Freud and the Modernist Aesthetic', in Peter Collier and Judy Davies (eds) *Modernism and the European Unconscious*, Oxford: Polity Press.

Finneran, Richard J. (1983) *Editing Yeats's Poems*, London: Macmillan.

Foucault, Michel (1972) *The Archaeology of Knowledge*, trans. Alan Sheridan, London: Tavistock.

—— (1981) *The History of Sexuality: Volume I*, trans. Robert Hurley, Harmondsworth: Penguin.

Frank, Manfred (1989) *What is Neostructuralism?*, Minneapolis: Minnesota University Press.

Fraser, Nancy (1990) 'The Uses and Abuses of French Discourse Theories for Feminist Politics', *Boundary* 2, 17: 2.

Freud, Sigmund (1940) *Gesammelte Werke Vol. XIII*, London: Imago.

—— (1955) *Standard Edition Vol. X*, trans. James Strachey, London: Hogarth.

—— (1973) *New Introductory Lectures on Psychoanalysis*, Harmondsworth: Penguin.

—— (1979a) 'Notes Upon a Case of Obsessional Neurosis: The "Rat Man" ', in Angela Richards (ed.) *Case Histories II*, Harmondsworth: Penguin.

—— (1979b) 'From the History of an Infantile Neurosis: The "Wolf Man" ', in Angela Richards (ed.) *Case Histories II*, Harmondsworth: Penguin.

—— (1984) *Beyond the Pleasure Principle*, in Angela Richards (ed.) *On Metapsychology: the Theory of Psychoanalysis*, Harmondsworth: Penguin.

Fricker, Miranda (1991) 'Reason and Emotion', *Radical Philosophy* 57: 14–19.

Fridja, Nico H. (1986) *The Emotions*, Cambridge: Cambridge University Press.

Gadamer, Hans-Georg (1979) *Truth and Method*, London: Sheed & Ward.

Gardiner, Muriel (1973) *The Wolf-Man and Sigmund Freud*, London: Hogarth Press.

Gasché, Rodolphe (1986) *The Tain and the Mirror: Derrida and the Philosophy of Reflection*, Cambridge, Mass.: Harvard University Press.

Gilbert, Sandra M. and Gubar, Susan (1988) *No Man's Land: the Place of the Woman Writer in the Twentieth Century, Vol. I*, New Haven, Conn.: Yale University Press.

Graves, Robert (1955) *The Greek Myths*, vol. 1, Harmondsworth: Penguin.

Green, André (1983) 'The Logic of Lacan's *objet (a)* and Freudian Theory: Convergences and Questions', in Joseph H. Smith and William Kerrigan (eds) *Interpreting Lacan*, New Haven, Conn.: Yale University Press.

Grosskurth, Phyllis (1986) *Melanie Klein: Her World and Her Work*, London: Hodder & Stoughton.

Grubracker, Marianne (1988) *There's a Good Girl: Gender Stereotyping in The First Three Years of Life: a Diary*, trans. Wendy Philipson, London: Women's Press.

Habermas, Jurgen (1983) 'Modernity: an Incomplete Project', in Hal Foster (ed.) *Postmodern Culture*, London: Pluto Press.

—— (1987) *The Philosophical Discourse of Modernity*, trans. Frederick Lawrence, Cambridge, Mass.: MIT Press.

Harré, Rom (1986) *The Social Construction of Emotions*, Oxford: Basil Blackwell.

Harvey, David (1989) *The Condition of Pure Modernity: An Enquiry into the Origins of Cultural Change*, Oxford: Blackwell.

Hearn, Jeff (1987) *The Gender of Oppression: Men, Masculinity and the Critique of Marxism*, Brighton: Harvester.

Heath, Stephen (1982) *The Sexual Fix*, London: Macmillan.

—— (1987) 'Male Feminism', in Alice Jardine and Paul Smith (eds) *Men in Feminism*, London: Methuen.

Hegel, G.W.F. (1892) *The Logic of Hegel*, trans. William Wallace, Oxford: Clarendon Presss.

—— (1971) *Philosophy of Mind*, trans. William Wallace and A.V. Miller, Oxford: Clarendon Press.

—— (1977) *Phenomenology of Spirit*, trans. A.V. Miller, Oxford: Oxford University Press.

Heidegger, Martin (1962) *Being and Time*, trans. John Macquarrie and Edward Robinson, Oxford: Blackwell.

Heller, Agnes (1979) *A Theory of Feelings*, Assen: Van Gorman.

Henke, Suzette (1990) *James Joyce and the Politics of Desire*, London: Routledge.

Hillman, James (1968) 'C.G. Jung on Emotion', in Magda B. Arnold (ed.) *The Nature of Emotion: Selected Readings*, Harmondsworth: Penguin.

—— (1970) 'C.G. Jung's Contributions to "Feelings and Emotions": Synopsis and Implications', in Magda B. Arnold (ed.) *Feelings and Emotions*, New York: Academic Press.

Hite, Shere (1981) *The Hite Report on Male Sexuality*, New York: Knopf.

Hodson, Philip (1984) *Men: an Investigation into the Emotional Male*, London: BBC.

Hollway, Wendy (1984) 'Gender Difference and the Production of Subjectivity', in Julian Henriques, Wendy Holloway, Cathy Urwin, Couze Venn and Valerie Walkerdine *Changing the Subject: Psychology, Social Regulation and Subjectivity*, London: Methuen.

—— (1989) *Subjectivity and Method in Pyschology: Gender Meaning and Science*, London: Sage.

Horn, Maurice (1982) *The World Encyclopedia of Comics*, New York: Avon.

Hulk (1978) *Rampage Monthly* 4, New York: Marvel.

—— (1981) *The Incredible Hulk* 269, New York: Marvel.

—— (1986) *The Incredible Hulk* 319, New York: Marvel.

—— (1988) *The Incredible Hulk* 344, New York: Marvel.

Hume, David (1969) *A Treatise of Human Nature*, ed. Ernest C. Mossner, Harmondsworth: Penguin.

Humphries, Martin and Metcalf, Andy (1985) *The Sexuality of Men*, London: Pluto Press.

Hyde, Lewis (1983) *The Gift: Imagination and the Erotic Life of Property*, New York: Random House.

Ingham, Mary (1985) *Men: The Male Myth Exposed*, London: Century.

Jacobus, Mary (1990) ' "Tea Daddy": Poor Mrs Klein and the Pencil Shavings', *Women: A Cultural Review* 1, 2: 160–79.

James, Henry (1966) *The Golden Bowl*, Harmondsworth: Penguin.

—— (1978) *The Wings of the Dove*, ed. J. Donald Crowley and Richard A. Hocks, New York: Norton.

—— (1984) *The Awkward Age*, ed. Vivien Jones, Oxford: Oxford University Press.

James, William (1950) *The Principles of Psychology, Vol. 2*, New York: Dover Reprint.

Jameson, Fredric (1984) 'Postmodernism, or The Cultural Logic of Late Capitalism', *New Left Review* 146.

Jardine, Alice (1985) *Gynesis: Configurations of Woman and Modernity*, Ithaca, NY: Cornell University Press.

Jardine, Alice and Smith, Paul (1987) *Men in Feminism,* London: Methuen.

Jay, Martin (1985) 'Habermas and Modernism', in Richard J. Bernstein (ed.) *Habermas and Modernity*, Oxford: Polity Press.

Johnstone, Keith (1981) *Impro: Improvisation and the Theatre*, London: Eyre Methuen.

Joyce, James (1971) *Ulysses*, Harmondsworth: Penguin.

—— (1988) *A Portrait of the Artist as a Young Man*, London: Paladin.

Kant, Immanuel (1933) *Critique of Pure Reason*, trans. Norman Kemp Smith, London: Macmillan.

—— (1952) *The Critique of Judgement*, trans. James Creed Meredith, Oxford: Oxford University Press.

—— (1974) *Anthropology from a Pragmatic Point of View*, trans. Mary J. Gregor, The Hague: Nijhoff.

Kauffman, Linda (1989) *Gender and Theory: Dialogues on Feminist Criticism*, Oxford: Blackwell.

Kearney, Richard (1984) *Dialogues with Contemporary Continental Thinkers: The Phenomenological Heritage*, Manchester: Manchester University Press.

Kenner, Hugh (1972) *The Pound Era*, London: Faber.

Kimmel, Michael S. and Messner, Michael A. (1989) *Men's Lives*, New York: Macmillan.

Klein, Melanie (1986) *The Selected Melanie Klein*, ed. Juliet Mitchell, London: Penguin.

Kohut, Heinz (1978) *The Search for the Self: Selected Writings of Heinz Kohut 1950–1978*, ed. Paul H. Ornstein, New York: International Universities Press.

Kolb, David (1986) *The Critique of Pure Modernity: Hegel, Heidegger and After*, Chicago: University of Chicago Press.

Koonz, Claudia (1988) *Mothers in the Fatherland: Women, the Family and Nazi Politics*, London: Methuen.

Kristeva, Julia (1983) 'Within the Microcosm of "The Talking Cure" ', in Joseph H. Smith and William Kerrigan (eds) *Interpreting Lacan*, New Haven, Conn.: Yale University Press.

—— (1987) *Tales of Love*, trans. Leon S. Roudiez, New York: Columbia.

Lacan, Jacques (1975) *Le Séminaire de Jacques Lacan, Livre XX: Encore*, Paris: Seuil.

—— (1977) *Ecrits: A Selection*, trans. Alan Sheridan, London: Tavistock.

—— (1979) 'The Neurotic's Individual Myth', *Psychoanalytic Quarterly* 48.

—— (1988) *The Seminar of Jacques Lacan Book I: Freud's Papers on Technique 1953–1954*, ed. Jacques-Alain Miller, trans. John Forrester, Cambridge: Cambridge University Press.

Lang, Jeffrey S. and Trimble, Patrick (1990) 'Whatever Happened to the Man of Tomorrow? An Examination of the American Monomyth and the Comic Book Superhero', *Journal of Popular Culture* 24: 157–73.

Lanyi, Ronald Levitt (1983) 'Idea and Motive in Jack "King" Kirby's Comic Books: a Conversation', *Journal of Popular Culture* 17/2.

—— (1984) 'Comic Books and Authority: An Interview with "Stainless Steve" Englehart', *Journal of Popular Culture* 18/2.

Lawrence, D.H. (1968) *Phoenix II: Uncollected, Unpublished and Other Prose Works*, ed. Warren Roberts and Harry T. Moore, London: Heinemann.

—— (1981) *The Rainbow*, (ed.) John Worthen, Harmondsworth: Penguin.

Leavis, F.R. (1936) *Revaluation: Tradition and Development in English Poetry*, London: Chatto & Windus.

Leavitt, David (1987) *The Lost Language of Cranes*, London: Penguin.

Lechte, John (1990) 'Art, Love and Melancholy in the Work of Julia Kristeva', in John Fletcher and Andrew Benjamin (eds) *Abjection, Melancholia, and Love: the*

Work of Julia Kristeva.

Lehman, David (1991) *Signs of the Times: Deconstruction and the Fall of Paul de Man*, London: André Deutsch.

Lessing, Doris (1973) *The Golden Notebook*, London: Granada.

Leverenz, David (1989) *Manhood and the American Renaissance*, Ithaca, NY, and London: Cornell University Press.

Levinas, Emmanuel (1969) *Totality and Infinity: An Essay on Exteriority*, trans. Alphonso Lingis, Pittsburgh, Pa: Duquesne University Press.

Lloyd, Genevieve (1984) *The Man of Reason: 'Male' and 'Female' in Western Philosophy*, London: Methuen.

Long, Michael (1988) 'The Politics of English Modernism: Eliot, Pound and Joyce', in Edward Timms and Peter Collier (eds) *Visions and Blueprints*, Manchester: Manchester University Press.

Lukacs, Georg (1963) 'The Ideology of Modernism', in *The Meaning of Contemporary Realism*, trans. John and Necke Mander, London: Merlin.

Lyons, William (1980) *Emotion*, Cambridge: Cambridge University Press.

Lyotard, Jean-François (1984) *The Postmodern Condition: A Report on Knowledge*, trans. Geoff Bennington and Brian Massumi, Minneapolis: University of Minnesota Press.

MacCabe, Colin (1979) *James Joyce and the Revolution of the Word*, London: Macmillan.

McCumber, John (1989) *Poetic Interaction: Language, Freedom, Reason*, Chicago: University of Chicago Press.

MacEwan, Ian (1988) *The Child in Time*, London: Picador.

McGill, Michael E. (1985) *The McGill Report on Male Intimacy*, New York: Harper & Row.

MacIntyre, Alasdair (1985) *After Virtue: A Study in Moral Theory*, London: Duckworth.

Mahony, Patrick J. (1986) *Freud and the Rat Man*, London: Yale University Press.

Mann, Thomas (1955) *Tonio Kroger*, trans. H.T. Lowe-Porter (with *Death in Venice* and *Tristan*), Harmondsworth: Penguin.

Marcus, Stephen (1984) *Freud and the Culture of Psychoanalysis: Studies in the Transition from Victorian Humanism to Modernity*, Boston: Allen & Unwin.

Mason, Steve (1986) 'Men Overcoming Violence, *Men's Antisexist Newsletter.*

Masters, Brian (1986) *Killing for Company: The Case of Dennis Nilsen*, London: Coronet.

Meisel, Perry (1987) *The Myth of the Modern: A Study in British Literature and Criticism after 1850*, New Haven, NJ: Yale University Press.

Melchiori, G. (1970) 'The Dome of Many-Coloured Glass', in R.J. Finneran (ed.) *W.B. Yeats: The Byzantium Poems*, Columbus, Ohio: Merrill.

Mercer, Kobena (and Isaac Julien) (1988) 'Race, Sexual Politics and Black Masculinity', in Rowena Chapman and Jonathan Rutherford (eds) *Male Order: Unwrapping Masculinity*, London: Lawrence & Wishart.

Metcalf, Andrew and Humphries, Martin (1985) *The Sexuality of Men*, London: Pluto Press.

Michaels, Barbara (1987) *Search the Shadows*, London: Bantam.

Middleton, Peter (1986a) 'The Academic Development of *The · Waste Land*', in Samuel Weber (ed.) *Glyph Textual Studies, Vol. I: Demarcating the Disciplines*, Minneapolis: Minnesota University Press.

—— (1986b) 'Wittgenstein and the Question of Masculinity', *The Oxford Literary Review* 8: 133–42.

—— (1988) 'Portrait of an Unknown Man', *Temblor: Contemporary Poets* 7.

—— (1989a) 'Linguistic Turns', *The Oxford Literary Review* 11/2: 137–68.

—— (1989b) 'Socialism, Feminism and Men', *Radical Philosophy* 53: 8–19.

—— (1989c) 'Why Structure Feeling?', *News From Nowhere* 6: 50–7.

—— (1990) 'Vanishing Affects: the Disappearance of Emotion from Postmodernist Theory and Practice', *New Formations* 12: 125–42.

—— (1991) 'Nurture and Culture: Reading and Readers in H.D.'s *Helen in Egypt*', *Textual Practice* 5/3: 352–62.

Mill, John Stuart and Taylor, Harriet (1990) 'On the Subjection of Women', in John Gray (ed.) *On Liberty and Other Essays* Oxford: Oxford University Press.

Miller, Frank (1990) Interview with Frank Miller, *Comics Interview* 82: 5–33.

Miller, Stuart (1983) *Men and Friendship*, London: Gateway.

Millett, Kate (1977) *Sexual Politics*, London: Virago.

Mitchell, Juliet (1971) *Woman's Estate*, Harmondsworth: Penguin.

—— (1974) *Psychoanalysis and Feminism*, Harmondsworth: Penguin.

Mitchell, Juliet and Rose Jacqueline (eds) (1982) *Feminine Sexuality: Jacques Lacan and the 'école freudienne'*, London: Macmillan.

Mitchell, Stephen (1988) *Relational Concepts in Psychoanalysis*, Cambridge, Mass.: Harvard University Press.

Modleski, Tania (1988) *The Women Who Knew Too Much: Hitchcock and Feminist Theory*, New York: Methuen.

Monk, Ray (1990) *Ludwig Wittgenstein: the Duty of Genius*, London: Cape.

Moretti, Franco (1983) *Signs Taken for Wonders*, London: Verso.

Mossner, Ernest C. (1980) *The Life of David Hume*, Oxford: Oxford University Press.

Mulvey, Laura (1985) 'Film and Visual Pleasure', in Gerald Mast and Marshall Cohen (eds) *Film Theory and Criticism: Introductory Readings,* 3rd edn, Oxford: Oxford University Press.

Murray, Michael (1978) *Heidegger and Modern Philosophy: Critical Essays*, New Haven: Yale University Press.

Nagel, Thomas (1986) *The View from Nowhere*, Oxford: Oxford University Press.

Naifeh, Steven and Smith, Gregory White (1987) *Why Can't Men Open Up:Unlocking the Intimate Man*, London: Sphere.

Nietzsche, Friedrich (1968) *Twilight of the Idols/ The Anti-Christ*, trans. R.J. Hollingdale, Harmondsworth: Penguin.

Nikki (1986) *Nikki* 50, 1 February.

Nye, Andrea (1987) 'Woman Clothed with the Sun: Julia Kristeva and the Escape from/to Language', *Signs* 12/4.

Olson, Charles (1983) *The Maximus Poems*, ed. George Butterick, Berkeley: University of California Press.

Osherson, Samuel (1986) *Finding Our Fathers: How a Man's Life is Shaped by His Relationship with His Father*, New York: Fawcett.

O'Sullivan, Sue and Ardill, Susan (1986) 'Upsetting an Applecart: Difference, Desire and Lesbian Sadomasochism', *Feminist Review* 23.

Oxenhandler, Neal (1988) 'The Changing Concept of Literary Emotion: a Selective History', *New Literary History* 20/1: 105–22.

Pippin, Robert (1989) *Hegel's Idealism: The Satisfactions of Self-Consciousness*, Cambridge: Cambridge University Press.

Plato (1973) *Phaedrus*, trans. Walter Hamilton, Harmondsworth: Penguin.

—— (1974) *The Republic*, trans. Desmond Lee, Harmondsworth: Penguin.

Pleck, Joseph (1981) *The Myth of Masculinity*, Cambridge, Mass.: MIT Press.

Porter, Carolyn (1981) *Seeing and Being: The Plight of the Participant Observer in Emerson, James, Adams and Faulkner*, Middletown, Conn.: Wesleyan University

Press.

Pound, Ezra (1952) *The Spirit of Romance*, London: Peter Owen.

—— (1975) *The Cantos*, London: Faber.

—— (1977) *Selected Poems*, London: Faber.

Price, A.W. (1989) *Love and Friendship in Plato and Aristotle*, Oxford: Clarendon Press.

Prynne, J.H. (1988) 'English Poetry and Emphatical Language', *Proceedings of the British Academy* LXXIV: 135–69.

Pynchon, Thomas (1975) *Gravity's Rainbow*, London: Picador.

Radway, Janice (1984) *Reading the Romance: Women, Patriarchy and Popular Literature*, Chapel Hill: University of North Carolina Press.

Rainer, Yvonne (1974) *Work 1961–73*, New York: New York University Press.

Rapp, Carl (1984) *William Carlos Williams and Romantic Idealism*, London: University Press of New England.

Reed, Gail S. (1984) 'The Antithetical Meaning of the Term "Empathy" in Psychoanalytic Discourse', in Joseph Lichtenberg, Mehrin Bornstein and Donald Silver (eds) *Empathy I*, Hillsdale, NJ: The Analytic Press.

Restuccia, Frances L. (1989) *Joyce and the Law of the Father*, New Haven, Conn., and London: Yale University Press.

Richardson, Dorothy (1979) *Pilgrimage* (4 vols), London: Virago.

Ricoeur, Paul (1970) *Freud and Philosophy: An Essay on Interpretation*, trans. Denis Savage, New Haven and London: Yale University Press.

—— (1986) *Fallible Man*, trans. Charles A. Kebley, New York: Fordham University Press.

Riley, Denise (1988) *'Am I That Name': Feminism and the Category of "Woman" in History*, London: Macmillan.

Rilke, Rainer Maria (1987) 'The Second Elegy', from *The Duino Elegies* in Stephen Mitchell (ed. and trans.) *The Selected Poetry of Rainer Maria Rilke*, London: Pan.

Roberts, Les (1989) *An Infinite Number of Monkeys*, London: Hodder & Stoughton.

Roberts, Yvonne (1984) *Man Enough: Men of Thirty-Five Speak Out*, London: Chatto.

Rorty, Amelie Oksenberg (1980) *Explaining Emotions*, Berkeley: University of California Press.

Rose, Jacqueline (1986) *Sexuality in the Field of Vision*, London: Verso.

Ross, Andrew (1986) *The Failure of Modernism: Symptoms of American Poetry*, New York: Columbia University Press.

Russell, Bertrand (1921) *The Analysis of Mind*, London: Unwin.

Rutherford, Jonathan (1992) *Men's Silences: Predicaments in Masculinity*, London: Routledge.

Ryan, Michael (1989) *Politics and Culture: Working Hypotheses for a Post-Revolutionary Society*, London: Macmillan.

Sabo, Don (1990) 'The Myth of the Sexual Athlete', in Franklin Abbott (ed.) *Men and Intimacy: Personal Accounts Exploring the Dilemmas of Modern Male Sexuality*, Freedom, Calif.: The Crossing Press.

Sacks, Oliver (1986) 'The President's Speech', in *The Man Who Mistook His Wife for a Hat*, London: Picador.

Safransky, Sy (1990) 'Some Enchanted Evening', in Franklin Abbott (ed.) *Men and Intimacy*, Freedom, Calif.: The Crossing Press.

Sartre, Jean-Paul (1963) *Sketch for a Theory of the Emotions*, trans. Philip Mairet, London: Methuen.

Satris, Satris (1987) *Ethical Emotivism*, Dordrecht: Nijhoff.

Scherer, Klaus R., Wallbott, Harold G. and Summerfield, Angela B. (1986) *Experiencing Emotion: A Cross-Cultural Study*, Cambridge: Cambridge University Press.

Scott, Bonnie Kime (1990) *The Gender of Modernism: A Critical Anthology*, Bloomington: Indiana University Press.

Sedgwick, Eve Kosofsky (1985) *Between Men: English Literature and Male Homosocial Desire*, New York: Columbia University Press.

Segal, Lynne (1987) *Is the Future Female? Troubled Thoughts on Contemporary Feminism*, London: Virago.

—— (1989) 'Slow Change or No Change: Feminism, Socialism and the Problem of Men', *Feminist Review* 31: 5–21.

—— (1990) *Slow Motion: Changing Masculinities Changing Men*, London: Virago.

Seidler, Victor J. (1989) *Rediscovering Masculinity: Reason, Language and Sexuality*, London: Routledge.

—— (1991) *Recreating Sexual Politics: Men Feminism and Politics*, London: Routledge.

Shell, Susan Meld (1980) *The Rights of Reason*, Toronto: Toronto University Press.

Simpson, Hilary (1982) *D.H. Lawrence and Feminism*, London: Croom Helm.

Smith, John H. (1989) 'The *Transcendence* of the Individual', *Diacritics* 19/2: 80–98.

Smithson, Robert (1979) 'A Museum of Language in the Vicinity of Art', in Nancy Holt (ed.) *The Writings of Robert Smithson*, New York: New York University Press.

Solomon, Robert (1979) 'Paul Ricoeur on Passion and Emotion', in Charles Reagan (ed.) *Studies in the Philosophy of Paul Ricoeur*, Columbus: Ohio University Press.

—— (1983) *In the Spirit of Hegel*, Oxford: Oxford University Press.

Somerville, Jennifer (1989) 'The Sexuality of Men and the Sociology of Gender', *The Sociological Review* 37/2: 277–307.

Spinoza, Baruch (1986) *Spinoza's Ethics*, trans. Andrew Boyle, London: Dent.

Stearns, Peter N. (1987) 'Men, Boys and Anger in American Society, 1860–1940', in J.A. Mangan and James Walvin (eds) *Manliness and Morality: Middle-Class Masculinity in Britain and America 1800–1940*, Manchester: Manchester University Press.

Stearns, Peter N. with Stearns, Carol Z. (1985) 'Emotionology: Clarifying the History of Emotions and Emotional Standards', *American Historical Review* 90/4: 813–36.

Stevenson, Charles L. (1944) *Ethics and Language*, New Haven, Conn.: Yale University Press.

Strean, Herbert S. (1988) *Behind the Couch: Revelations of a Psychoanalyst*, New York: Wiley.

Supergirl (1973) *Supergirl* 2/5, June.

Superman (1987) *The Greatest Superman Stories Ever Told*, New York: DC Comics.

Suttie, Ian D. (1988) *The Origins of Love and Hate*, London: Free Association.

Taussig, Michael (1987) *Shamanism, Colonialism and the Wild Man: a Study in Terror and Healing*, Chicago: Chicago University Press.

Tavris, Carol (1982) *Anger: the Misunderstood Emotion*, New York: Simon & Schuster.

Taylor, Charles (1975) *Hegel*, Cambridge: Cambridge University Press.

Theweleit, Klaus (1985) *Male Fantasies I: Women, Floods, Bodies, History*, trans. Stephen Conway, Erica Carter and Chris Turner, Oxford: Polity Press.

Umphlett, Wiley Lee (1983) *Mythmakers of the American Dream: The Nostalgic Vision in Popular Culture*, Lewisburg, Ohio: Bucknell University Press.

Walczak, Yvette (1988) *He and She: Men in the Eighties*, London: Routledge.

Webster (1971) *Webster's Third New International Dictionary*, London: G. & C. Merriam.

White, Stephen K. (1988) *The Recent Work of Jurgen Habermas: Reason, Justice and Modernity*, Cambridge: Cambridge University Press.

Williams, Raymond (1977) *Marxism and Literature*, Oxford: Oxford University Press.

—— (1979) *Politics and Letters: Interviews with New Left Review*, London: New Left Books.

—— (1988) 'David Hume: Reasoning and Experience', in *Writing in Society*, London: Verso.

Williams, William Carlos (1986) *The Collected Poems of William Carlos Williams: Vol. I 1909–1939*, ed. A. Walton Litz and Christopher MacGowan, New York: New Directions.

Wilson, Elizabeth (1982) 'Yesterday's Heroines: On Rereading Lessing and De Beauvoir', in Jenny Taylor (ed.) *Notebooks/Memoirs/Archives: Reading and Rereading Doris Lessing*, London: Routledge and Kegan Paul.

Wimsatt, W.K. Jr and Beardsley, Monroe C. (1967) 'The Affective Fallacy', in *The Verbal Icon: Studies in the Meaning of Poetry*, Lexington: University of Kentucky Press.

Winnicott, D.W. (1958) 'Aggression in Relation to Emotional Development', in *Collected Papers: Through Paediatrics to Psycho-Analysis*, London: Tavistock.

Wittgenstein, Ludwig (1961) *Tractatus Logico-Philosophicus*, trans. D.F. Pears and Brian McGuinness, London: Routledge and Kegan Paul.

—— (1976) *Philosophical Investigations*, trans. G.E.M. Anscombe, Oxford: Blackwell.

Worthen, John (1991) *D.H. Lawrence: the Early Years 1885–1912*, Cambridge: Cambridge University Press.

Yeats, W.B. (1978) *A Vision*, London: Macmillan.

—— (1980) 'The Symbolism of Poetry', in A. Norman Jeffares (ed.) *Selected Criticism and Prose*, London: Pan Books.

—— (1984) *The Poems*, ed. Richard J. Finneran, London: Macmillan.

INDEX

Abbott, Franklin, *Men and Intimacy* 7
Achilles Heel 123–4, 25
Adams, Parveen 130, 134–5
Adler, Dr Alfred 87
Adorno, Theodor W. and Max
  Horkheimer 205, 206, 211; *Dialectic
  of Enlightenment* 169
aesthetics 57; *see also* sublime
affective anaesthesia 228
aggression 95, 139
American Marvel 23
Anderson, Benedict 200
anger 40–1, 86, 116, 122, 200, 205;
  acceptability 33; Archie Bunker
  example 174, 177; God's 56
Aristotle 25, 60; *Nicomachean Ethics*
  203–4
art 45–6, 50, 77, 196; theory 227
Astrachan, Anthony 123,131; *How
  Men Feel* 6
Auden, W.H. 66
Austen, Jane, *Emma* 174
autobiography 113

Baker, G.P. and P.M.S. Hacker 222
Barrett, Michele, *Women's Oppression
  Today* 134
Barker, Martin 23
Barthes, Roland 138
Batman 4–6, 25, 44; and conflict 29–34
Baumli, Francis, *Men Freeing Men* 7
Beano 28
Beauvoir, Simone de, *The Second Sex*
  113
Beckett, Samuel 52, 65
Beneke, Tim 123, 139, 191
Benhabib, Seyla 134, 149–50, 164
Benjamin, Jessica 181

Bernstein, Charles 216–18; 'The Klupzy
  Girl' 217–18
Blake, William 185
Bloom, Harold 58, 59, 157
Bly, Robert, *Iron John: A Book about
  Men* 6, 120
Bond, Edward, *The Woman* 200–1
bonding, male 121
Boone, Joseph Allen 161
Booth, Wayne, *The Rhetoric of Fiction*
  173–4
Bowie, Andrew, *Aesthetics and
  Subjectivity* 159
boys/boyhood 13, 59, 181, 231; and
  comics 23–4; and mothers 190;
  recollections 17–20, 21; relation to
  men 39–42; rituals 23; transition
  from 56
Brittan, Arthur and M. Maynard
  Sexism, Racism and Oppression 150;
  Masculinity and Power 7
Brooks, Cleanth 172
Browning, Robert, *Bishop Blougram's
  Apology* 46–7; *Sordello* 46

Cameron, Deborah and Elizabeth
  Frazer 195
Cartesian model 71–2
cartoon images 23, 25, 38, 191–2
catharsis 169, 181–4, 223–4
cathexis 63,143, 153, 158; libidinal 81
'Changing Identities' (conference) 145,
  168
childhood 21, 22–3, 79; access to 226;
  separation in 118; trauma 86
Chodorow, Nancy 124, 128–30; *The
  Reproduction of Mothering* 127–8
'chora' 191, 220

244

245

INDEX